CAMBRIDGE

Brighter Thinking

The Tudors: England, 1485–1603

A/AS Level History for AQA Student Book

Hannah Dalton

Series Editors: Michael Fordham and David Smith

CAMBRIDGE
UNIVERSITY PRESS

University Printing House, Cambridge CB2 8BS, United Kingdom

Cambridge University Press is part of the University of Cambridge.

It furthers the University's mission by disseminating knowledge in the pursuit of education, learning and research at the highest international levels of excellence.

www.cambridge.org
Information on this title: www.cambridge.org/ukschools/9781316504321 (Paperback)
                               www.cambridge.org/ukschools/9781316504345 (Cambridge Elevate-enhanced Edition)

First published 2015

A catalogue record for this publication is available from the British Library

ISBN 978-1-316-504321 Paperback
ISBN 978-1-316-504345 Cambridge Elevate-enhanced Edition

Additional resources for this publication at www.cambridge.org/ukschools

Message from AQA

This textbook has been approved by AQA for use with our qualification. This means that we have checked that it broadly covers the specification and we are satisfied with the overall quality. Full details of our approval process can be found on our website.

We approve textbooks because we know how important it is for teachers and students to have the right resources to support their teaching and learning. However, the publisher is ultimately responsible for the editorial control and quality of this book.

Please note that when teaching the A/AS Level History (7041, 7042) course, you must refer to AQA's specification as your definitive source of information. While this book has been written to match the specification, it cannot provide complete coverage of every aspect of the course.

A wide range of other useful resources can be found on the relevant subject pages of our website: www.aqa.org.uk

Contents

About this Series

Cambridge A/AS Level History for AQA is an exciting new series designed to support students in their journey from GCSE to A Level and then on to possible further historical study. The books provide the knowledge, concepts and skills needed for the two-year AQA History A Level course, but it's our intention as series editors that students recognise that their A Level exams are just one step to a potential lifelong relationship with the discipline of history. This book has further readings, extracts from historians' works and links to wider questions and ideas that go beyond the scope of an A Level course. With this series, we have sought to ensure not only that the students are well prepared for their examinations, but also that they gain access to a wider debate that characterises historical study.

The series is designed to provide clear and effective support for students as they make the adjustment from GCSE to A Level, and also for teachers, especially those who are not familiar with teaching a two-year linear course. The student books cover the AQA specifications for both A/AS Level. They are intended to appeal to the broadest range of students, and they offer challenges to stretch the top end and additional support for those who need it. Every author in this series is an experienced historian or history teacher, and all have great skill in conveying narratives to readers and asking the kinds of questions that pull those narratives apart.

In addition to high-quality prose, this series also makes extensive use of textual primary sources, maps, diagrams and images, and offers a wide range of activities to encourage students to address historical questions of cause, consequence, change and continuity. Throughout the books there are opportunities to criticise the interpretations of other historians, and to use those interpretations in the construction of students' own accounts of the past. The series aims to ease the transition for those students who move on from A Level to undergraduate study, and the books are written in an engaging style that will encourage those who want to explore the subject further.

Icons used within this book include:

 Key terms

 Developing concepts

 Speak like a historian

 Voices from the past/Hidden voices

 Thematic links

 Chapter summary

About Cambridge Elevate

Cambridge Elevate is the platform which hosts a digital version of this Student Book. If you have access to this digital version you can annotate different parts of the book, send and receive messages to and from your teacher and insert weblinks, among other things.

We hope that you enjoy your AS or A Level History course as well as this book, and wish you well for the journey ahead.

Michael Fordham and David L Smith
Series editors

1 Henry VII, 1485–1509

In this section we will examine the nature of political authority in England between 1485 and 1547, consider some of the changes that Henry VII implemented and how well he managed to secure a Tudor dynasty. We will look into:

- Henry Tudor's consolidation of power: character and aims; establishing the Tudor dynasty.
- Government: councils, parliament, justice, royal finance, domestic policies.
- Relationships with Scotland and other foreign powers; securing the succession; marriage alliances.
- Society: churchmen, nobles and commoners; regional division; social discontent and rebellions.
- Economic development: trade, exploration, prosperity and depression.
- Religion; humanism; arts and learning.

Introduction

Henry VII's victory at the Battle of Bosworth against the unpopular – and now infamous – Richard III has been presented, by some historians, such as GR Elton (1955), as a watershed in British history. Henry VII's reign marked a period of 'new monarchy' as the turmoil of the Wars of the Roses was bought to a close. The

Key terms

Lancastrian: often associated with a Red Rose. The Lancastrians were descended from John of Gaunt, who was the third son of Henry III and made the Duke of Lancaster. They were a powerful family with claims to the English throne. Henry of Bolingbroke (later, Henry IV) was the first Lancastrian to assert his claim when he deposed Richard II in 1399. The Lancastrian throne was weakened when Henry VI succeeded the throne as an infant. Another family, also descended from Henry III's first and fourth sons, challenged the Lancastrians for the throne in wars that became known as 'The Wars of the Roses'.

Yorkist: the Yorkist family were descended from a branch of the Plantagenet family tree. They claimed the English throne and three of its members became English kings in the 15th century. The last Yorkist king was Richard III who lost his life in battle to Henry Tudor in 1485.

Tudors themselves manufactured this myth: that Henry VII had begun something 'new' in statecraft or royal governance. Early historians of the period (Hall in 1547 and Bacon in 1622) celebrated Henry VII's achievements too, painting him as the unifier of a war-torn land bringing justice and financial stability to the Crown. More recently, historians such as John Guy (1988) and John Lander (1980) have suggested that 1485 was significant only in dynastic history, for the Tudors would rule over England for over a century. Henry VII himself ruled England for almost a quarter of a century, quite an achievement given his dubious claim to the throne and the manner by which he usurped Richard III. Arguably, the perils of civil war would define his reign as he frequently faced threats of claimants to the throne until 1506. Historians have vigorously debated whether Henry VII was a successful monarch and whether he truly 'innovated' aspects of governance, but still there is no consensus on this. However, Williams's (1963)[1] assessment of Henry VII as a great 'adaptor' seems convincing. Henry VII was a ruthless pragmatist, as medieval monarchs needed to be; he managed to defend his title against several claimants to the throne and pass the baton on to his son, Henry VIII. Establishing the Tudor dynasty was undoubtedly more important to Henry VII than offering a new kind of governance to the country and in this he was surely a success.

Henry Tudor's consolidation of power

When Henry, Earl of Richmond, was born on 28 January 1457 in Pembroke Castle, just a few miles away from where he would eventually launch his campaign for the Crown, it would have seemed unlikely that he would ever become King. He was born into a country tarnished by war and plague. The Hundred Years War (1337–1453) had been fought in France in pursuit of English kings' claims to the French throne, but it was followed by war on English soil. The Wars of the Roses were a struggle for the throne between two branches of the ruling Plantagenet family, the Houses of York and Lancaster. King Henry VI, of the House of Lancaster, was a weak monarch and was utterly dominated by his advisers and his wife, Margaret of Anjou. Lack of leadership from the king left a political vacuum that powerful noble families attempted to fill. At first, Henry VI had no heir, and the Duke of York tried to topple him. This led to internecine conflict between **Yorkists** and **Lancastrians** from 1455 onwards. However, it was not only dynastic wars that had ravaged England. Sporadic outbreaks of plague had greatly reduced the population; even the young Henry's father, Edmund, had fallen victim three months before he was born. His mother, Lady Margaret Beaufort, was a widow aged just 14 when she gave birth to him, and had been imprisoned in a Yorkist dungeon (because she was a Lancastrian). It was in these circumstances Henry entered the world.

By 1461, due to a catastrophic defeat for the Lancastrians at the Battle of Towton, England had a Yorkist King in the form of the charismatic Edward IV, only 18 years old when he took the crown from the mentally ill Lancastrian, Henry VI. The political uncertainties of the 1450s had been largely settled by the assertive Edward IV and he had seemingly assured his dynasty as he had ten children, including two surviving sons. By the time he was aged 40, however, his insatiable appetite for wine had caught up with him and he died in 1483. Henry meanwhile had been sent to Brittany in 1471, aged 14, with his uncle Jasper Tudor, for his own safety. Edward IV had executed Henry VI, the Duke of Somerset and Henry VI's son in 1471, leaving the half-blood Henry with a stronger claim to the throne (see Figure 1.1). Henry was transferred from fortress to castle, never settled, and always patiently waiting for an opportunity to return to England.

Hereditary rules for monarchs:

1. The claim must descend lineally, therefore sons of the monarch's eldest son have priority over the monarch's other sons and their children.
2. Males are given preference over females.
3. Male sons of subsequent marriages take precedence over daughters of previous marriages.

Discussion points:

1. Where does Henry VII's 'Royal Blood' come from?
2. What made Henry VII's claim to the throne stronger in 1471?
3. Why do you think Henry VII married Elizabeth of York?
4. How strong was Henry's claim to the throne? Did others have stronger claims?

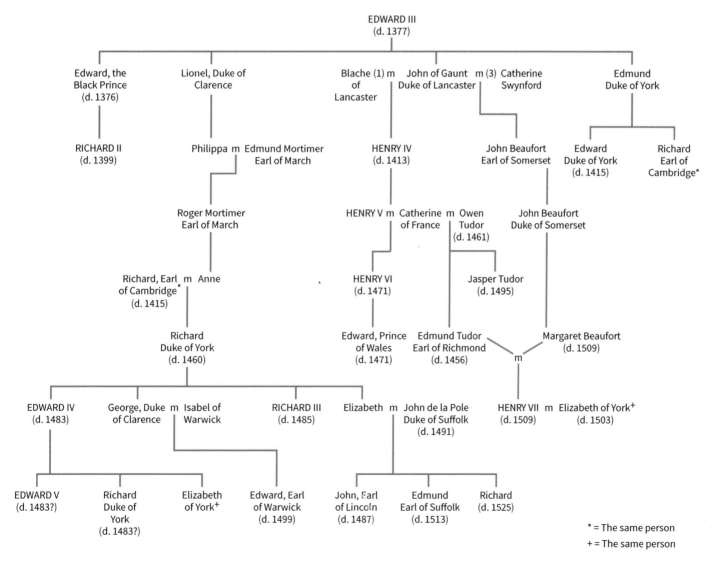

Figure 1.1: Family tree showing Henry VII's claim to the English throne.

Speak like a historian: internecine

The adjective 'internecine' is used by historians to describe wars that are highly destructive to both sides involved in the conflict. The Wars of the Roses have been described as internecine not so much because of the material destruction they caused, but because of the destabilising effect that lawlessness and the weakening of the Crown had on the social structure.

While Henry learnt about court and politics in France, the elder of Edward IV's two sons, Edward Prince of Wales, was named his heir upon his death, but he was only 12 years old. Edward IV's younger brother, Richard Duke of Gloucester, pronounced himself King and imprisoned the two princes in the Tower of London. A publicity campaign was mounted to declare Edward IV's marriage invalid, then endorsed by an assembly of lords and commoners, rendering the children illegitimate and invalidating any claims they could have to the throne. Richard arrested and executed leading members of the family of Elizabeth Woodville (Edward IV's wife) and crowned himself Richard III. The princes were never seen again. Richard's usurpation of the apparently rightful heir to the throne, coupled with the widely held belief that he had arranged the murder of the princes in the Tower made him extremely unpopular. He had also failed to win the loyalty of the nobility, and plots to overthrow him were formed almost immediately.

Lady Margaret Beaufort opened negotiations through a priest and an astrologer to arrange the marriage of her son to Elizabeth of York, the eldest of Edward IV's daughters. A pact was agreed, upon Henry's successful return from Brittany. If Henry married the daughter of the former king, he could be presented as the successor to Edward IV (this was flawed logic, as Edward had nearly obliterated the Lancastrians for good at Towton). However, bringing together the House of Lancaster with the House of York was symbolically very powerful indeed and would add legitimacy to his reign. Henry's mother saw the potential for Henry to be seen as the unifier of two great families, and therefore of the rest of the country.

Henry VII had planned to seize the throne much earlier than he did. He was lucky that the first plot to bring him to England failed because of bad weather, as Richard III had quickly routed his co-conspirators and beheaded the Duke of Buckingham who had led the rebellion. Rumours reached Henry that Richard was busy arranging marriages between his own knights and the daughters of Edward IV, he was even rumoured to have his eye on Henry's betrothed, Elizabeth of York. Henry and his advisers quickly scrambled to raise loans and assemble an army. He managed to find almost 5000 French mercenaries and, on 1 August 1485, set sail towards Milford Haven. By 22 August Henry and his troops had reached Bosworth Field, and faced Richard's forces. Richard III had amassed the largest army England had ever seen, of up to 15 000 men.

Richard's nobles refused to advance against the young usurper, perhaps because they lacked loyalty towards Richard. Therefore Richard was left with a much-reduced army. In the midst of the battle, monarch (Richard) and pretender (Henry) fought face to face. Henry was saved by Sir William Stanley, Henry's uncle by

Hidden voices

Margaret Beaufort

Lady Margaret Beaufort was an extraordinary woman of her time. Jones and Underwood's (1993) scholarly account paints her as a highly influential figure in the government of Henry VII. She married four times, but only had one child, Henry, when she was aged just 14. A shrewd political operator, she managed to avoid Edward IV's wrath following two battles, which saw him wipe out many of the Lancastrian clan. Her marriage to Thomas Stanley enabled her to return to court under Edward IV where she orchestrated a planned marriage between her son Henry and Elizabeth of York, which had the potential to unite the two houses.

marriage, who swept Richard away, battering him to death. Lord Thomas Stanley, Henry's stepfather, who had done little during the battle to support the would-be King, helped to mop up the remainder of Richard's defences. Finding Richard's circlet in a thorn bush, Stanley placed it on his stepson's head and pronounced him King of England. And so it was that on 22 August 1485 Henry claimed the throne.

Henry Tudor's character and aims

Henry VII claimed the throne when he was 28 years old. He died on the throne aged just 52 and yet he has traditionally been painted as an old man, particularly by perhaps his most prolific biographer, Francis Bacon. Historians do seem to agree that his formative experiences as a youth, spending significant time in exile and in danger of execution, taught him self-restraint and to veil his purposes from others. Perhaps the most important lesson Henry VII had learnt while in Brittany, was that to maintain his position on the throne he would have to end the Wars of the Roses once and for all. For Henry VII this did not mean merely defeating those hostile towards him, but healing the deep wounds left by the wars.

Once he had obtained the throne, Henry VII aimed to show **clemency** and resolution towards his subjects. His first instinct seems to have been to bring former enemies into the court – perhaps where he could keep an eye on them – but he was also reluctant to take extreme measures against those who had been involved in plots because he was aware that further conflict was a possible consequence. He was not particularly kind-hearted and few ever described him as weak. He was a man of action and a soldier who had fought for his crown and, knowing the true cost of conflict, tried to avoid them thereafter. No procrastinator

Key term

clemency: term used to describe mercy or lenience shown by a monarch or leader when punishing enemies or traitors.

Voices from the past

Aldo Brandini

In 1496 a Florentine named Aldo Brandini who had visited the Court of Henry VII, said of him:

The King is feared rather than loved, and this was due his avarice … The king is very powerful in money, but if fortune allowed some Lord of the blood royal to arise and he had to take the field he would fare badly owing to his avarice; his people would abandon him.

Source: Lander JR. *Government and Community: England 1450–1509*. London: Edward Arnold; 1980. p. 331.

either, he swiftly and tenaciously set about stabilising his kingdom and securing his dynasty almost as soon as he returned from Bosworth. He surrounded himself with the brightest in the land, namely Cardinal Morton, Bishop Fox, Sir Reginald Bray and Sir Thomas Lovell, Richard Empson and Edmund Dudley, all of whom were exceptionally clever, loyal and zealous servants of their master. Even though these men may have been the architects of much of the successes of Henry VII's reign, it was Henry himself who was in control. He was an active and interested monarch. Of all those who had claimed the crown before, Henry may well have been the most prepared and best equipped to keep it.

Establishing the Tudor dynasty

On 3 September 1485, Henry VII entered London in triumph. The young Henry must have known, however, that with the battle done, the real challenge was only just beginning. He had a precarious claim to the throne and no large family who could support him; Edward IV had seen to that. Henry VII also had virtually no experience of government and was therefore reliant upon Yorkist nobles, whose allegiances really lay with his betrothed. The threat of another civil war was a distinct possibility. Henry VII (as he was crowned on 30 October 1485) knew he had to establish a new dynasty, which would merge his family name with royal authority. It was under these circumstances that he began his reign.

On both sides of his family, Henry's lineage was Lancastrian. On his mother's side, Henry could trace his bloodline back to the magnificent John of Gaunt, Duke of Lancaster. The Pope and Richard II had legitimised John's Beaufort descendants from his marriage to Katherine Swynford, even though she was only his mistress when they were born. However, Henry IV had written them out of the line of succession, through an Act of Parliament and the Yorkists disparaged them as bastards. Henry's paternal grandfather had secretly married Catherine of Valois, the widow of Henry V, giving the Tudors a connection with the Lancastrians, but Henry had no English royal ancestry through the male line. In fact, the young Earl of Warwick who was Edward IV's nephew had the best claim to the throne (see Figure 1.1).

Henry was, for obvious reasons, reluctant to base his claim to the throne on his impending marriage to Elizabeth of York, daughter of Edward IV, and he therefore had to establish another way of legitimising his reign. This he had to do on his own terms, and he chose a simple solution: he simply declared that he was King, for there was no authority that could prevent him from doing so. Henry delayed

Voices from the past

Francis Bacon

Francis Bacon (1561–1626) was a scientist and philosopher who served as the Attorney General and Lord Chancellor under James I (also known as James VI of Scotland). Bacon wrote about Henry VII in 1622 under James I, probably to flatter his king. Bacon painted Henry VII as being master of his realm and unifier of warring houses, just as he thought James had attempted to unite England and Scotland. How much historical research Bacon did is debated, since it only took him several weeks to complete.

the marriage to Elizabeth until 18 January 1486, when the ceremony took place in Westminster Abbey. He delayed the crowning of his new wife even further, until 25 November 1487, two years after his own coronation. Henry must have been mindful of Elizabeth's sisters Cecily, Anne, Catherine and Bridget, who would undoubtedly have children were they to marry, thereby producing claimants to the throne. Henry was therefore delighted and relieved when Elizabeth gave birth to their first son (20 September 1486). Wishing to ground the legitimacy of the Tudors in potent national myths, he named him Arthur in emulation of the legendary king. Henry and Elizabeth went on to have another six children, helping to secure the Tudor Dynasty and providing a clear line of succession: Margaret, Queen of Scots (28 November 1489–18 October 1541), Henry VIII of England (28 June 1491–28 January 1547), Elizabeth Tudor (2 July 1492–14 September 1495), Mary, Queen of France (18 March 1496–25 June 1533), Edmund Tudor, Duke of Somerset (21 February 1499–19 June 1500) and Katherine Tudor (2 February 1503–10 February 1503). It should be noted here that Henry VII was unlucky that he survived so many of his children. The deaths of Edmund and Arthur certainly affected him. Historians have noted that the last years of his reign were marked by intensely personal governance of a despotic nature, and many have attributed this to the deaths of his sons and his wife, Elizabeth, in 1503.

Extension activity: Carry out some research into portraits painted of other European kings at the time. How does Henry VII compare?

During the first few months of his reign, Henry VII had to establish himself as rightful King of England in the eyes of his subjects. Therefore, he called Parliament to session on 7 November 1485, as Henry IV had done in 1406, and announced that he had received the Crown through inheritance – using intentionally vague terms – and that God had divinely intervened at the Battle of Bosworth to allow him to be victorious. This also had the benefit of enabling Henry to denounce Richard III as a usurper, although Edward IV and Edward V had to be accepted as rightful kings as his wife's father and brother. Henry VII did not need to summon Parliament, but he did so because he wanted to follow tradition and to quash any doubt whatsoever that he was the rightful king and, more importantly, thereby establish his heirs as the rightful successors to his throne. Like several of the Tudors after him, he found it better to put a matter beyond doubt by having it written down.

Henry VII declared that his reign started on 21 August 1485, a day before Bosworth, so he could swiftly deal with those who had supported Richard III during the battle. Henry was fortunate that less than a quarter of England's temporal (non-church) peers fought against him at Bosworth; the rest had been killed or imprisoned already. Therefore the matter of dealing with 'traitors' was manageable and a certain degree of clemency could be shown to those willing to accept him as their sovereign. No legal action was taken against any man for supporting Richard III. Henry preferred to use Parliament to make adjustments to **Acts of Attainder**. A great many Yorkist attainders were repealed (both those that had been passed under Edward IV and Richard III) and an **Act of Indemnity** was passed securing Henry's followers against any legal action for their campaigns before Bosworth (see the section on Nobles). Only 30 of Richard's supporters had attainders passed against them, but this was a fairly modest number. Consequently, Henry gained the duchies of Gloucester and Norfolk, which aroused

Figure 1.2: Henry VII by an unknown artist (1505). Henry VII probably never posed for this portrait. Why do you think he is holding a rose?

 Key term

Act of Attainder: a statute (law) used by monarchs to punish without trial nobles or magnates who had committed an act of treason or serious crime against the Crown. Punishment could include revoking their property and hereditary titles, and typically the right to pass them on to their heirs. Attainders (meaning 'corruption of blood') could be reversed upon promises of loyalty: for example, Edward IV had reversed 86 of 120 when he claimed the throne.

Key term

Act of Indemnity: a statute (law) passed to protect someone who has committed an illegal act from legal penalties. They were used by monarchs to show clemency to those who had fought against them.

some protest from the nobles, but they were in no position to quarrel with the new king.

Henry VII dealt with the immediate threats to his throne in a relatively benevolent manner. The greatest threat to his throne was undoubtedly the Earl of Warwick, the ten-year-old nephew of Richard III. He was sent to the Tower of London almost immediately, although he was given relatively comfortable apartments there. The Earl of Surrey, who had fought for Richard III at Bosworth, was imprisoned until 1489 when Henry felt satisfied he could be trusted to remain loyal. The Earl of Northumberland, Henry Percy, had accompanied Richard to Bosworth although refused to commit his soldiers during the battle. Therefore Percy was briefly imprisoned, although he swore his allegiance to the new king. Consequently, Henry gave him the opportunity to prove his loyalty by returning to the North to take up his titles and posts later in 1485 on condition that he maintain the peace there.

From the outset, Henry VII made it clear that he was willing to employ prominent Yorkists as well as his personal adherents. On 7 October the Great Seal was entrusted to John Alcock (Bishop of Ely) and the Privy Seal to the Bishop of Exeter, both of whom had been loyal servants of Edward IV. For his personal secretary Henry chose a former exile, Richard Fox. There was no major shift in power in the localities of England or any attempts by Henry to pursue personal vendettas against those who had served another monarch. Only in the household appointments – which Richard had filled with personal, loyal servants – was there a complete change in personnel.

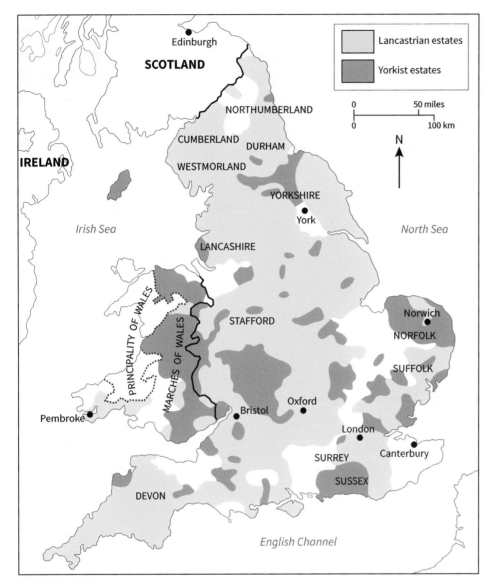

Figure 1.3: The division of England between Lancastrians and Yorkists during the Wars of the Roses 1455–85.

Conspiracies

It is generally agreed among historians (such as Carpenter (1997), Loades (1999) and Elton (1955)) that the first few conspiracies to depose the king, up until 1486, were feeble because they had no cause. The only two possible heirs to the throne were either locked up in the Tower of London, like the Earl of Warwick, or had declared loyalty to Henry VII and worked in the King's Council, such as John de la Pole, the Earl of Lincoln. Nevertheless, the new king was anxious about the North, which was a Yorkist stronghold. In March 1486 Henry made his first progress throughout the kingdom to show himself to his subjects. As he reached Lincoln, Henry heard that Lord Lovell, friend of Richard III, planned to attack York along with Sir Humphrey Stafford and his brother Sir Thomas, who schemed to seize Worcester. However, York welcomed Henry and Lovell's forces melted away when Henry promised to pardon their behaviour. Lovell sought refuge in Flanders at the

> **Speak like a historian: Cadwallader**
>
> During his coronation, Henry VII evoked the red dragon of Cadwallader, a medieval king, said to be the last in an ancient line to hold the title King of Britain. Tales of Cadwallader were popularised by Geoffrey of Monmouth who wrote the largely fictional *History of the Kings of Britain* around 1152, creating the national myth of King Arthur. King Arthur supposedly epitomised the kind of king England needed: adored by his subjects, strong in battle and just in law and order. During the Wars of the Roses, both the Yorkists and Lancastrians used images of a red or white dragon to associate themselves with Cadwallader.

court of Margaret of Burgundy. The Staffords took **sanctuary** at Culham Abbey but were nonetheless arrested and put in the Tower of London. The elder of the brothers, Humphrey, was executed but Thomas was pardoned.

In September 1486 Elizabeth of York gave birth to Arthur Tudor, which seemed to secure the dynasty. Given that Henry was only 30 years old, it was likely he would live long enough to see his heir come of age. However, a more serious conspiracy was afoot. Rumours about the princes in the Tower still circulated around much of the country, and one Oxford priest, Richard Symonds, seemingly decided to exploit this. He chose a young, unassuming boy named Lambert Simnel to be a pretender to the throne. Simnel was chosen to pretend to be the Earl of Warwick, who according to rumour had died in the Tower. This was helpful to the plotters because the government would not be able to exhibit the real heir and thereby disprove the claim. It was likely that John de la Pole (the same Earl of Lincoln who professed loyalty to Henry after Bosworth) was behind the scheme. The Earl of Lincoln was a natural leader of the Yorkist claimants, being the nephew of Edward IV and Richard III and Richard's chosen successor.

Margaret of Burgundy, sister of the Yorkist kings and Aunt of Lincoln, was central to this plot. She had many reasons to want to depose Henry. It was her brother, Richard III, who had been usurped. She had lost lucrative trading rights, and France – Burgundy's rival state – had seemed to gain those rights, having supported Henry. Margaret of Burgundy raised forces numbering 2000 men and sent the exiled Lord Lovell and the new plotter, the Earl of Lincoln, over to Ireland to meet with the Earl of Kildare, a strong Yorkist supporter and the most powerful magnate in Ireland, in May 1487. Having gained reinforcements from Kildare and proclaiming Simnel king, the pretenders landed in Lancashire on 4 June 1487. Henry VII had called a Great Council in February 1486 and raised an army, which marched to Stoke to meet the rebels. Henry himself was willing to fight with his 12 000 soldiers, against the rebels' 8000.

On 16 June 1487 Henry was victorious at Stoke and the Earl of Lincoln was killed, while Lovell died soon after. Simnel was given a job in the royal kitchens and the 25 or so Yorkist followers were given significant fines through an Act of Attainder. There were notably few executions as Henry tried to play down the threat Simnel had posed. Kildare made haste to repent, and the king, knowing he lacked the resources to strengthen his authority in Ireland, accepted his apology.

Historians have argued over the magnitude of the threat this posed; Carpenter (1997) has suggested that Henry was well supported in the campaign and therefore had little to fear, whereas Elton (1955) suggests that this scheme demonstrates the magnitude of Henry's problem in securing his throne. John Guy (1988) declared this was one of the most serious revolts because it had dynastic intentions and came so soon after Bosworth. Even Carpenter acknowledges that the Simnel plot was a serious threat, given who had supported it. It is perhaps no coincidence, that Henry, feeling unsettled, decided to crown Elizabeth of York as his queen on 25 November 1487 in an attempt to unite the nation. The Battle of Stoke rebellion marked the end of the Wars of the Roses according to almost all historians. Although Henry VII still had to face conspiracy and rebellion, he never again had to face an army in the field on English soil.

Perkin Warbeck

Undoubtedly the most threatening of the pretenders to the throne was the enigmatic Perkin Warbeck from Tournai in France. In 1491 he arrived in Cork, dressed in the finest silk clothes, making a great impression on the local population, which included many Yorkists. They took him for the Earl of Warwick, whose whereabouts was still the subject of rumour. He was received by Charles VIII of France in 1492. This was not wholly surprising, given that Henry was at war with France at the time (see the section on France). In the Treaty of Étaples with France in 1492, Henry VII made Charles promise not to protect any claimants to the English throne, so Warbeck had to find new lodgings. He was subsequently recognised by Margaret of Burgundy as her nephew Richard, Duke of Shrewsbury, one of the missing princes in the Tower. Henry responded by breaking off all trade with Flanders for two years, even though the English cloth trade depended on it. Late in 1493, Warbeck found an even more powerful protector, in the form of Maximilian, the newly elected Holy Roman Emperor. Maximilian recognised Warbeck as Richard IV, rightful king of England, and promised him full support in recovering the Crown. Luckily for Henry, Maximilian failed to back up his promises with sufficient arms or funding.

What made Warbeck's attempts more dangerous, were his English followers. Sir Robert Clifford, who went to Flanders to join the pretender (although there is some debate about whether he was merely spying for Henry) broke news of the conspiracy to Henry. One important man implicated in the Warbeck plot was Sir William Stanley, Henry's uncle by marriage, who had been crucial in his victory at Bosworth. He had been made Chamberlain of the King's Household and therefore the depth of the betrayal was significant. Stanley was executed in 1495, along with Lord Fitzwalter (a steward) and a number of lesser men. Despite the executions and arrests, Warbeck still attempted to invade. While his forces landed in Deal in July 1495, Warbeck stayed on the ship. Henry's soldiers were waiting and routed the invaders, leaving Warbeck to flee to Ireland. After a failed attempt to besiege Waterford for 11 days, Warbeck fled to Scotland. James IV was ready to offer Warbeck assistance. In 1496 a Scottish force crossed the border, burning and looting as they went, horrifying the young pretender, but Henry threatened James IV with invasion, forcing him to retreat (see the section on Scotland).

After returning to Ireland and finding the Earl of Kildare now loyal to Henry, Warbeck set sail for Cornwall, hoping to take advantage of a recent uprising

Key term

sanctuary: a safe haven, usually in a church. Fugitives from the law could take refuge in a sanctuary because the Church laws forbade anyone to be arrested within their walls. Under Henry VII, the Court of the King's Bench decided that sanctuary was a matter for common law and not the Pope. Therefore Henry VII was able to arrest and try the Staffords for treason. A **papal bull** was later issued vindicating Henry's actions and limiting the right of sanctuary in cases of treason.

ACTIVITY 1.2

The statements below could all be associated with a strong and secure monarchy. For each statement, discuss how far you think each is true about Henry VII. If you can, try to find examples from your notes to support your claims.

1. The king was a charismatic leader.
2. The king had a strong/ legitimate claim to the throne.
3. The king had an effective working relationship with the nobility.
4. The king was well supported by able men to help him govern.

Key term

Parliament: The highest court in the realm. Parliament's decisions were binding on all other courts and parliamentary statute overrode a judge's ability to interpret the law.

(see the section on Social Discontent and Rebellions). Again, he was driven out of Exeter and Taunton after very few joined him. Warbeck claimed sanctuary at Beaulieu Abbey, but in August 1497 signed a full confession, placing himself at Henry's mercy. Not wanting to make a martyr of Warbeck, Henry showed clemency. However, Warbeck tried to abscond in 1498 and this time, he was put in the stocks to be publicly humiliated, then placed in the Tower of London. Perkin Warbeck was executed in 1499 by hanging. A week later, the Earl of Warwick was beheaded; it seems his very existence was just too threatening to Henry, despite his having been on the throne for some 14 years by this time.

The Earl of Suffolk

On the execution of Warwick, one Yorkist claimant remained. He was Edmund de la Pole, Earl of Suffolk, brother of the rebellious Earl of Lincoln who had died at Stoke in 1487 and nephew of the Yorkist Edward IV and Richard III. Suffolk had reconciled himself to Henry's rule in 1485, at least on the surface. Elton (1955) described him as a 'romantic but unimpressive figure'[2] who was allowed to live at Henry's court, under the king's watchful eye. Suffolk held deep-seated reservations about Henry for refusing to elevate him to the dukedom his father had held. In July 1499 Suffolk fled to Guisnes, near the port of Calais, without licence. Though he returned to court after the King's messengers had persuaded him, and remained superficially loyal, it was not long before he broke away again. In October 1501, while assisting in the journey of Catherine of Aragon to England, he and his brother Richard fled to the court of Maximilian, the Holy Roman Emperor.

Once more a group of Yorkists gathered in Flanders, ready to invade. This might not have worried the king quite so much had his son Edmund not died in 1500, followed by the heir to his throne, Prince Arthur, in April 1502. Henry VII was left with the ten-year-old Prince Henry, who many contemporaries regarded as a weak child. Perhaps this explains Henry VII's ruthless actions. He rounded up and imprisoned any remaining relatives of Suffolk and in January 1504 persuaded **Parliament** to pass Acts of Attainder against 51 of them. This was the largest number of attainders passed by any parliament during his reign. There were still relatively few executions; the most significant was probably Sir James Tyrell, who was accused of murdering the princes in the Tower – whether this was true or not is still not known.

Henry VII used his spies to surround Suffolk and send information back to England. Henry managed to convince Maximilian to sign a treaty in June 1502 in which the Emperor agreed to expel the earl from his dominions in return for £10 000. Suffolk fled to Aix-la-Chapelle in 1504 but Henry continued to pursue the earl, clearly not satisfied the matter was over until he was imprisoned in England. At last in 1506 the Archduke Philip of Burgundy agreed to surrender the earl if Henry spared his life. The Earl of Suffolk was imprisoned in the Tower of London until 1513 when Henry VIII had him executed.

The Suffolk problem was dealt with effectively and demonstrates the firm grasp Henry had on the Crown after 17 years on the throne. It must not have felt that way for the king himself, however, for there was every reason to suggest that the safety of the Tudor dynasty depended too much on Henry's own life. There is evidence to suggest that in discussions about the succession in 1504, the claims of both

Buckingham and Suffolk were mentioned over that of Prince Henry. However, as Guy (1988) observes, the dynastic threat must not be exaggerated, as 'the striking feature of the period is not the prevalence but the absence of males of the royal blood'[3]. There were few serious rival claimants and most of the rebellions he faced were not dynastic in nature.

Government

Fifteenth-century government primarily centred around the person of the king and his immediate circle of advisers. The scope of government was limited. Expectations of government had been established in the 14th century as defending the realm, providing justice, peace and creating conditions for prosperity. Government under Henry VII consisted of increasingly formalised departments: the royal household, the Signet and Privy Seal offices, the Chancery, the Exchequer, the courts of King's Bench, Common Pleas, the assizes, justices of the peace and sheriffs offices. However, Lander (1980) suggests that their staff, numbering no more than 1500 men, were exceedingly small, and powers in enforcement extremely limited as there was no police force. The formal institutions of government were almost exclusively financial (the Exchequer) and legal (the Chancery, Privy Seal and Signet Offices).

Historians have long debated the extent to which Henry VII was a 'new monarch' who governed in a more modern manner than his predecessors. This has perhaps been because of a temptation to trace the origins of the vast changes undertaken by Henry VIII back to this reign. More modern historians, such as Chrimes (1977) have tended to play down any reforms made under Henry VII and have attributed these to a political evolution or in reaction to events, rather than forming part of any programme of modernisation. In fact, historians have suggested that Henry's methods of governing became more tyrannical and less modern, because of his ever-increasing reliance upon a small band of trusted advisers as he discovered more sedition. Figure 1.4 shows how the government of the country worked.

ACTIVITY 1.3

Use your notes to annotate the diagram (and add in departments where they fit) with whether the government was likely to help Henry VII restore law and order or to hinder him.

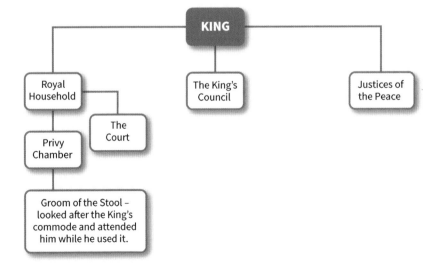

Figure 1.4: How Henry VII's government operated.

Key term

demesne: refers to the land held by the king or nobles not let out to tenants, effectively their great personal estates.

Key term

factions: power blocs within the court. Factionalism plagued many monarchs as personalities at court sought to group together to further their own careers, usually at the expense of others.

The Court

Attachment to the Royal household had been used as a way of gaining power and influence since Henry IV, but Henry VII (and the Tudors who followed him) made it a central element in assuring loyalty to the monarch. Henry VII used the demesne-based magnates Hastings, Daubeney and Herbert (see the section on Nobles) as his Lord Chamberlain of the Household. Other men who dominated their localities were used after 1471 as senior officers at court, for example Lord Willoughby de Broke became Lord Steward under Henry. Even those given no office but used in ceremonies conducted at court, such as the Earl of Derby, were recognised as being influential, because most saw the court as a place where the nobility could counsel, and therefore influence, the king. Henry VII followed Edward IV and Richard III's example by recruiting the gentry to service in the royal household.

Francis Bacon popularised the view that Henry VII avoided factionalism at court (something that later Tudor monarchs were criticised for). However, the historian Steven Gunn (1995) suggests that intrigues such as Attorney General Sir James Hobart's resignation in 1507 was as a result of factional politics. The downfall of Sir William Stanley, the Lord Chamberlain, was as a result of factional politics according to historian Roger Lockyer (1983). Stanley was found to be in treasonable communication with the pretender to the throne, Perkin Warbeck, and as a result Henry VII took steps to improve his security by establishing stricter controls on the Privy Chamber – his innermost sanctum – during the 1490s.

Privy Chamber

The king sought privacy, therefore created a private set of rooms with only select members of staff in attendance. However, the quest for royal favour followed him no matter how much he tried to retreat from it. Hugh Denys (Henry VII's Groom of the Stool) amassed a small fortune by accepting monies to mention suitors to the king in more vulnerable moments. In some ways, the influence that Henry VII accrued made central politics more difficult to control, because it caused an intensification of pressure on the king from those wanting his power deployed to further their own standing.

Other principal offices

Perhaps one of the more extraordinary features of Henry VII's government was the long tenure of office enjoyed by those whom the king had appointed. It is clear Henry would only appoint those he trusted and saw no reason to change them as long as they remained loyal. Only four Chancellors were appointed throughout Henry's reign, and two of these – John Morton and William Warham – held the office for almost 20 years between them. Both the first two Chancellors appointed were men who had experience of rule under the Yorkist king, Edward IV. John Morton took the office from 1487 and remained in post until his death in 1500. Two Treasurers held office across the whole reign. Thomas Howard, Earl of Surrey was rehabilitated, remarkably, after he had fought for Richard III at Bosworth in 1489 and was later given responsibility for the North (after Northumberland's murder). His military achievements in the Yorkshire rising secured Henry's favour and served as Lord High Treasurer from 1501 to 1522. He was another man of clear political ambition and aptitude and his appointment demonstrates Henry's talent for selecting the most valuable servants, not just the most loyal.

Some historians have criticised Henry VII for concentrating power in the hands of a few, and running his government through his household, instead of the traditional institutions. However, it is clear that the conspiracies to claim the throne had taken their toll on the king. The depth of Stanley's betrayal seems to have affected the king a great deal and he began to retreat into his Privy Chamber more often to avoid government officials. Withdrawal from the public was not uncommon for medieval kings who felt under threat and Henry VII was reverting to this fairly common practice.

Councils

King's Council

It has been suggested that Henry VII innovated by professionalising the Council because he hired men on the basis of their talent, not their nobility. Many historians now agree that Henry VII followed precedents established by the Yorkist monarch Edward IV, both in the patterns of organisation of the Council and, to an extent, personnel (30 had served under Edward IV and Richard III). Henry surrounded himself with those whom he felt he could trust, although it is clear that Henry did appoint nobles on the Council. The Earl of Oxford was appointed Lord Chamberlain and his former opponent at Bosworth, the Earl of Surrey, was appointed Lord Treasurer. Of the total number of councillors, it seems there were 43 peers, 45 courtiers, 61 churchmen, 27 lawyers and 49 men classed as 'officials'. What was new was the amount of power the 'new men' wielded. They were mostly of the gentry, typically trained in the law, and had either been in exile with Henry or had served under Edward IV.

The King's Council advised the king over matters of state and acted on his behalf in a judicial capacity. Henry was often but not always present at meetings, although it is clear from documents taken from the time that he was very much in control of what was discussed there. Different areas of business were dealt with by what would be known today as sub-councils or sub-committees but it is important to note that most of these were never formalised under Henry: for example, the Star Chamber was named thus because of where those councillors met – in the Chamber with a highly decorated ceiling – rather than being reflective of any specific duties performed there. Over 240 men were eligible to sit on the Council: in reality regular attendees numbered between six and eight in the smaller meetings and approximately 40 across all the smaller groups. The most important

 Hidden voices

John Morton

John Morton was a key figure in Henry VII's government, although there has been scant research carried out about his life. Davies (1987) suggests that they built a trusting relationship in 1483–85 in planning Richard's usurpation, even though they probably never met during this time.

It is clear from documents at the time, such as accounts of meetings in the Council Learned in the Law, that he was an astute politician and perceptive lawyer. The fact he served under Yorkist, **Lancastrian** and Tudor Kings suggests he was able to adapt to new regimes and act cautiously making good use of his resources.

ACTIVITY 1.4

1. Create a diagram like the one in Figure 1.5 for yourself and annotate it to show what each group/committee was responsible for. There will be overlap in some cases.

2. Then shade each committee to show whether it was primarily concerned with the administration of finance or legal matters.

attendees who sat in several 'sub-committees' were the clerics Bishop Morton (the Chancellor, who probably presided) and Richard Fox, Lord Daubeney, Lovell (a knight), lawyer Edmund Dudley and Reginald Bray (an administrator).

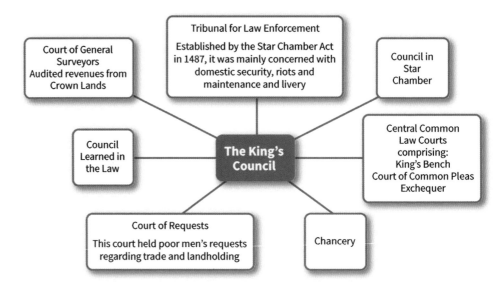

Figure 1.5: The separate committees that formed the King's Council.

Council in the Star Chamber

Once thought of as a new law court established to control the nobility of the realm, the Star Chamber was not a separate body from the King's Council and most of the business that came before it was as a result of disputes between subjects. Between four and 40 councillors met in the Star Chamber. The Council was dominated by the Lord Chancellor (John Morton, Archbishop of Canterbury 1487–1500 and William Warham who took the same offices 1504–15). The Chancellor was supported by the Secretary of State, Keeper of the Privy Seal and the Treasurer.

The punishment for rioting was a major concern of Henry VII – 59% of the cases adjudicated by the Council in the Star Chamber were private suits alleging rioting (of varying scale and magnitude). Several statutes were passed to deal with riots involving 40 or more people and these cases had to be sent straight to the Star Chamber, so they could mete out adequate punishment. Even so, punishments were relatively moderate – in the form of fines, or imprisonment if the fine could not be paid. Cases of criminal law were largely left to the common law courts and the Star Chamber was not seen as an instrument of coercion. Rather, it was a place where subjects went for speedy justice, which the King's Council had always been able to offer. The necessity of the Star Chamber also perhaps reveals the extent to which lawlessness still pervaded England under Henry VII.

Council Learned in the Law

Some of the councillors who sat in the Star Chamber might also form the Council of the Learned. However, it was the Council Learned that earned a specific identity in Henry VII's reign. Established in 1495 to deal with the king's finances, it reached its zenith around 1500 when members met almost daily. Guy (1988) has argued that the rule of Henry VII and the Council Learned was 'personal monarchy at its height'.[4] Henry used the Council Learned to supervise the collection of debts due from bonds and recognisances (see the section on Nobles), and it acted as a tribunal court. Not much is known about the membership or activities of this Council before 1500, however Sir Reginald Bray, a former servant of Margaret Beaufort, presided over it until 1503. Other prominent members included Richard Empson (who took over from Bray) and Edmund Dudley. There were also two bishops, Roger Leybourne and Robert Sherbourne who sat on this Council at one time or another. Nearly all of these men were councillors of the Duchy of Lancaster and were the King's most trusted advisers and executive officers. The fact that their power derived from their place on the Council demonstrates Henry VII's intense personal control over the governance of his realm.

There was undoubtedly some overlap in the work of the Star Chamber and Council Learned – particularly over the hearing of private suits. The distinction is clearer in the area of government prosecutions and the collection of Crown debts – the Council Learned was formed with this specific purpose in mind. The bulk of prosecutions ended with the imposition of fines, and it seems most cases were referred to this Council when action was needed swiftly, rather than waiting for the cumbersome common courts to hear the case. Perhaps unsurprisingly this Council was deeply unpopular and gained a reputation for being ruthless in the pursuit of monies for the Crown.

The Provincial Councils

In addition to the central King's Council, there were two other Councils that served a similar function in order to keep the peace in the distant parts of Henry's kingdom. The Council of Wales and the Marches, established in 1471, was based in Ludlow, Shropshire and was overseen by John Alcock. It was a challenging task. Poverty was widespread, cattle were easy to steal and sell and the plethora of courts, laws and customs meant that evading punishment was easy. It was not until Henry VIII that the Council was strengthened.

The Council of the North, which met intermittently during Henry VII's reign, was primarily concerned with preventing foreign invasion and maintaining law and order. This Council was run by the former ally of Richard III, the Earl of Northumberland, until his murder in 1489 (see the section on Social discontent and rebellions). He was employed extensively in the field of tax collection, and indeed this was his business when he was murdered. After Northumberland's death Henry divided responsibility for the work of the Council between Lord Dacre (a southern noble) and Thomas Howard, Earl of Surrey. It was clear that Henry VII was ensuring his own personal control by dividing the responsibility. In order to extend his royal authority in the provinces, he ordered the King's Council in London to monitor the provincial councils.

Parliament

Although recognised as a specific institution, Parliament was not part of the ordinary government of the country. It met only when the king called it, and Henry would not call it unless he had specific reason to do so. Parliament was called to obtain supplies of money in extraordinary circumstances or to pass statutes. Parliament had to consent if taxes were to be raised and laws passed by Parliament were superior to all others. Parliament consisted of two chambers that met separately: the Upper Chamber consisted of the Lords Temporal and Lords Spiritual – noblemen, bishops and abbots – while the Lower Chamber was made up of knights of the shire and representatives of the boroughs, who became known as the Commons. It brought together the most powerful people in the kingdom and was therefore a useful barometer for testing how royal initiatives would be received. Although Henry VII did not need parliamentary backing or approval, he certainly sought it, which perhaps demonstrates its evolution towards becoming an integral part of government.

The Commons were far less important than the Lords, who also constituted the Great Council, or Magnum Consilium, which the king might call to ask for advice. Henry VII called the Great Council five times during his reign, and although little evidence remains as to who attended or what was discussed there, these were significant meetings. One Great Council in June 1491 authorised an intended war against France and subsequent levy of a subsidy of a tenth (an extraordinary tax). This example demonstrates that the meetings of the Great Council were almost always concerned with the threat of war or rebellion, and therefore performed an indispensable function for Henry VII.

The Commons were strictly excluded from the Upper Chamber and had an official known as the Speaker to address the king there. Members of Parliament had to be knights or men of similar standing in society. Seventy-four knights for the shires and 222 burgesses for the boroughs were elected for each Parliament – 296 in total. The franchise in the shires was restricted to those who held freehold land worth more than 40 shillings, or £2, per annum, which was a fairly small number of people. In the boroughs the franchise could vary, including anything from a handful of people to all the male inhabitants. Each of Henry's seven Parliaments had a different Speaker: Thomas Lovell; John Mordaunt; Thomas Fitzwilliam; Richard Empson; Robert Drury; Thomas Englefield and Edmund Dudley. All of the Speakers were lawyers, except Dudley, and all received knighthoods from Henry for their services. Henry VII maintained practice already established under Yorkist kings with regard to the 'Commons' and there is little innovation of which to speak, in the way this part of Parliament was used.

Henry VII continued the pattern established by medieval kings for the most part. Parliament would be Henry's weapon, to employ and dispense with at his bidding. Henry called six Parliaments in 23 years; five of which were called in the first ten years of his reign and only one after 1497. Its sessions sat for a total of 21 months, in a reign that lasted nearly a quarter of a century. Henry used Parliament to recognise his title as king in 1485, pass Acts of Attainder and vote on taxes. In this way Parliament can be seen as a means by which Henry VII extended royal authority. Probably the most significant of parliamentary meetings was that held after the Battle of Stoke in 1487, where six statutes were passed to suppress sedition and disorder, as well as attainting (passing an Act of Attainder against) 28 rebels who had fought for Simnel. However, they also took votes on less significant statues that reformed a part of the administrative functions of governments. For example, Parliament was primarily concerned with acts that protected the English cloth industry, clarified the responsibilities of Justices of the Peace and to prevented the keeping of retainers (uniformed followers). Few of the statutes passed under Henry's reign can be regarded as historically significant or particularly modern in their outlook. After 1504 Henry expressly stated that he was not minded to call Parliament unless a great and urgent cause necessitated it, which perhaps demonstrates his change in attitude towards governance towards the end of his life.

Justice

The lasting damage caused by the Wars of the Roses was surely the erosion of law and order throughout the realm. Henry VII knew that to secure his dynasty he had to restore this. The vast majority of the work of the King's Council was associated with maintaining the king's peace. Lander (1980)[5] suggests that there was an 'impressive' hierarchy of law courts, ranging from maritime matters, equity courts to courts of chivalry and claims; however, some of these were rather obscure and hardly used. The vast majority of claims that went through the courts, and the single greatest problem that tested Tudor courts, was the use of violence that erupted over land disputes (Gunn, 1995). This was because the law surrounding land ownership was extremely complex – land was a major source of wealth and status, and those who disputed it were often the most powerful men in the land.

At the lowest level were manorial or local courts, which organised agricultural arrangements for the year and settled civil matters worth less than 40 shillings, criminal matters such as cattle wounding or damage to crops, assaults not leading to bloodshed and the damaging of timber. Here the leading townsmen often wielded control or arbitrated disputes, demonstrating the participatory nature of the early modern justice systems. Strangers and professional criminals – horse thieves or burglars – were treated extremely harshly, as were vagrants. Manorial courts were also able to produce by-laws that almost gave them the status of a mini-local parliament in some areas.

The Shire Courts, run by the Justices of the Peace (selected from the country gentry), could hear cases relating to land, debts and contracts. They could exercise jurisdiction for keeping the peace and could arrest people on suspicion, hearing all criminal matters from trespasses to murder. The JP sessions in the Shire Courts became the basis of criminal courts under Henry VII. Approximately nine-tenths of cases put before the King's Bench originated in cases bought to the JPs, demonstrating their increasing role in the justice system. However, complaints were bought before Parliament about JPs abusing their position just as much as had happened under previous kings, so law and order was probably no better organised under Henry VII.

There was no police force in Tudor England. Parish constables, Justices of the Peace and Sheriffs took on the role of maintaining the peace, although they varied greatly in ability and had pitiful resources. Even if the accused were caught, had an accurate writ bought against them and made it to trial, there was no certainty that justice would be done. Juries of 12 were drawn from the locality, and were therefore susceptible to bribery, intimidation or blackmail. Even if found guilty, the defendant often disappeared before punishment could be meted out and Sheriffs were open to bribes to 'lose sight' of defendants. Henry sought to remedy

Key term

bonds: written contracts of good behaviour given to nobles to ensure they kept the peace. Bonds specified a penalty (in the form of a fine) if the noble failed to maintain peace in their area and therefore bound the nobility to the king's wishes.

some of these problems by employing freelance informers to bring actions against Sheriffs who took bribes. A statute in 1504 made Sheriffs clearly responsible for the upkeep of county gaols, and fines were levied if prisoners escaped. JPs were given responsibility to watch over Sheriffs. In the same way he used patronage to reward good service (see the section on Nobles) Henry VII used the lure of royal favour to keep Sheriffs and JPs from abusing their positions, or at least from doing so conspicuously. In fact, dismissal for abusing one's position was very rare. Henry VII passed 21 statutes, enhancing the responsibility of the JPs and bestowing new powers upon them. Therefore the prestige surrounding the office of JP grew and made it a more attractive proposition for gentry to undertake. JPs could arrest suspects, bail them, take **bonds** from troublemakers, arbitrate in local issues and investigate crimes.

The principal courts of the realm were the King's Bench and the Common Pleas. The King's Bench heard a wide variety of civil cases, mostly based on acts of trespass causing damage to the plaintiff (the person who initiates a lawsuit). Both courts were presided over by a Chief Justice and sat for no more than three months in the year, somewhat limiting provision. The effectiveness of these courts was further restricted by the fact that judges only sat for three hours on a given day. However, twice a year the judges from central London courts set out on the assizes. The Justices of the Assize were organised into six circuits and were travelling courts, which visited towns on average twice a year. Cases could take between 18 months and several years to try and so the justice system was, at best, inefficient.

The Chancery grew in its business and functions during the Wars of The Roses, but expanded even further under Henry VII (and further again under Henry VIII). The Chancellors themselves, Archbishop John Morton 1487–1500 and William Warham 1504–15, were partly responsible for this. Cases were bought to the Chancery in part because litigants could deal with one of the king's chief ministers, giving it an aura of authority and esteem. Expert judges, led by the Chancellor himself, reached decisions based on evidence presented, rather than in the common courts in which lawyers engaged in extravagant verbal exchanges to try and win juries over. The Chancery largely took on work involving the enforcement of contracts, landholding arrangements and creating and interpreting wills and it could revise the decisions of lesser courts. The Chancery therefore gained a reputation under Henry VII for being flexible, speedy and powerful.

Finally, the King's Council itself arbitrated on disputes among the nobility, and was one of the chief ways in which Henry VII maintained peace in the countryside. It had taken on this arbiter role since the 14th century as an extension of the king's personal role as the fount of justice. The Council specialised in dealing with politically sensitive cases, such as landowners, including nobles, who could be summoned before the Council. For example, Lords Dudley and Grey of Powys were both imprisoned after the King's Council heard the case when they became involved in an affray. The Council was used when royal power was needed to impose a settlement, and Henry VII followed the Yorkists in their interest for and dynamism in judicial matters. Henry VII even took notes himself during witness depositions, as he did when Lord Dacre was called before the Council following the riot in 1489 (see the section on Social Discontent and Rebellions). Obviously the sheer mass of petitions calling for the intervention of royal justice meant that Henry VII could not oversee all of the cases, so his councillors would hear them in his absence.

Historians have also noted how moderate most forms of punishment were under Henry VII. Punishments were mainly given in the form of fines and it is suggested this is because the King chose to avoid direct confrontations in the courts. Guy (1988) has suggested that Henry VII did restore law and order to a large extent, although this was not really achieved through reform of the legislative process, but through his use of bonds and recognisances (see the section on Nobles). The use of bonds meant that Henry could personally determine the behaviour of the nobility and gentry without reference to the law. This was an undoubtedly calculated measure to ensure that nobles took responsibility for upholding order in their domains, but it also strengthened the authority of the Crown too.

Royal finance

Chrimes (1977) has suggested that no other king had succeeded the throne with so little financial experience or resources as did Henry VII. Henry has been described as shrewd and calculating, which he had to be – given his precarious position on the throne. Elton (1955) suggests that he was eager for money without being miserly, a trait that all the Tudors seem to share. Criticisms levelled at Henry for being miserly or greedy could perhaps be explained by his early life being reliant upon the charity of the Duke of Brittany, although it should be noted that Henry spent a fortune on a lavish court, which impressed foreign visitors and displayed liberality in giving gifts (as seen in the meticulous records his clerks kept).

Undoubtedly one of the most significant pressures facing Henry VII upon receiving the Crown was how to restore the royal position. Henry had learnt that the Lancastrian kings before him were weak because they were poor. Henry saw that strong kingship required an accumulation of wealth under the Crown. He did not set up any new sources of revenue but has been praised for the way in which he managed to exploit existing revenues in a more systematic way than had been achieved previously, particularly given his lack of experience. Again perhaps the only new thing about Henry's approach to financial administration was his sustained personal supervision of it.

Ordinary revenue: Crown lands and feudal dues

The need to tackle the issue of the management and accounting of revenue accrued from Crown lands was an urgent one, particularly after the Acts of Attainder and Resumption were passed, increasing the amount of land falling under the Crown's supervision considerably. Henry was shocked to find that there were no central records of exactly what the Crown owned. Significant reform of the **Exchequer** was needed. Henry achieved this by tightening measures that had been introduced by the Yorkist kings in what is known as the 'chamber system'. Collection of revenues from Crown lands, feudal dues and most other sources apart from customs was diverted from the Exchequer directly into Henry's own household. The Exchequer was slow moving because of its complex system of audits, but now local receivers became responsible for collecting revenues in cash and remitting them directly to the Chamber of the Household, where Henry

Key term

The **Exchequer**: a court that specialised in collecting the king's revenues. Only small amounts of litigation stemmed from this court since its primary function was administrative. The office of the Chancellor of the Exchequer was held for the whole reign by Sir Thomas Lovell, which he combined with the office of Treasurer of the Royal Household. There were only five Chancellors of the Exchequer throughout Henry VII's reign and so his reliance on trusted members of the court continued in areas of finance too.

could keep tighter control of them. As a result, collection of revenue became more efficient.

Historians have argued about whether the subsequent increases in Crown revenue was as a result of the increased size of royal lands or the better management of them. It is clear, however, that Henry VII enjoyed the greatest landed estate of any monarch since William the Conqueror. The revenue received from Crown lands increased from £22 000 in 1485 to almost £40 000 in 1509. Henry gained land throughout his reign. He benefited from his uncle Jasper Tudor's lack of an heir when he died in 1495. When Sir William Stanley was executed for treason in 1495 his lands were seized by the Crown, which also boosted revenue. Even the death of Prince Arthur in 1502 saw lands revert back to the Crown and this bought in a further £6000 to the household. Henry VII was far more reluctant than Yorkist kings to give land to foster loyalty among his nobles, and his consequent retention of land also strengthened the position of the Crown.

It is noted by Gunn (1995) that the expansion of the royal demesne, which had begun under Edward IV, led to Henry VII's holding five times more land than Henry VI by the end of his reign. What was remarkable was not really the amount of land per se, but that Henry VII was gradually tipping the balance between noble and royal landholdings, re-establishing the power of the Crown. Land was of course worth much more than the revenue it produced, since it bought lordship over men, as tenants could be called upon for military service or to sit on juries (see also the section on Acts of Attainder).

Henry VII and his agents exploited feudal dues with zeal and increasing efficiency (much to the disgruntlement of the nobility). In 1501 he declared all major landowners 'tenants-in-chief', which meant he could seize lands upon the death of a noble. Wardship (where the king could oversee land if the rightful heir was a minor) was exploited so that by 1503 a new post was created called Master of Wards. Henry charged 'livery' fines to recover lands from wardship upon nobles coming of age and 'relief', which was paid to the king as land was inherited. In 1502, Robert Willoughby de Broke had to pay £400 for livery of his lands. When land was seized from families due to disloyalty, 'Escheats' were charged as payment for the administration of it. Heiresses also had to pay marriage dues to the king, which brought in small but significant amounts to the Exchequer. In 1508 Henry created a new official post, although Empson and Dudley had been performing the task for years. The 'Surveyor of the King's Prerogative' investigated infringements upon the king's rights. In 1487 dues brought in less than £350 per annum, but by 1507 owing to the efforts of his agents, dues brought in over £6000 to the Exchequer. Feudal aid could also be levied on special occasions to pay for a particular event. For example when Prince Arthur was knighted in 1504 or when his daughter Margaret was married, Henry raised £30 000 from the nobility to contribute to the ceremony.

Bonds and recognisances (see the section on Nobles) were written agreements to ensure the good behaviour of the nobility. In 1491 the Marquis of Dorset signed bonds totalling £10 000 promising his loyalty and maintaining the peace. Fines levied by courts increased under Henry VII although records are much more sketchy on how much this brought in to the Exchequer, as fines were not usually collected in cash and amounts varied year on year for obvious reasons.

As his predecessors had done, Henry exercised his right to tax both imports and exports. Henry VII used two types of customs duties to pay for the defence of the realm, particularly the garrison permanently stationed at Calais. Prerogative duties were placed on the export of wool, leather and cloth. This was less lucrative than it might sound due to the decline in the wool trade during Henry VII's reign: it brought in £30 000 to the Crown – under Edward IV this had been as high as £70 000. Parliament granted him tonnage (on wine) and poundage (the right to tax goods) for life, as it had Richard III had before him. For the first ten years of his reign this brought in approximately £33 000 per year, increasing to £40 000 annually thereafter.

Extraordinary revenue including Parliamentary grants

Parliament sanctioned extraordinary grants in times when the realm needed defending or wars were to be fought abroad. In 1486 (and again in 1487) Parliament passed the Act of Resumption, which recovered on behalf of the Crown all properties that had been given away since 1455 (before the Wars of the Roses), which bought huge tracts of land under Henry's control. The traditional parliamentary grant was named the **Fifteenth and Tenth** and bought in a fixed sum from each community – approximately £30 000 in total each time it was levied. Theoretically this tax was levied on one-fifteenth the value of goods in rural areas and one-tenth the value in urban areas. Parliament granted eight of the Fifteenth and Tenths during Henry's reign, three in 1491 to assist in the invasion of France and two in 1496 to deal with the Scots (see the section on Relationships with Scotland and other foreign powers). Henry VII requested a parliamentary subsidy in 1489 to pay for archers to defend Brittany. This would be based on individual income and sparked the Northern rising, which resulted in the death of the Earl of Northumberland, the king's tax-collector in the North (see the section on Social discontent and rebellions). This subsidy only raised £25 000 out of the expected £100 000 as many simply refused to pay. However, over the course of his reign, Henry VII managed to raise £282 000 through parliamentary taxation alone, which was a substantial achievement.

Henry VII looked to other sources of extraordinary revenue as well. In times of crisis (see the section on Relationships with Scotland and other foreign powers) Henry could request a benevolence, which was effectively a grant with no repayment from his nobility. In 1491 he raised £48 500 to send an army to France this way. Similarly, the clerics could be forced to offer their help and in 1489 the Archdioceses of Canterbury and York voted £25 000 be donated towards the cost of the French war. Henry also sold church appointments (for example the Archdeaconry of Buckingham cost £300), and although this raised a lot less money it perhaps shows the detailed way in which the early Tudor government sought to exploit even the smallest revenue streams. Selling judicial offices was certainly in breach of custom, but Henry was bent on demanding a premium for offices of profit. For example, he twice sold the chief justiceship of the Court of Common Pleas for £333 and Dr John Yonge paid £1000 on appointment to the post of Master of the Rolls. Henry was fortunate in that several of his bishops died between 1500 and 1504: the king could receive the revenue that would fall to the bishop until he

Key term

Fifteenth and Tenth: a subsidy based on a fraction of the value of moveable, personal goods from each community. These were based in one fifteenth for rural inhabitants and one tenth for urban areas and royal demesne lands.

appointed a new one. Henry saw a bonus of £6000 per annum for the four years mentioned due to this. Perhaps the most significant form of extraordinary revenue was the French Pension that Henry received as part of the Treaty of Étaples in 1492 (see the section on Relationships with Scotland and other foreign powers). It was a sort of bribe offered by the king of France to remove English soldiers from French soil, which earned Henry a noteworthy £159 000 (to be paid at £5000 per annum).

None of the received myths surrounding Henry VII is more widely accepted than that which suggests he was miserly or given to avarice. Perhaps this stems from contemporary accounts, which suggest Henry kept hoards of cash in his Chamber. Chamber finance was run on cash receipts, and Henry's reputed bags of gold may have made him seem rich in comparison with monarchs whose income came in 'assignments' or credits. But in fact he was poor in relation to the leading monarchs of Europe – the Holy Roman Emperor enjoyed an annual income of approximately £1 100 000, whereas Henry's income is estimated at £113 000. Therefore, far from being a miser, Henry had to be lavish in his spending in order to display his wealth and maintain his standing on the European stage. He went further than previous monarchs in stamping his mark on his palaces. He spent thousands on decorating everything with the Beaufort portcullis, the 'Tudor Rose', the Richmond greyhound, the Cadwallader dragon and the Hawthorn Bush. Everything from ceilings to stained glass windows to flags, banners and horses' harnesses were emblazoned with these symbols. It is estimated that he spent just under £300 000 on jewels and gold plate. In 1503 he donated a vast amount of money to Westminster Abbey to build a chapel in his name (it was not completed in his lifetime). No other monarch, save perhaps Henry V, had spent so much on propaganda.

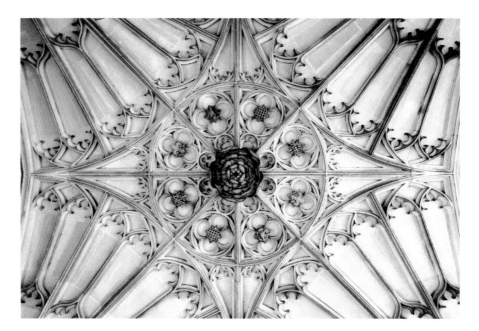

Figure 1.6: This ceiling features the Tudor Rose in the centre (a mix of the Yorkist white with Lancastrian red roses) surrounded by the portcullis, which was the symbol for the House of Beaufort. This is one of the many ways Henry used his wealth to demonstrate the power of the monarchy.

It is perhaps odd that Henry VII never spent money on a standing army, although he created the Yeomen of the Guard, whose number reached 200 by 1598. Henry also failed to find new sources of income for the Crown, as some historians have noted; it only took his son one war with France to completely wipe out all that he had accrued. The political costs of relentlessly pursuing revenues for the Crown have also been remarked upon by historians including Gunn (1995) and Carpenter (1997). Some historians have even suggested that Henry VII was fortunate to die when he did because there would almost certainly have been a major rebellion against revenue collection (see Chapter 2 on how Henry VIII countered this ill-feeling). However, Henry was successful in returning royal income, in real terms, to the levels of the later 14th century (it had collapsed under Henry VI) and managed to project an image as a wealthy monarch in the eyes of his contemporaries, which was perhaps his biggest achievement.

Domestic policies

Enclosure

Land had been farmed in an open-field system in the medieval period. Land surrounding villages was divided into strips and shared among villagers, and decisions about farming practices were decided collectively. Stretches of common land were left for the people to graze their animals. This practice was increasingly challenged during the 15th century by enclosure. This was occurring most frequently in the Midlands, where land was more suited to sheep farming than growing arable crops. In certain cases enclosures led to evictions and occasionally vagabondage (vagabonds were people without land or employment). The **engrossing** of farms was more common under Henry VII but was closely associated with **enclosure** and thought of as unjust by many contemporaries.

Henry VII passed two pieces of legislation against enclosures in 1489. An act forbidding engrossing on the Isle of Wight was aimed at limiting depopulation and is thought to have had a strategic aim, given the importance of having a population capable of defending the island. A second act, applicable to the whole country, forbade converting arable land to pasture and the destruction of dwelling places. This was probably a response to worries about depopulation, loss of tax revenue and social unrest. The enforcement of this act was left to landlords, the very ones who stood to gain the most from enclosure, so perhaps unsurprisingly it was poorly enforced. Wood (2002) has suggested that outbreaks of violence increased at the turn of the 16th century and were an increasing problem for all the Tudor monarchs, although much less so for Henry VII.

Vagabonds and beggars

Along with the social ills caused by enclosure, Henry VII sought to moderate some of the harsher penalties that had been imposed on vagabonds and beggars in the reign of Richard II. He reduced the punishment for vagabonds to being put in the stocks for three days and nights with only bread and water as sustenance, after which they should be sent away from the parish. He later implemented a further reduction to one day and one night in the stocks. Beggars who were not able to work were to be sent back to the 'hundred' (a division of a county) where they had previously lived, were best known or were born.

Key terms

engrossing: a practice that consolidated two or more farms to increase the profit of a unit.

enclosure: the fencing off of common land. Once enclosed, these uses of the land become restricted to the owner, and it ceased to be land for commons.

Relationships with Scotland and other foreign powers

Henry VII has been criticised for pursuing a reactive foreign policy, which was subordinate to other more pressing domestic issues. This view sees him used as a pawn in the great European plays for power. However, Chrimes (1977), Storey (1968) and Lockyer (1983) have highlighted similarities between Henry's domestic and foreign policy; that his primary concern was his security. Henry's diplomatic actions were all designed to further his own dynasty, and therefore he was willingly defensive. More recently, historians such as Arthurson (1994) and Currin (1993) have challenged this view and have suggested that Henry VII was not very peaceful and that he was willing to spend money on promoting his royal image abroad.

Figure 1.7: Europe in 1485. England was an island and therefore vulnerable to attack, particularly because England had no military forces at her disposal. Calais was still controlled by England and remained a vital foothold on the continent. Antwerp played an essential role in the cloth industry, which was vital to the economy of England.

France

Traditional hostilities towards France were far from dead when Henry VII acceded to the throne in 1485. Although Henry initiated a one-year truce with France in 1485, which was later extended to last until January 1489, tensions still simmered. Materially, England still possessed Calais, a foothold in France, which created tension between the two nations. These factors, along with his drive to secure recognition for his dynasty, led Henry to secure a marriage alliance for his son Arthur with Catherine (the younger daughter of Ferdinand of Aragon and Isabella of Castile, whose marriage united the territories that became known as Spain). Spain was extremely ambitious and had designs on French territory in the Pyrenees. In exchange for marriage, Henry had to promise his support against the French, should the Spanish monarchs require it. It was a quarrel over the small territory of Brittany (Henry's shelter when he was an exiled claimant) that was to drag England into European affairs for the first time since the Wars of the Roses began. France was surely the most powerful of the European nations in the latter part of the 15th century, with a sizeable population of 15 million and a highly professionalised army. When Charles VIII acceded to the throne aged 13, his sister Anne of Beaujeu, acting as his regent, set France's sights on recovering the valuable Duchy of Brittany. The Duke of Brittany (Francis II) was desperate to preserve Breton independence, but was elderly and only had two daughters. Henry VII agreed on intervention to prevent French expansion, but in order to share the burden of providing aid, he made alliances with the Holy Roman Emperor, Maximilian of Austria (who belonged to the Habsburg Dynasty), and Ferdinand of Aragon, who were also keen on limiting French supremacy.

Anne of Beaujeu raised an army to send to Brittany in 1487, prompting Maximilian to commit 1500 troops to Brittany's aid, along with Ferdinand's 1000. Henry was in an awkward position, since if the French gained complete control of the southern shore of the English Channel, England's security would naturally be threatened. However, Henry had signed a truce with France and he did not want to jeopardise this. The compromise was to send a few hundred volunteers under Lord Scales to Britanny's aid, while attempting to mediate a truce. The French resoundingly defeated the Bretons at Saint-Aubin-du-Cormier in July 1488, and Francis died some months later. Henry VII attempted a diplomatic solution by allying with Maximilian and Ferdinand. The Treaty of Redon was signed with Brittany in 1489 committing Henry to supplying 6000 men to defend the territory if the Bretons paid their expenses. Henry tried to raise the £100 000 necessary through parliamentary subsidy, but it provoked a rising in Yorkshire. His allies also proved unreliable as Maximilian had committed troops in Hungary and Spanish soldiers were recalled to take part in the conquest of Granada. Therefore the small-scale expedition to Brittany was a failure. In December 1491 Charles VIII captured Rennes and married Anne of Brittany. Charles also retaliated by bringing Perkin Warbeck to his court. War seemed certain.

Henry planned to invade France in early June 1492 with help from Maximilian and additional financial support from Parliament. It became clear fairly quickly that Maximilian would not honour his commitments. In these circumstances Henry had to launch a limited assault that would allow him to salvage some honour. In October of 1492 he besieged Boulogne with 26 000 men, while trying to negotiate with the French. Charles quickly offered peace terms with Henry as he was anxious to pursue a conflict in Italy. On 3 November 1492 the Treaty of Étaples was signed, agreeing Henry's withdrawal, if Charles paid an indemnity of approximately £159 000 in total (or £5000 per year). Crucially, Charles VIII promised not to support any Yorkist claimants to the throne again.

The rapprochement with France was fairly easily retained. When Henry joined the Holy League, initially formed to combat French conquests in Italy, he made it clear he had no intention of fighting against France and in 1497 signed a commercial treaty with Charles VIII (see the section on Trade). Ferdinand begged Henry to attack France with him in 1502, but Henry would not countenance the idea.

Scotland

Scotland had been particularly hostile to England since Edward IV's acquisition of Dunbar and Berwick (two border towns). Scotland's natural alliance with France also made it a significant threat, especially given the border raids and invasions, which were perfunctory during times of English instability. The 'Auld Alliance' dates back to 1295 with the death of Scotland's seven-year old queen, which left Edward I of England with an opportunity to declare his authority over Scotland. The Council of Twelve left in charge of Scotland sought French support as an obvious way of protecting themselves. In 1486 Henry signed a three-year truce with James III of Scotland and tried, unsuccessfully, to arrange a marriage alliance between the two realms. However, in 1488 James III was murdered by Scottish nobles. His heir, James IV, was a minor and his regency was fought over by Scottish nobles, only some of whom were Anglophiles. Despite the renewal of a truce in 1493, when James IV came of age in 1495 he immediately welcomed Perkin Warbeck to his court, even offering him the hand of his cousin Lady Catherine Gordon in marriage. In 1496 the Scottish raided the northern border towns of England as the ally of Warbeck. Although the raids failed to stir rebellion in the North, James IV had made his intentions clear. Henry prepared for a large offensive (of about 20 000 men and 70 ships) against Scotland in 1496 and agents were sent to Flanders to recruit mercenaries. The Parliament of 1497 secured Henry grants of £120 000 and loans of £51 000. Alarmed at the prospect of an English invasion, James quickly negotiated the Treaty of Ayton (30 September 1497), which paved the way for more agreeable relations between the two countries. In 1502 the Treaty of Perpetual Peace was signed, agreeing the marriage of Margaret Tudor and James IV.

Securing the succession: marriage alliances

Henry successfully negotiated the marriage alliance of Catherine of Aragon and Prince Arthur under the Treaty of Medina del Campo in 1489 The marriage went ahead in October 1501, although Arthur died shortly after in 1502. The Spanish alliance not only bought Henry support from a mighty country, but from the Netherlands too, as Joanna (heiress to Spain) was married to Maximilian's son, Archduke Philip of Burgundy, who was their ruler. Prince Arthur's death in 1502 came as a huge shock. Guy (1988) argues that mortality dominated foreign policy after the deaths of Arthur and then Elizabeth of York in 1503. As a widower, Henry VII used his own freedom to marry again as a potential means for furthering dynastic union with other European rivals. Henry sought the hand of Queen Joanna of Naples, niece to Ferdinand of Aragon, then Margaret of Savoy, daughter of Emperor Maximilian, and finally Joanna, widow of Philip of Burgundy (who died in 1506).

Although he failed to secure himself another marriage, he did secure terms in June 1503 for Catherine of Aragon to marry Prince Henry. A full papal dispensation was needed because Catherine (in her previous marriage to Arthur) had become related to Prince Henry. The Pope granted the dispensation on condition that the marriage be delayed until Henry reached the age of 14, in 1505.

Foreign policy: an assessment

Henry VII was never in a position to dominate foreign relations or assert England as a European power. However, there is plenty of evidence to suggest Henry made the best of what small resources he had, and seemed to impress foreign visitors. This perhaps explains why so many of the European powers sought alliances with him, in the hope of inducing him to fight with them. Henry VII did have to endure indignities of facing pretenders to the throne who were supported by his foreign rivals on several occasions. However, he was astute in appreciating England's limited resources and never overcommitted himself, with the result that most forays into diplomacy benefited him. Henry's success can be judged by the extreme weakness of his position in 1485, compared with the substantial strength towards the end of his reign.

Society

The advent of Henry VII's reign did not itself bring any great change to the fabric of society and what held it together. However, there were marked developments in the second half of the 15th century to the social order: the growth of education and new challenges to religion. Professional bureaucrats, appointed on merit rather than birth, populated the increasingly sophisticated organs of state and new cultural movements spread throughout Europe changing the way people perceived the world around them. Yet, much of the medieval survived too. Bubonic plague was still the number one cause of death in Europe and could devastate populations. Medieval incarnations of paradise and hell still struck fear into the heart of most people. The mass of the population remained largely illiterate, without property or political power, and still struggled to survive most of the time. Perhaps most significantly, the position of one's place in society was defined in relation to land ownership. This did not change under Henry VII.

ACTIVITY 1.5

List as many historical figures as you can and see where they fit into society during Henry VII's reign. The nobility included dukes, counts, earls, marquesses and barons. The gentry were knights and yeomen, and the commoners were everyone else.

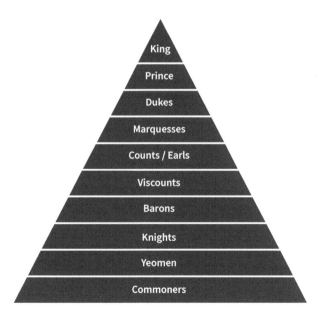

Figure 1.8: The hierarchy of society at the turn of the 16th century.

Churchmen

The single largest landowner in the country, alongside the king, was the Church. In England in 1485 the vast majority of the population were Roman Catholics, who owed spiritual allegiance to the Pope in Rome. The Church was a powerful organisation, consisting of the regular clergy (monks and nuns), numbering approximately 10 000, and the secular clergy (priests and other clerics), numbering up to 35 000. The Church had its own system of law courts and privileges and can therefore be referred to as a state within a state. In many ways the authority of the Church rivalled that of the king, and it was essential for Henry to maintain a peaceful coexistence with the Church.

Henry had an excellent relationship with the Church in the main, and the clergy supplied many of his leading ministers and servants. It is notable that among Henry's closest advisers were those who had been trained in the Roman and canon law. The most notable of these were John Morton, Richard Fox and Thomas Savage, who all became royal councillors. Morton was made Chancellor and Archbishop of Canterbury and remained in both posts until his death in 1500. Richard Fox became the Bishop of Durham (1494–1501) a powerful position from which he looked after the king's interests in the North. He was also Bishop of Winchester for 27 years and exercised what Gunn (1995) calls total 'dominance'.[6] Thomas Savage was from the gentry and his family were allied in marriage to the Stanleys. He was made Bishop of Rochester, then of London, then of York from 1501. He was president of the King's Council for six years until 1502.

However, Henry VII did weaken the religious leadership of the bench of bishops. He appointed 16 bishops who were lawyers and just six who were theologians, which marked a significant shift from Edward IV's reign, where almost 40% of his bench had a theological background. Most of Henry's theologians were also administrators too. Henry was willing to risk damaging the Church to ensure a transformation in the balance of power; bishoprics became rewards for those who had performed administrative services. For example, Richard Redman of Exeter had to pay £100 per annum merely to have permission to reside in his diocese, which simply served to demonstrate that the state came first. Guy (1988) argues that this was a deliberate strategy to encourage more service to the state instead of the papacy.

Rome

Pope Innocent VIII gave Henry VII considerable support in his early years as king, probably due to Archbishop John Morton's influence. In March 1486 Pope Innocent formally recognised Henry as rightful king of England in a **papal bull**, which Henry gladly printed and circulated throughout the kingdom. In the same document the Pope called upon all churchmen to denounce conspirators against the king's person or estate, threatening the 'great curse' would fall upon them. The Pope then acted against the Irish bishops by excommunicating them, following their support for Lambert Simnel – the first pretender to the throne in 1486 – which was a gesture of huge significance.

Pope Innocent also supported Henry in dealing with ecclesiastical (Church) immunities. In 1487 the Pope agreed that the king had the right to remove from

Key terms

papal bull: an official letter or document issued by the Pope.

praemunire: law prohibiting the assertion of papal jurisdiction over that of the monarch.

sanctuary any felon who had committed treason. In 1489 Henry VII decided to restrict 'benefit of the clergy', an age-old grievance of the general population. This practice had been established after Thomas Becket's murder in 1170 and exempted clergy from punishment by secular courts. The test of clerical status was to read a passage of Latin, and lay judges would determine the strength of the claim, but clearly this practice was open to corruption and abuse. The 1489 Act meant that the privilege of the clergy could only be used once; this Act was extended in 1497 depriving those not in holy orders of benefit in cases involving murder. Henry also attacked ecclesiastical jurisdiction in the form of **praemunire**. Praemunire prohibited the assertion of papal jurisdiction over that of the monarch. James Hobart (Attorney General and member of the Council Learned) began to prosecute praemunire cases, particularly after 1495. Hobart vexed the Bishop of Norwich in 1504, who was accused of excommunicating men who refused to attend church courts in disputes over **tithes**. Penalties for praemunire were severe and could range from attainder to life imprisonment. Hobart was eventually removed from his post, so vociferous were complaints made against him for carrying out Henry's orders. When, during Henry VIII's reign, Edmund Dudley was put on trial for treasonable offences (see Chapter 2), he wrote a confession about all of his actions in the Council of the Learned. In it he listed ecclesiastical cases, in which 17 out of the 84 people indicted (and in his words – ill-treated) by Henry VII were churchmen; in at least two instances, the charge of praemunire was responsible (Guy, 1988).

Nobles and commoners

Nobles

It was essential that Henry VII gained the respect and loyalty of the nobility if he was to remain their feudal Lord, for he remembered well that as a usurper with tenuous claims to the throne, he was vulnerable to others attempting a similar coup. As much as he might have liked to, Henry VII did not attempt to rule without the nobility, since such ideas would have been 'wildly eccentric' as Lander (1980) puts it[7]. As Elton (1955) and Pollard (2001) assert, the Crown had been weakened during the Wars of the Roses and the nobility strengthened. However, under Henry VII it is now argued by Davies (1987) and Grant (1985) that under Henry VII not only was the size of the nobility reduced during his reign, but their relative power too. Significantly, it was the number of major peers (dukes, marquesses and earls) or as they have been referred to, 'super-nobles', that saw a reduction from 16 in 1485 to just 10 by 1509. The two major magnate families – the Stafford dukes of Buckingham and the Percy earls of Northumberland – were kept under control. Edward Stafford, third Duke of Buckingham was seven years old in 1498; and Henry Percy, fourth Earl of Northumberland, was killed in the riot of 1489, leaving a ten-year-old son. Henry was fortunate that he did not have to contend with 'super-nobles' to anything like the extent previous kings had.

Patronage

Patronage had long been used by medieval kings to buy loyalty from the nobility. Henry VII was innovative here in that he gave patronage as a result of (and not in the hope of) loyal or effective service. This was a form of meritocracy and was applied to both the nobility and the gentry. Those who were loyal to Henry

Key term

tithes: annual payments of an agreed proportion of the yearly produce of the land. Tithes were payable by parishioners to their local parish church, to support it and its clergyman.

when he was in exile and at Bosworth were rewarded handsomely. Jasper Tudor (Henry's uncle) was made the Duke of Bedford and Chief Justice of Wales, Constable of all the castles in the Welsh Marches, and Lord Lieutenant of Ireland. Lord Stanley (who married to Henry's mother) was made the Earl of Derby and retained control of Lancashire and Cheshire. John Morton, Bishop of Ely (who had resisted Richard's usurpation in 1483), was appointed Chancellor and Archbishop of Canterbury in 1486. The Earl of Oxford (John de Vere) was given lands in East Anglia and Lord Willoughby de Broke was given a seat on the King's Council, appointed High Sheriff of Devon and of Cornwall, made steward of the Crown's goldmines in Devon and was given lands in Warwick, Salisbury and the Duchy of Lancaster. Others were rewarded for their good service once Henry had become king. George Talbot, Earl of Shrewsbury, became one of Henry's closest councillors, Lord Daubeney was promoted to the peerage after his success in dealing with the Cornish rebellion in 1497 and Sir Reginald Bray accumulated land worth in excess of £1000 per annum thanks to Henry's patronage.

Henry also used the Order of the Garter as a form of patronage. The Order of the Garter was established in 1348 by Edward III and was an honour reserved for those who had served the sovereign personally. Henry VII created 37 Knights of the Garter, including the Earl of Oxford, Giles Daubeney and Reginald Bray. Henry favoured this kind of reward because it gave the recipient prestige without added power or the land that a peerage might offer.

Acts of Attainder

Acts of Attainder had been established in 1321 to allow the monarch to withdraw land from the nobility. They were a form of punishment, as a loss of land would surely signal financial and social ruin. However, under Henry they acted as incentives too. Lander (1980) argues it was a sanction for good behaviour as Henry reversed attainders if loyalty was shown, although for men of lower ranks he charged high prices for the reversal. In this respect Henry's use of attainders could be called a kind of 'cat and mouse' policy (Davies, 1987). Thomas Howard, the Earl of Surrey, who had fought for Richard III at Bosworth, was attainted in 1485 and imprisoned. In January 1489 he took an oath of allegiance to Henry VII and was restored to his earldom, with a promise that the attainder would be reversed. By April 1489 Howard had helped Henry to quell the Yorkshire rising for which he was rewarded with the return of most of the Howard estates. He was never, however, reinstated as the Duke of Norfolk. Henry VII was more severe than Edward IV had been in his use of attainder – which can account for the swelling in royal

 Hidden voices

Reginald Bray

Reginald Bray began his career as a servant of Henry VII's mother, Margaret Beaufort. He was used as an executor of wills by many of the nobility because of his influence with the king. He was granted **annuities** by eight nobles, including Northumberland, Devon and the Duke of Bedford (Henry's uncle). He was given land in the localities to enhance his authority, often taken from the redistribution of estates that had been confiscated under Acts of Attainder. Bray built up sizeable estates in the Thames Valley and Midlands as a result of this.

demesne. Even though numerically Henry VII passed 138 Acts of Attainder (against Edward IV's 140) and reversed 46 (Edward reversed 42) almost all the attainders Henry VII passed against nobles, totalling nine, had special features attached. Some 51 Acts of Attainder were passed after 1504, something that historians have used to demonstrate Henry's increasing attempts to bring the nobility into line, perhaps because the threat to the dynasty frightened him in his latter years after Prince Arthur's death in 1502.

Bonds and recognisances

Henry VII used bonds and **recognisances** throughout his reign. First introduced by Henry V, they were drawn up by the Council Learned from 1495 onwards. They bound nobles to good behaviour upon the threat of a financial penalty in what the historian Lander (1980)[8] calls a 'terrifying system of suspended penalties'. While bonds were the written agreements in which they promised loyalty, the recognisances were the formal acknowledgement of a debt or obligation (to keep the peace, for example). Enforcement was entrusted to the Council Learned because common law courts would take too long to claim the monies. Another advantage of bonds and recognisances was that they spread the burden of law enforcement, as those who were bound needed guarantors for the money. The king's real purpose was to enforce obedience to his new dynasty through financial coercion.

Out of the 62 families belonging to the peerage, it is estimated that 46 were bound under this scheme. However, it should be noted that most bonds and recognisances were implemented following the death of Prince Arthur in 1502, when fears for the succession resurfaced. Although some at the time accused Henry of avarice (greed) only £30 000 of £220 000 was collected according to the accounts kept by Dudley. Bonds were given for causing an affray: for example, the Earl of Northumberland and the Archbishop of York were charged £2000 each to keep the mutual peace. Lord Mountjoy was forced into 23 recognisances and even Henry's close adviser the Earl of Shrewsbury had to guarantee bonds of £500 for several of his friends, putting him at risk of owing £5000. Empson and Dudley (chief administrators in the Council of the Learned after 1504) earned themselves a reputation for ruthlessness in pursuing these claims (to see what happened to them see Chapter 2, in the section on Empson and Dudley).

Livery and maintenance

Henry had learnt from the Wars of the Roses that the military relationship between the monarchy and nobility had to change as the Wars of the Roses had shown Henry. After the Battle of Stoke in 1487, it was no longer felt necessary that a king should risk his own person in battle. Of course delegation to professional knights had always occurred. However, the Lancastrian and Yorkist Kings had learnt at high cost that the simple arrangement of **retaining** (or as it is sometimes referred to, **livery** and **maintenance**) through which nobles could raise a private army in service to the king could all too easily become disloyal and threatening. Therefore Henry VII tried to tackle retaining in two key ways, although it is important to note he did not try to abolish it altogether, perhaps because he recognised the vital role it played in helping him maintain peace within the realm. For example in 1486 it was the Earl of Northumberland's army that saved the king in Yorkshire.

Key terms

annuities: a fixed sum of money paid to someone each year, often acting as pensions or rewards for loyal servants of the Crown.

recognisances: sums of money pledged to fulfil an obligation.

Key term

retaining: a medieval practice in which nobles maintained bands of followers who would take up arms for them if necessary. Retainers wore **livery** (a uniform or badge) to show which noble family they served.

Figure 1.9: This portrait of Henry VII (centre) confiding with Sir Richard Empson (left) and Sir Edmund Dudley demonstrates how close Henry was to his advisers, whom he trusted implicitly. Both these men carried out the king's system of taxation, and consequently became very unpopular, although arguably many at court were simply jealous of their access to the king.

> ### 🔑 Key term
>
> **primogeniture:** a principle by which the first-born son inherits the estate or title of the father.

Henry VII began his attack on retaining at the beginning of his reign, forcing members of Parliament to swear that they would observe the existing limits on retaining. In 1504 Henry's proclamations ensured that nobles had to obtain licences or 'placards' to retain. These licences were given out by the king himself, and supported by the promise of financial ruin for failing to obtain a king's licence, extending his personal control over the nobility further. The 1504 Act had a penalty of £5 per month per illegal retainer; this was applied to Lord Bergavenny in 1506 who was fined £70 550 (although this was shared between him and 36 others) no doubt spelling the threat of financial strife for his family for years after. It has been suggested by Carpenter (1997) that the substantial penalty doled out to Bergavenny might have been due to his suspected involvement in the Cornish Rebellion of 1497. The Earl of Devon was also charged in 1506 when he broke his promise of recognisance (made in 1494) not to retain illegally. Even the Earl of Oxford, who was a close adviser to Henry, was fined £15 000 for illegally retaining men at his castle in Henningham. Evidence suggests that some nobles such as Buckingham and Northumberland employed many more men on their estates than was necessary, which could have been for the purposes of retaining. This perhaps suggests that Henry's actions were not wholly successful in reducing the power of the nobility.

Henry VII insisted that he consulted individuals about his choice, but he never lost sight of the fact that the local influence of the nobility was essential to the peace and stability of the realm. When a crisis threatened, such as that of 1486 in the case of Lambert Simnel or in 1487 (see the section on Social discontent and rebellions), the king summoned his peers to a Great Council without hesitation. He almost always heeded their advice and relied upon their retainers to support him in the field: they had far too much territorial power to be ignored.

The gentry

The gentry consisted of knights (there were approximately 500 during Henry VII's reign), esquires, of which there were around 800, and gentlemen, numbering about 5000. The gentry had status by virtue of their ownership of land and there was no great expansion in this class until the mid-16th century. Political status separated the nobility from the gentry. Peers had the privilege of being personally called to Parliament by the king, and could pass on their titles according to the principle of **primogeniture**. The gentry relied heavily on the patronage of the nobility. Henry VII was inclined to reward merit in appointing officials within his government, so this period saw the elevation of members of the gentry to posts of considerable political importance. Very few gentry families became nobility, however.

Commoners

There were no social surveys in Tudor England, so historians have had to build their own impressions of Tudor society at the time. There was an increasingly complex order of social classes by the time Henry VII claimed the throne in 1485. Much of the description historians have of England comes from Polydore Vergil, a papal tax collector, who first visited England in 1502. Vergil suggested there were 39 counties and around 700 towns in England and generally described the country as prosperous. There were under three million people living in Tudor England at

Speak like a historian: Christine Carpenter/JR Lander

Christine Carpenter has been called a 'revisionist' historian, in that she has questioned traditional views of Henry VII and in many ways is rather critical of his achievements.

That meant that behind the enforcement of the King's commands by the local officials, themselves in most cases members of the local gentry, lay the unspoken military power of the locality. They [the nobility] needed his [the King's] power, and needed to make it work to protect their own land, an easily damaged commodity, on which their wealth and their power depended … [I]n this chain of private power that enabled the chain of public administrative power to work, the nobility had an immensely influential role: they were unlikely to attack or undermine a system that made them what they were. The King had neither to force nor to buy their loyalty; he had it automatically by virtue of being King. Only a usurper, whose continued tenure of the throne was uncertain, needed to use threats or blandishments. Thus, the polity over which the king presided was one in which the private and the public were closely intermeshed; but the intermeshing went further than this.

Source: Carpenter C. 'Henry VII and the English polity'. In B Thompson (ed.) *The Reign of Henry VII,* Stamford; 1995. p. 20.

However, JR Lander sees Henry's policies towards the nobility differently.

Though the use of bonds and recognizances was well established at all levels of society during the fifteenth century, the degree to which Henry drove the system had been unprecedented since the days of King John. His combination of fiscal measures through haphazard, arbitrary 'exquisite means' with his measures *in terrorem* over a great many people was producing an intense backlash of resentment by the time of his death … Lord Mountjoy and Sir Thomas More, freed from fear and restraint, excoriated the system and its vile corruptions and rejoiced in its end in the prospect of new and more liberal times to come. Edward IV, Richard III and Henry VII all to a greater of lesser degree came to be condemned for tyranny.

The whole system sounds revolting. Indeed it was! But how else, perhaps, other than by fear, could Edward IV and Henry VII have controlled such a mob of aloof, self-interested magnates? After all, the entire justification for the presence of the nobility lay in its potential fidelity and its governing capacity. If its loyalty were not willingly given there could be no alternative to coercion.

Source: Lander JR. *Government and Community: England 1450–1509.* London: Edward Arnold; 1980. p. 360.

Discussion points:
1. What are each of these historians arguing?
2. How are these two interpretations different? Is there anything they agree on?
3. Can you find any evidence from your notes that support either of these two historians' claims?
4. Which of the historians do you find most convincing regarding Henry's relationship with the nobility?

ACTIVITY 1.6

Henry VII used a range of ways to increase his control of the nobility, sometimes he used incentives (a 'carrot') and sometimes he threatened sanctions (a 'stick'). Go back over your notes and draw in the margin whether you think each action Henry VII took represented an incentive or sanction (carrot or stick).

the turn of the 16th century and most of these people were engaged in agricultural practices, earning perhaps £2 per year at the lower end. Those who had supplementary incomes through weaving cloth or who had small landholdings could expect to fare better, mainly because they could grow their own food on their land. Society was far more mobile than has traditionally been suggested, with large numbers of people moving around the country in search of work, as parish records show.

Death loomed large in a commoner's life, as paintings and jewellery decorated with skulls illustrate. Infant mortality rates were high; it is estimated that more than one in ten infants did not survive until their first birthday. The frequent recurrence of the plague and other epidemics such as sweating sickness (a virulent influenza) decimated populations. Many considered that these epidemics were sent by God to punish sin, and the fact that one such epidemic broke out in 1485 saw many people forecasting bad omens for Henry VII, demonstrating the prevalence of superstition among villagers.

Merchants

England experienced a substantial increase in trade under Henry VII and this promoted an expansion of the merchant class. Merchants worked in various trading companies, each specialising in particular commodities. For example, the Mercers were associated with silk, the Grocers with spices, the Merchant Adventurers with woollen cloth and the Merchant Staplers with raw wool. Merchants demonstrated their status in society through building magnificent town houses, wearing fine clothes and, where they could, investing in land. Merchants began to organise themselves into groups during the 15th century and became known as Merchant Adventurers. Together they often dominated local trade and became a powerful political lobby group. In 1505 Henry VII granted the Merchant Adventurers of London a charter that allowed them to appoint a governor and hire 24 assistants to support their organisation.

Regional division

London and the towns

London's economic importance as the country's leading port added complexity to its relationship with the Crown. Loans from livery companies and individual merchants were invaluable in crises, and made Londoners worth courting. On the other hand, Henry VII's financial initiatives disproportionately affected wealthy Londoners and generated ill-will, expressed in chroniclers' denunciations of Empson and Dudley. Henry VII also intervened in London politics, backing the Merchant Tailors against other livery companies, which was detrimental to the good order of the city. Henry VII was particularly fearful of unrest here in the last year of his life.

Ireland

Ireland presented a rather different problem to Henry VII than London. As King of England Henry was also Lord of Ireland. However, it was not ruled in conjunction with a council. The king appointed a Lord Lieutenant in his place, although really this was no more than an honorary position. The work of governing Ireland was carried out by a Lord Deputy, and a difficult job it was. Only in the English Pale, which was a narrow band of territory about 50 miles long to the north and west of Dublin, was the king's authority really felt. Throughout the rest of Ireland the effective rulers were Anglo-Irish lords, who were descendants of English settlers, and Irish chieftains with their own family loyalties. Of these, the Geraldine and Butler families were the most powerful, and totally out of reach of the English kings. When Henry claimed the throne, the Geraldines held the position of Lord Deputy and Chancellor of Ireland. Henry VII learnt quickly that their loyalty was not secured when the Earl of Kildare supported Lambert Simnel in his claim to the throne. In 1492, after Kildare had supported Warbeck, Henry removed his title of Lord Deputy. Henry forced them to seek his pardon in person before he would restore their titles.

In 1494 Henry VII attempted to reorganise Irish government to encourage obedience to England. The infant Prince Henry was made Lord Lieutenant and Sir Edward Poynings was his Deputy. Poynings' task was to bring the rebellious region of Ulster under royal control and to impose a constitution on Ireland that would ensure its loyalty to the English Crown. Although he had only limited success in subduing Ulster, he managed bring about some profound constitutional changes. In 1494 the Irish Parliament passed the statutes that became known as Poynings' Law. These decreed that an Irish parliament could only be summoned on the king's approval. No legislation could be discussed unless Henry had already approved it and any law made it England would automatically apply to Ireland. Poynings' Law destroyed the independent legislative power of the Irish Parliament. However, realistically, Henry VII could not afford to impose his will in Ireland and he was forced to reinstate Kildare as Lord Deputy, who remained loyal to his king.

Wales
Wales was not a military frontier zone like Ireland. The Welsh gentry did not, for the most part, live in defensible dwellings and did not include any of the 'super-nobles' Henry VII feared. Henry VII therefore appointed Jasper Tudor, his uncle, to govern Wales and in 1493 placed his infant son Arthur in charge of the Council. Henry's familial links with Wales, which were highlighted and celebrated by native poets and writers, ensured him the support of the population. He appointed Welshmen to key positions in Wales, for example Sir Rhys ap Thomas was appointed to govern south-west Wales and William ap Gruffydd ruled the north on Henry's behalf.

Social discontent and rebellions

It was an accepted principle that monarchs should only tax the people for the needs of war or defending the realm. An act passed in 1483 confirmed that taxes had to be approved by Parliament before they could be levied. The most common form of tax was the Tenth and this assessed how much communities could afford to pay. Henry VII began what became common practice under the Tudors to raise subsidies by reassessing how much individuals could pay. At the local level, anger roused by taxation could provoke sporadic outbreaks of violence against tax collectors. In the period 1485–1547 there were 11 assaults recorded on tax collectors in London alone, and probably more that never reached the courts. More common were the forcible rescue of goods seized by collectors, of which there were 112 cases recorded. The new system of levying subsidies appeared arbitrary to many individuals and can explain two of the rebellions that broke out under Henry VII.

With hindsight, historians have played down the danger these posed for the king; however, the timing of these rebellions must be considered.

Northern Tax Rebellion 1489

The Northern Rebellion (sometimes referred to as the Yorkshire Rebellion) was sparked by Henry's levying of a parliamentary subsidy of £100,000 which was needed in 1489 to aid Brittany against the French (see the section on Relationships with Scotland and other foreign powers). Henry VII had only been king for four years and had just overcome the Lambert Simnel rebellion, which had culminated in the Battle of Stoke in 1487. The Earl of Northumberland, who was Lieutenant General of the Marches, was tasked with collecting the enormous subsidy on Henry's behalf in the North. A group of people in Cleveland, led by Sir John Egremont, were resolved to protest against the new tax, so Northumberland dutifully rode out to meet them. He was assassinated almost immediately – although he was the only person killed in the rising. Henry raised a large army to march north, which unnerved the rebels who dispersed as the king's men – led by Thomas Howard, Earl of Surrey – arrived at York. Henry VII issued a pardon to most of those taken prisoner, as a conciliatory gesture. Egremont had already fled to Flanders, fearing for his life. Despite his efforts, Henry appears to have raised only £27 000 of the total granted, perhaps demonstrating how badly it was received. According to Fletcher (2004) the Yorkshire Rebellion was a genuine expression of popular anger about taxation, rather than it being an attempt to depose the king. This rebellion may also demonstrate that Henry VII, having spent so much of his life abroad, was unfamiliar with the structures of consent on which English government rested.

Cornish Rebellions 1497

The spring of 1497 saw two rebellions in Cornwall: the first was almost certainly sparked by taxation. Henry VII needed money to raise an army against the pretender to the throne, Perkin Warbeck, who had received support from James IV of Scotland. Parliament granted Henry £120 000 from a subsidy and two Fifteenths and Tenths – the largest sum ever levied by the king. Parliamentary grants tended not to exceed £31 000, only in 1492 when £56 311 was paid in taxation were larger amounts collected. The burden fell on the whole population, not all of whom were threatened by an invasion from Scotland. Coupled with the new tax, Henry VII had interfered with the tin-mining industry, which was central to the local economy. Angry people from St Keverne and Bodmin were encouraged by Thomas Flamank and Michael Joseph An Gof to direct their anger towards the king's 'evil advisers' Sir Reginald Bray and Cardinal Morton. The 15 000 or so Cornishmen, led by Flamank and the impoverished Lord Audley, set out to present their grievances to the king and reached Blackheath on 16 June 1497. This was rebellion of a more frightening nature, and their anger was such that they had crossed the south of England meeting little resistance. The army of 8000 that had been raised to march to Scotland under Lord Daubeney had to be quickly diverted south. Henry also gathered forces at Henley to see them off. Once the rebels realised their leaders were not prepared to fight, approximately 5000 of them deserted. This left 10 000 rebels, against the king's 25 000 strong army, to fight it out at Blackheath. Fletcher (2004) estimates 1000 rebels were killed in battle and the rest fled swiftly thereafter. Audley was beheaded – a noble execution – and Flamank and An Gof were hanged, drawn and quartered, but hundreds of fines were systematically issued following the rebellion.

The fines probably explain the second rebellion, which broke out later in 1497. This time Perkin Warbeck was directly involved, staging his last attempt to capture Henry's kingdom. In what can be described as pure opportunism, Warbeck arrived in Cornwall just 11 weeks after the defeat at Blackheath, and was proclaimed King Richard IV at Bodmin. Initially raising forces of 6000 men, Warbeck tried to capture Exeter, but failed. It seems Warbeck lost his nerve thereafter and was arrested and taken to London. Henry VII collected approximately £15 000 in fines from Devon and Cornwall that year due to the rebellions, which impoverished many. Cornwall would become a troublesome region for later Tudors, as Henry VII's harsh treatment of them was not forgotten.

Economic development

Crucial in developing royal authority were commerce and a robust commercial economy. Henry VII was aware that trade had suffered badly during the Wars of the Roses due to the instability of the throne, but he believed that the relative prosperity of his subjects would lead to an increase in their support for him as they would credit him for their increased wealth. Henry, therefore, supported the development of the country's commercial base, especially overseas trade. England's main industries in the 15th century were cloth, mining, salt production, fishing, metalworking and building.

Trade

Wool and cloth trade
The emergent cloth industry had a significant impact on trade and employment, which coincided with a growing population. Most communities engaged in the woollen cloth trade also farmed on a small scale too, therefore total unemployment was less feared because they were not completely dependent on agriculture. The three main districts for woollen cloth production were the West Riding of Yorkshire, East Anglia and the West Country. There were a few families such as those in Wiltshire, who were almost wholly dependent on the cloth trade for their incomes.

Hanseatic League
The majority of England's trade was conducted through the Hanseatic League, an organisation of German merchants that had managed to secure special trading privileges in Germany, Scandinavia and Russia and monopolies on the purchase and carriage of particular goods. England traded wool, cloth, tin and coal with the Hanse merchants in exchange for fish, furs and soft woods. The League had a privileged position in England too because it was exempt from customs duties. Operating the length of England's east coast, the merchants had a base in London called the Steelyard. Henry VII tried to secure similar privileges for English

---

ACTIVITY 1.7

One of the key debates historians of this period are engaged in surrounds how secure Henry VII was on his throne. Go back through the notes you have made on this chapter and consider whether Henry was ever secure on his throne, and if so, when? Make a table using the following three headings and fill in the evidence:

Evidence that Henry VII was secure on the throne.

Evidence that could be argued either way.

Evidence that Henry VII was not secure on the throne.

merchants abroad, which would undermine the operations of the Hanseatic League. In 1485 and 1489, Henry VII passed Navigation Acts to prevent the carriage of certain imported goods in foreign ships. The acts forbade English merchants from exporting their goods using foreign ships if English ships were available. In 1489 this law was extended, stating that only English ships were allowed to be used to import goods (and only if these were not available could foreign ships then be used). Henry's aim was to protect the English market – even if it was at the expense of endangering future trade with the Hanse merchants.

Henry VII attempted to put pressure on the Hanse by allying with other rivals of theirs, but this was only short-lived as the Hanse were too strong a body to be outmanoeuvred in this way. In 1504 Henry VII capitulated and restored the Hanse to the favourable position they had enjoyed under Edward IV through an act of parliament. Historians debate why he did this. Perhaps Henry was concerned that the Hanse would seek revenge by supporting the Earl of Suffolk, who was travelling the continent looking for support to challenge the English throne. Nevertheless the act was a significant commercial loss for England.

Burgundy

Henry VII was keen on maintaining trade with Antwerp, in the Burgundian-ruled Netherlands. However, the exploits of the pretenders to the throne and changing relations with foreign powers meant that other markets had to be found throughout Henry's reign. In 1493, due to Margaret of Burgundy's harbouring of Perkin Warbeck, Henry issued a trade embargo against the Netherlands and ordered English merchants to move to Calais. In retaliation, a counter-embargo was placed on English trade. Since this embargo benefited no one, it was lifted in 1496 under the *Magnus Intercursus,* a treaty that stated that English merchants could sell their goods wholesale anywhere in the Duke of Burgundy's lands without paying customs duties, except in Flanders. This treaty did not solve the continued conflicts between English merchants and Duke Philip, as he continued imposing import duties and then tried to confine their trade to Antwerp.

In 1506 a twist of fate saw Henry gain the upper hand in trade with the Duke of Burgundy. A ferocious storm occurred on the duke's route to Spain, forcing him to take refuge in the English port of Weymouth. As Henry's guest, Philip was persuaded to agree to the *Malus Intercursus,* which established free trade between England and the Low Countries. The treaty also entailed Philip's subjects having to pay the customary English duties, set up in 1496. Unfortunately for Henry, Philip died soon after the agreement was signed and the *Magnus Intercursus* was once again adopted.

Spain and Portugal

Trade with the newly united Spain was a lucrative business, particularly given her dominant role in the voyages of exploration to the New World (see the section on Exploration). England already had an established commercial link with Portugal, which Henry renewed in 1489, but now he sought the bigger prize. He signed the Treaty of Medina del Campo in 1489, and although it is remembered for the marriage alliance between Prince Arthur and Catherine of Aragon, it had significant commercial impact. From 1489 both England and Spain traded on equal terms, receiving the same rights in each other's country and fixing duties at a low rate.

The navy

Henry VII could no more keep a navy than a regular army, because it was too expensive to maintain. However, the tensions between trade and defence were obvious so he had to encourage merchants to build vessels that could be transformed into fighting ships. He encouraged English merchants to build ships of more than 80 tonnes, which could be swiftly converted if necessary. In doing so, he established the basis of a formal navy. Henry VII bequeathed only nine ships to his son, but they were of a high quality. Henry VII's ships were large, well-equipped and more efficiently administered than in previous periods. An example of this was the 600-tonne *Regent*, which could carry 225 cast-iron guns and was the forerunner of the effective warships associated with Elizabeth I's reign. Henry VII also constructed the navy's first fortified base at Portsmouth, from which his son and granddaughter would benefit.

Exploration

The 15th century was a great age in exploration. Henry VII has been criticised by some historians for failing to give patronage to Christopher Columbus in 1486, but evidence suggests that it was the King's Council who rejected the navigator's idea of crossing the ocean in an attempt to reach the Far East. Henry's later patronage of John Cabot could therefore be explained by his regret upon hearing of Columbus' successful voyage to what was thought to be Asia (but subsequently recognised as the **New World**). John Cabot was an Italian sailor who arrived in England in 1495 to seek support from Henry for a voyage across the Atlantic. He believed he could shorten the distance to the Far East by sailing in a more northerly latitude than Columbus had done. The prospect of profits from increased eastern trade in exotic luxuries and spices was too alluring for Henry and so he authorised the voyage. The king offered £50 in the first instance, but would commit more if the voyage proved successful. After a disastrous first journey, which was scuppered by stormy weather, Cabot finally reached land in 1497. It is likely he landed in Newfoundland – as he commented in his log that there were plentiful cod in the waters. However, Cabot sadly died on the return journey.

In 1509, just before his death, Henry VII supported Sebastian Cabot (John's son), who sought north-west passage around America to Asia. Although by now it was generally accepted that America was a continent distinct from Asia, it was not known that the seas to the north of it were blocked with ice. Cabot believed that he had discovered a new channel leading to the Far East, although historians now suspect he had discovered the Hudson Strait. When Cabot returned, Henry VII was dead and his son, the new King Henry, was not so enamoured by exploration. Owing to Henry VII's patronage, England gained more knowledge of North America than any other European state. Sadly this was not exploited by his son and it was not until Elizabeth I that maritime activity resumed again.

 Key term

New World: the term applied to the Americas and Caribbean islands. Although a few Vikings had set foot there, the Americas were essentially unknown to Europeans until the voyage of Christopher Columbus in 1492.

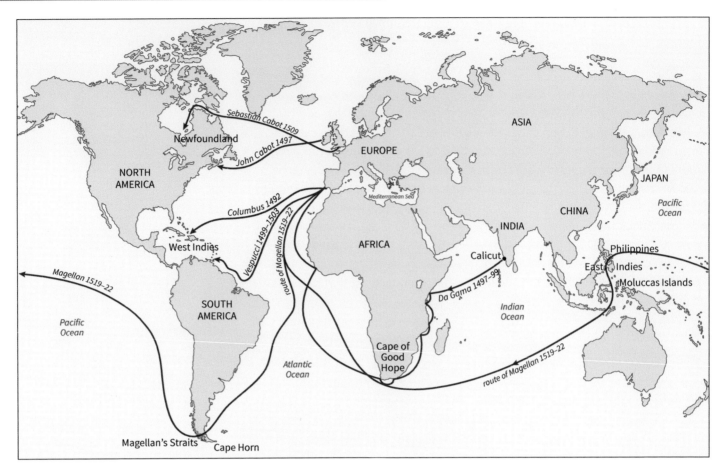

Figure 1.10: This map illustrates the exploration undertaken by Spanish, Portuguese and English explorers during the late 15th and early 16th century.

Prosperity and depression

England's prosperity was, in large part, dependent upon the wool trade, so much so that the Lord Chancellor sat on a symbolic woolsack in Parliament. England exported the highest quality wool in a raw state to be worked by the weavers of Antwerp, arguably the centre of the Flemish cloth trade. Kings had always levied heavy duties on the export of wool and it had been highly profitable for the Crown. However, when Henry VII took the throne the export of wool had halved and was being subsumed by that of woollen cloth. During Henry VII's reign England experienced a 60% increase in the export of cloth and a 30% decrease in the export of raw wool, with a corresponding increase of 50% in imports. The increase in imports perhaps reveals how dependent England was on foreign industry.

Religion, humanism, arts and learning

Religion

Guy (1988)[9] has argued that Henry VII was 'ostentatiously pious', founding three religious houses and contributing to church building and poor relief. However, Henry VII well understood the uses of piety as a tool to further safeguard his status. He therefore sought to demonstrate his commitment to the Church, and built a chapel at the east end of Westminster Abbey – at huge expense. The Church was an essential tool for any monarch, because priests taught their congregations about the order of society, that everyone had to accept their place. The 'Great Chain of Being' was a concept clearly expressed in Church **doctrine** and was taught as part of normal church services. The 'chain' conveyed the contemporary idea of a God that punished those who rebelled against their king, which was treason, or who questioned the authority of the Church, which was heresy. Therefore the Church was a fundamental pillar in maintaining control throughout the kingdom.

Although Henry VII was not personally interested in theology, he was intolerant of heresy. The key heretical idea of the medieval period was **Lollardy**. Led by John Wycliffe, the Lollards wanted reform of the Catholic Church and laid stress on lay piety, that is, that the reading of the Bible by ordinary people should be encouraged. Wycliffe minimised the importance of the priesthood and the **sacraments**. He even questioned the accepted notion of transubstantiation – the doctrine that the communion bread and wine really become the body and blood of Christ during the celebration of the Eucharist. Over 73 suspects were tried in Church courts during his reign, although only 11 were burned for their crimes. Henry VII can be judged as taking an orthodox approach to ecclesiastical affairs, gaining the Pope's ear via the appointment of a Cardinal Protector (Francesco Piccolomini, the future Pope Pius III).

Humanism

A dramatic cultural movement, called the 'Renaissance', originating in Florence in the 1450s, was spreading through Europe when Henry VII claimed the throne. The Renaissance (meaning 'rebirth') was a movement that focused on a renewal of interest in classical civilisations. In art, architecture and literature, scholars began to both imitate and reflect on Roman and Greek techniques. The hub of the Renaissance was Italy, but literary forms of the Renaissance, known as **Humanism**, reached England by the 1470s. Humanism encouraged a return to studying classical, particularly Roman texts, as well as teaching the humanities to create a civilised society. Humanism was a reaction to the medieval movement of **Scholasticism**, which promoted a narrower philosophy. The most celebrated Humanist scholar, Erasmus, visited England in 1499. He visited John Colet, the Dean of St Paul's Cathedral and founder of St Paul's School, and was impressed by the standards of classical teaching there. However, there is little to show that this development was occurring anywhere else in the country.

The Humanists challenged the orthodox theology that man was born sinful and only through repentance and divine intervention could he be redeemed. Humanists preferred to place destiny in human hands, believing instead that each individual can choose virtuosity. Erasmus adopted a scientific approach to studying sacred texts; instead of interpreting ecclesiastical texts, he decided to study the scriptures in their earliest form. As a result he published the Greek New Testament, but also revealed the disparity between the original sources and religious traditions. Humanists placed emphasis on a religion that was less ritualistic, and criticised **transubstantiation** and tithes. They highlighted how texts could be interpreted in radically different ways. In this respect, Humanists have been seen as the link between Catholicism and Protestantism.

 Key terms

doctrine: stated set of beliefs held and taught by the Church.

Lollardy: a heretical movement, originating in the 1380s under the Oxford scholar, John Wycliffe.

sacraments: Christian rite of particular importance. The Catholic Church teaches that there are seven sacraments. During the 16th century, Protestants argued that there were only two sacraments instituted by Christ – the Eucharist and Baptism.

Humanism: refers to a movement that promoted the study and recovery of classical texts and the teaching grammar of, rhetoric, poetry, history and moral philosophy.

Scholasticism: refers to a medieval movement that taught arithmetic, geometry, astronomy and music.

transubstantiation: Catholics believe that the bread and wine are changed into the blood and body of Christ, whereas Protestants believe they are symbolic.

Speak like a historian: Roger Lockyer

The historian Roger Lockyer has suggested the Church was strong under Henry VII.

Henry VII clearly found the doctrine and ceremonies of the Ecclesia Anglicana – the English branch of the Catholic Church – sufficient for his spiritual needs, and the same seems to have been true of the great majority of his subjects. The Church played a central part in the activities of the English people at all levels. Daily attendance at mass was not uncommon, especially in urban areas, and guilds and brotherhoods dedicated to Jesus or Corpus Christi or a particular saint were widespread. The English enjoyed and took for granted a rich religious culture which had as its focus the parish churches, and they showed their commitment by embellishing, enlarging and rebuilding these on a massive scale in the late fifteenth century and early sixteenth centuries. The Church had serious faults, of which pluralism and non-residence were glaring examples, but it seemed to be firmly rooted in the affection and respect of its congregations. At the time of Henry VII's death there was little to suggest that the Ecclesia Anglicana was about to undergo radical transformation.

Source: Lockyer R. *Henry VII* (2nd edn). Harlow; 1983. p. 57.

Discussion points
1. What are the 'obvious flaws' Lockyer refers to?
2. Can you give other examples of where Henry VII demonstrates his allegiance to the Church?
3. Do you agree with Lockyer overall?

Arts and learning

Perhaps the most historically significant event of the period was the advent of the printing press, which would make books increasingly affordable to the public. The press was brought to England by William Caxton, a rich wool merchant, in 1476 from Germany where it had been invented. Between 1476 and 1491 nearly 100 books were published by Caxton's press, covering a wide range of topics. Besides the clergy, Caxton catered for the tastes of kings, aristocrats and landowners. In common with most mercers, Caxton supported the Yorkist side of the Wars of the Roses. In a surviving copy of *The Recuyell of the Histories of Troye*, his first English book, an engraving can be found showing Caxton presenting the book to Margaret of York, Duchess of Burgundy, the sister of Edward IV, to whom he was especially close.

Caxton lost his powerful friends at court with the death of Edward IV in April 1483, the murder of Edward's two sons in the Tower of London and the fall of the Woodville family. In around April 1484 he dedicated to Richard III his translation of the *Book of the Ordre of Chyvalry or Knyghthode*. Only some three years later did Caxton manage to get closer to the court again, receiving a commission from Margaret Beaufort to translate and print the romance *Blanchardyn and Eglantine*. John de Vere, the Earl of Oxford, was instrumental in obtaining for him a commission from Henry VII for an English translation of Christine de Pisan's *Faits d'armes et de chevalerie,* which he completed on 14 July 1489 and in 1490 he dedicated to Arthur, Prince of Wales, his English translation of a French courtly romance, *Eneydos*. Caxton's new connections with the court also brought him the job of printing the statutes passed by the first three Parliaments of Henry VII, which were printed in English rather than the legal French normally used for such documents.

Despite Caxton's success in printing, one should not overestimate the spread of literacy across the country. As late as 1560 as many as 92 of the leading 146 gentry of Northumberland could not sign their own names. Primary and grammar schools did exist, and as statutes drawn up in 1518 show, St Paul's school certainly expected entrants to read and write. Other than this, very little is known about the curriculum in such schools or how widespread they were. It is likely almost all schools were tied to local churches or cathedrals, but instruction was often arranged privately and informally.

Arts and architecture

King's College Chapel was perhaps the greatest architectural achievement of the age. It was designed in the perpendicular style, fashionable at that time, and work on its foundations had begun in 1446 under Henry VI. Due to the disruption of the Wars of the Roses, work did not resume on the chapel until 1480, and it was not completed until Henry VIII's reign. Generally, building on such a grand scale was rare during this period, perhaps because the fortunes of the aristocracy fluctuated. However, churches continued to be the focus of grand adornments in the form of spectacular woodwork, rood screens and sumptuous decoration. Henry VII had established royal workshops for the artists and craftsmen he employed and commissioned buildings of his own: the chapel at Westminster Abbey, the nave at St George's Chapel in Windsor, Christchurch Gate at Canterbury and a new palace at Richmond were all begun during his reign. They were constructed in the **Gothic style** and were visible symbols of Tudor power. In many ways the buildings that

Key term

Gothic style: The Gothic Style characterises much of the architecture developed in the medieval era. Key features include pointed arches, heavily buttressed tower walls, ornate façades and vaulted ceilings.

ACTIVITY 1.8

1. Why do you think 'new learning' (Humanism) had taken a long time to appear in England?

2. Carry out some research on John Colet, William Grocyn, Thomas Linacre, Thomas More and John Fisher. Who were they and what did they contribute to Humanism?

3. How useful is the Erasmus source to the historian studying Humanism in 15th century England?

Voices from the past

Erasmus

This extract is taken from a letter written by Desiderius Erasmus to Robert Fisher in Rome, 1499.

… But how do you like our England, you will say. Believe me, my Robert, when I answer that I never liked anything so much before. I find the climate both pleasant and wholesome; and I have met with so much kindness and so much learning – not hackneyed and trivial, but deep, accurate, ancient Latin and Greek – that but for the curiosity of seeing it, I do not now care so much for Italy. When I hear my Colet I seem to be listening to Plato himself. In Grocyn who does not marvel at such a perfect round of learning? What can be more acute, profound and delicate than the judgement of Linacre? What has Nature ever created more gentle, more sweet, more happy than the genius of Thomas More? I need not go through the list. It is marvellous how general and abundant is the harvest of ancient learning in this country … From London, in haste, this fifth day of December.

Source: *The Epistles of Erasmus*, ed. FM Nicholas. London; 1901, Vol. 1. p. 225–56.

survived him are reflective of his reign: they were essentially medieval in nature, but with hints of a new flamboyancy that would become synonymous with his son.

Henry VII: an assessment

Henry VII consciously spent the first ten years of his reign acting with clemency towards his subjects. He attempted to cultivate a strong government with more efficiency in providing law and order across the realm and greatly improved the finances for the Crown. The unexpected death of Prince Arthur in 1502 aged only 16 proved to be something of a turning point in the deterioration of Henry's character. This is not entirely surprising. Henry VII was mercenary in his pursuit of dynastic security, it had aged him and he did not believe his son Henry Tudor was at all prepared for kingship. Therefore after 1502 the security of his throne rested on a knife-edge, or at least it probably appeared so to him. This could explain the retreat into the Privy Chamber towards the end of his reign, and at times excessive reliance upon a small handful of trusted ministers to do his bidding. Penn (2012) has argued that despite the challenges he faced, Henry VII was a still a cunning and secretive man who kept notes on the nobility, to help him to decide who he should reward. When he died on 21 April 1509, it was reported that Londoners celebrated by burning bonfires and dancing in the streets. The miserly king was dead and his athletic, handsome and charismatic son, Henry VIII, would succeed him. The fact that this happened without challenge is surely Henry VII's lasting legacy. He had taken a kingdom that had suffered after 30 years of warfare and brought it peace and a degree of stability.

	Domestic matters	**Foreign matters**
1485	Henry defeats Richard III at the Battle of Bosworth	
1486	Henry VII marries Elizabeth of York Begins first progress across the kingdom Arthur (first son) is born	Truce signed between England and Scotland
1487	Second Parliament opens	Lambert Simnel crowned king in Dublin Brittany Crisis
1489		Henry signs the Treaty of Medina del Campo with Spain
1491	Henry (second son) is born	Perkin Warbeck appears in Ireland
1492		Treaty of Étaples
1494		
1495	Execution of Sir William Stanley Fifth Parliament opens	

	Domestic matters	Foreign matters
1496		Invasion of Scots led by James IV and Warbeck
1497	Cornish Rebellion	
1499	Warbeck beheaded	
1501		
1502		
1503	Elizabeth of York dies	
1506		
1509	Henry VII dies and his son, Henry VIII, is crowned king	

Practice essay questions

1. 'Henry VII increased the power of the monarchy during his reign.' To what extent do you agree with this statement?
2. With reference to the extracts in the section on nobility and your understanding of the historical context, which of the two extracts provides the more convincing interpretation of the effectiveness of Henry VII in dealing with the nobility?
3. 'Rebellions in the years 1489 and 1497 stemmed from the weakness of central government.' Assess the validity of this view.

Chapter summary

By the end of this chapter, you should be able to:

- describe the threat posed by pretenders to the throne
- assess how well Henry VII responded to challenges he faced during his reign
- explain why Henry VII's foreign policy has been criticised by some
- evaluate how successful Henry was at restoring the power of the monarchy.

Further reading

For an intriguing read about the latter years of Henry VII's reign, Thomas Penn's *Winter King: The Dawn of Tudor England*; 2012 is riveting.

Christine Carpenter's 1997 book *The Wars of the Roses: Politics and the Constitution in England c. 1437–1509* is a radical revision of English politics during the Wars of the Roses, but also of Henry VII's reign. It requires you to understand a lot

ACTIVITY 1.9

The timeline outlines some of the main events that took place under Henry VII.

1. Go back through your notes and add the missing events.
2. When you have completed the timeline, use different colours to identify the kinds of problems Henry VII had to deal with: securing the dynasty, threats from abroad, modernising England, economic problems, securing his own throne.
3. As an extension activity write a paragraph explaining how successful Henry VII was in dealing with each of the problems he faced.

about Henry's reign already as she takes an analytical approach, but it is well argued throughout.

End notes

1   Williams PP. 'A Revolution in Tudor History: The Tudor State.' *Past and Present*: 25(1); 1963. p. 39–58.

2   Elton GR. *England under the Tudors.* London: Folio Society; 1955. p. 37.

3   Guy J. *Tudor England.* Oxford: OUP; 1988. p. 58.

4   Guy J. *Tudor England.* Oxford: OUP; 1988. p. 58.

5   Lander JR. *Government and Community: England 1450–1509.* London: Edward Arnold; 1980. p. 35.

6   Gunn SJ. *Early Tudor Government, 1485–1558.* London: Palgrave Macmillan; 1995. p. 31.

7   Lander JR. *Government and Community: England 1450–1509.* London: Edward Arnold; 1980. p. 35.

8   Lander JR. *Government and Community: England 1450–1509.* London: Edward Arnold; 1980. p. 35

9   Guy J. *Tudor England.* Oxford: OUP; 1988. p. 78.

2 Henry VIII, 1509–1547

In this section we will examine the nature of King Henry VIII's reign and consider some of the changes that were taking place in politics and religion and how these changes began to affect the relationship between the people and the monarchy. We will look into:

- Henry VIII: character and aims; addressing Henry VII's legacy.
- Government: Crown and Parliament, ministers, domestic policies including the establishment of Royal Supremacy.
- Relationships with Scotland and other foreign powers; securing the succession.
- Society: elites and commoners; regional issues and the social impact of religious upheaval; rebellion.
- Economic development: trade, exploration, prosperity and depression.
- Religion: renaissance ideas; reform of the Church; continuity and change by 1547.

Introduction

'The limit of our slavery, the beginning of our freedom, the end of sadness, the source of joy.' So wrote Thomas More in 1509.[1] Among other court poets, he clamoured to show that the beginning of Henry VIII's reign signalled the end of the Wars of the Roses, the end of winter, the end of injustice and a new beginning for England. The first 20 years of Henry VIII's reign could be characterised as stable, and in many ways, by a continuation of policies that had been established by his father, Henry VII. Yet there were marked differences between these two Tudor kings. This was demonstrated most obviously when Henry VIII took a personal interest in governance. Rather than pursuing a defensive policy, as his father had, Henry VIII longed for the glory that Henry V had acquired at Agincourt. Henry VII could hardly have imagined what his son would do to the English Church in the pursuit of providing an heir to the throne.

Henry VIII

Character and aims

Figure 2.1: This portrait of Henry VIII was painted in c. 1520. It is difficult to tell how accurate a likeness it is because most of these panels were completed by travelling artists who may not have spent much, if any, time with the king.

Born in Greenwich on 28 June 1491, Henry Tudor could hardly have imagined that he would succeed to the throne on the death of his father, on 21 April 1509. As the younger brother of Prince Arthur, he was not expected to become king, and therefore spent much of his childhood with his sisters, Margaret and Mary, at Eltham Palace. Educated by the poet, John Skelton, under the supervision of his grandmother, Lady Margaret Beaufort, he was schooled in the standard works of Homer, Virgil, Cicero and Tacitus. He excelled in languages and playing music and was given religious instruction by the Bishop of Rochester, John Fisher. Interestingly, unlike his elder brother, Arthur, Henry was never given any responsibility in his youth. Whereas Arthur was sent to the Welsh Marches to acquire political experience, for reasons unknown Henry was never given any apprenticeship. Therefore, according to the acclaimed historian Scarisbrick (1997), Henry VIII acceded to the throne 'unseasoned and untrained in the exacting art of kingship.'[2] However, the very fact that Henry VIII's accession was a peaceful one was a triumph for his father's policy; he was unquestionably the rightful King of England.

The scramble for lucrative offices and land began almost as soon as the old king had been laid to rest. Henry VIII had been bequeathed a fortune few English kings had ever inherited, and he was willing to spend it. George Talbot, Earl of Shrewsbury and Lord Steward, secured a valuable chamberlainship of the exchequer, and the Earl of Oxford was awarded many grants. The Lord Chamberlain, Charles Somerset, Lord Herbert, was given confirmation of his Welsh offices and awarded innumerable new ones. Richard Weston, who had been a personal attendant of Henry VII, regained the old family office of Captain of Guernsey, and was made keeper of Hanworth, a royal house near Richmond. Even Lady Margaret Beaufort, Henry's grandmother, was given the manor of Woking, which she had been forced to surrender to her son, Henry VII in 1503. Henry's patronage upon his accession was markedly different from the actions of his father in 1485, who needed to win over Yorkists to secure his throne. Although Henry VIII was clearly courting popularity by restoring members of the nobility to favour, he did this with a self-assured confidence that there was no one who could really provide a serious threat to his throne. Henry VIII had learnt from his father the importance of bearing a son who could succeed the throne. This could perhaps explain his hurry to marry Catherine of Aragon in 1509. John Guy (1988) suggests that Henry VIII was pressured into marrying Catherine of Aragon by his Council shortly after his father's death to maintain the relationship with Spain. However, Thomas Penn (2012) argues that Henry was single-minded about marriage: he knew it was needed and Catherine was acceptable, so he personally arranged the marriage in a hasty fashion. Evidence would suggest that Henry VIII was a devoted husband during the early years of their marriage and played the part of a courtly suitor excellently.

Date	Marriage	Surviving offspring	Fate of wife
11 June 1509	Catherine of Aragon	Mary: 18 February 1516	1533 no longer Queen. May 1534 placed under house arrest. Died 7 January 1536.
25 January 1533	Anne Boleyn	Elizabeth: 7 September 1533	Beheaded for adultery, May 1536.
30 May 1536	Jane Seymour	Edward: 12 October 1537	Died October 1537.

Date	Marriage	Surviving offspring	Fate of wife
6 January 1540	Anne of Cleves	None	Marriage annulled 9 July 1540.
28 July 1540	Catherine Howard	None	Beheaded for adultery 13 February 1542.
12 July 1543	Catherine Parr	None	Outlived Henry VIII, died 1548.

Table 2.1: Henry's marriages and children.

Historians have debated what kind of man Henry VIII was and have reached varying conclusions. Most now agree that over a period of 38 years he certainly changed a great deal. When he acceded to the throne, the Venetian ambassador Sebastian Giustinian described him as 'the handsomest potentate I ever set eyes on'.[3] An energetic young man, Henry was devoted to sports and jousting and enthusiastically threw banquets, pageants and masques. His good character was often remarked on. In 1529 Erasmus referred to Henry as 'a man of gentle friendliness, and gentle in debate; he acts more like a companion than a king'.[4] Gwyn (1990) asserts that accounts from the time almost all concur that the young Henry was utterly mesmerising and portrayed all the attributes of a chivalrous Renaissance King.

As he grew older, Henry's character changed. He became quicker to anger and carried out legendary acts of cruelty towards those who had been close to him. Smith (1971) argues that Henry 'invariably over-reacted to any stimulus … [and] Unfortunately the English king rarely looked before he leaped.'[5] Scarisbrick (1997) goes further to suggest that Henry VIII was 'highly strung and unstable; hypochondriac and possessed of a strong streak of cruelty'.[6] Guy (1988)[7] characterises Henry VIII's aims as 'imperial': he spoke of his rightful inheritance to the French throne and longed for the same sort of glory afforded Henry V at Agincourt. For these reasons, his policies were always going to differ from those of his father.

Addressing Henry VII's legacy

Many reigns began amidst an atmosphere of jubilant expectation, but Henry VIII's accession was especially heralded. For the courtiers and nobility, Henry VIII promised deliverance from an oppressive and unreasonable regime. There is some suggestion that, unlike his father, who had always kept his distance, even from his most trusted councillors, those at court felt that Henry VIII was open to persuasion. The extraordinary optimism that greeted Henry VIII can also be seen as an expression of dissatisfaction with the governmental and financial methods of his father. Henry VIII had been angered by tales of two particular ministers' wrongdoing, and swiftly took steps to provide a clean break with the previous reign.

Empson and Dudley

Henry VIII was astute enough to recognise that a gesture was needed to mark a difference between him and his father. An emphatic statement was to be made, that this regime would not be like the old. Richard Empson and Edmund Dudley had risen to dizzy heights under Henry VII, but were associated with the most repressive and arbitrary activities of his reign: both were prominent members of the much-hated Council Learned in the Law. They were most associated with collecting bonds and **recognisances**, universally dreaded by the nobility. They also received a percentage of the proceeds when prosecutions brought money into the Treasury, which aroused jealousies at court and among their neighbours in London. The chance for Henry VIII to win popularity with the nobility and send a clear message regarding his authority was too tempting, and Empson and Dudley were offered up as scapegoats. The round-ups began on 24 April 1509, just three days after Henry VII's death. John Camby and Henry Toft, both of whom had sat on Empson and Dudley's carefully chosen juries, were arrested, as were Empson and Dudley themselves, and all were carted off to the Tower of London.

The charge against Dudley was that on 22 April, he had 'conspired with armed forces to take the government of the King and realm'. The charge seems absurd; Dudley had thrived under the reign of Henry VII and surely must have been hoping to do the same under that of his son. Gunn (1995) suggests that Dudley and Empson might have summoned armed men to London, although it was either out of fear of their political enemies or in anticipation of political instability following the death of their master. After 16 months languishing in the Tower, they were finally executed on 17 August 1509. The speed with which Henry VIII had Empson and Dudley arrested perhaps reveals much about his character; that he was willing to take dramatic actions in the name of expediency with little regard for the fallout. As Elton (1955) asserts, there was something 'strikingly different from his father's clemency'.[8]

Break with the past?

Henry VIII's subsequent meetings with the Royal Council were designed to repudiate his father's most unpopular policies. Most notably, bonds and recognisances were put on a new footing. The Council also swept away the courts of Wards and Surveyors and the Council Learned in the Law. However, as Penn (2012) points out, the reforms were not so much about abolishing Henry VII's system of government, as consolidating it. It was politically expedient to cancel the bonds of magnates such as the Duke of Buckingham or Earl of Northumberland, but Henry VIII was not seeking a reversal of the overwhelming gains in royal authority his father had achieved. All debts or claims that had not been explicitly cancelled were now grounded firmly in law, and bonds were still collected and prosecuted. It is important to note that even though his father's tribunals were abolished, their practices and personnel continued more or less unchanged, with the exception of Empson and Dudley.

Henry VIII issued a general pardon to his people as his first official act as king on 25 April 1509. Although this was common practice, and before his death, Henry VII had also issued a similar general pardon, Henry VIII asserted that judges should minister justice freely, and that trade and manufacture should be free from forfeiture. This was a concession specifically to the merchants of London, with whom his father had poor relations due to his relentless policies of tax collection. Many of Henry VII's political prisoners were released, the most famous example being William Courtenay, who had been imprisoned in 1503 for supporting Edmund de la Pole, Earl of Suffolk. The earl himself remained in the Tower, however. The pardon represented the move away from the avaricious old monarch to the new, generous one.

Government

Crown and Parliament

Throughout his reign Henry VIII had an institutional council to advise him and to act in an executive capacity. It is also true that he depended heavily on individual ministers and, for more than a third of his 38-year reign, on one minister in particular (see the section on Thomas Wolsey). Yet Henry was no mere figurehead and held direct responsibility for war and diplomacy, if nothing else. According to Ives (1995), Henry did take a keen interest at an executive level in a range of issues; from the policy towards the Duke of Bavaria to sanctions for fraudulent cloth manufacture in the North. However, his threshold for boredom was alarmingly low. Despite this, he was not given to hand over total responsibility to others, even for those matters he found tedious. Henry VIII was well aware that the system waited on him, and he was happy to let matters wait. Henry VIII also exercised a personal form of government in appointments, because the power to reward was seen as a major political asset. He appointed his Council and his ministers, whom he allowed to assume the role of chief executive when it suited. How Henry VIII operated is an area of debate, not least because his personality and attitudes seem to shift seismically during his reign. Historians do agree, however, that royal favour was the basis of the power of any individual or group.

Parliament

Henry VIII thought Parliament a priority. He was in London for 19 of the 27 parliamentary sessions held in his reign and present for part of six more. Quite clearly he felt his presence was vital to proceedings: he often left Westminster on the day of dissolution. However, in the first 14 years of Henry's reign, when Thomas Wolsey dominated the political scene (see the section on Ministers) the House of Commons was used as little more than a tool to grant subsidies. Henry VIII was occupied with the impending invasion of France in 1511; at a time when war was costing upwards of £100 000 per annum, demands for subsidies came thick and fast. In 1513 Parliament granted £160 000 but only £50 000 was collected, therefore supplementary grants were made to raise the remainder. This process was repeated in 1515, but by 1523 Wolsey had grown tired of this lengthy process and so implemented a series of forced loans on strict individual assessments, raising over £350 000. It seemed to Wolsey that it was more advantageous to apply direct pressure than to use constitutional methods. By 1525, Henry VIII wanted to invade France again and tasked Wolsey with raising the necessary funds for the war chest. Wolsey proposed the optimistically titled 'Amicable Grant' in March 1525, which demanded one-sixth of the incomes of laymen and one-third of the equivalent wealth of the clergy. This provoked widespread spontaneous uprisings and Henry VIII was forced to retreat.

Aside from a clash over subsidies, the other major issue undertaken by Members of Parliament during Henry's early years was **anticlericalism**. In 1512 Parliament had passed an Act limiting the **benefit of clergy** to men in holy orders. By the time Parliament met again in 1515 the Hunne Case was the burning issue of the day and it was inextricably linked to the Benefit statutes. Richard Hunne, a London merchant clashed with the clergy over the payment of fees for spiritual services. He brought an action to the king's court and was arrested on charges of heresy. He was later found hanging from a beam in the Bishop of London's prison. The Church declared it had been suicide, but it looked to contemporaries like murder. Bishop Fitzjames of London elevated the issue by appealing for clerical immunity for those clergy implicated in the murder. Although royal disputation found in favour of the clerical lobby, later in the year the issue raised its head again; this time, however, judges found that clerics were encroaching on the king's regality, and were found guilty of **praemunire**. Wolsey, as symbolic leader of the clergy, was forced to kneel before Parliament and beg the king's pardon. This political clash between the clergy and laity might explain why there were fewer parliaments during the decade that followed.

In 1529, failure to obtain an annulment of Henry's marriage to his first wife, Catherine of Aragon, led to the downfall of Wolsey. In the confused political situation that followed there was no acceptable replacement, but Henry was determined to secure his succession by marrying Anne Boleyn. It was in these circumstances that he called the 'Reformation Parliament'. It should be noted that this title was not coined until the 20th century, although contemporaries were aware that its objectives were to reform the abuses of the Church. The work of this Parliament can be divided into three stages:

- Between 1529 and 1531 members turned their attention to the abuses in the Church, such as **non-residence** by the clergy and the exaction of excessive fees by officials in Church courts. It is important to note that the King had no intention of permitting Parliament to initiate policy, nor were members allowed to discuss the divorce.
- From 1532 to 1534, as the divorce became more urgent and Thomas Cromwell came to dominate royal policy, Parliament was directed to ensure the supremacy of the Crown over the affairs of the Church. Therefore the central business of Parliament was concerned with charges of praemunire made against the whole clergy. Following this, policy was directed towards disendowment of the Church, which included the dissolution of the monasteries.
- When Henry established the Royal Supremacy in 1534 (see the section on Royal Supremacy) he was careful to confine Parliament to discussing Church affairs and fixing penalties for those who transgressed the laws. Parliament's own authority was augmented by Cromwell under the Franchises Act of 1536. The act extended Parliament's jurisdiction into property rights, an area previously occupied by the king's prerogative. This culminated in the acts dissolving the monasteries (see the section on Dissolution of the Monasteries).

Key term

anticlericalism: opposition to the Church. At the turn of the 15th century this focused on the Church's independent jurisdiction, its wealth and abuses such as payment of fees for spiritual services.

Key term

benefit of clergy: enabled clerics to be tried in an ecclesiastical court. By the 16th century it was being successfully claimed by those who could simply read a couple of verses of the first psalm, enabling them to escape severe punishment.

Key term

praemunire: a law prohibiting the assertion of papal jurisdiction over that of the monarch.

Key term

non-residence: refers to an abuse by clerics who held positions in several parishes or bishoprics but never visited their congregations, and merely lived off the proceeds. This issue was linked with pluralism – where clergy held multiple ecclesiastical offices. Wolsey is one such example as he held the Bishopric of Lincoln and the Archbishopric of York.

The development of Parliament is perhaps one of the most significant consequences of the Reformation. Its composition was changed considerably as a result of the dissolution of the monasteries, with the disappearance of abbots and a slight increase in number of bishops. Overall the number of peers increased to 55 by 1534, making the clergy a minority in the House of Lords. In the Commons, 14 new boroughs elected MPs for the first time and this chamber gained status and significance under Cromwell. Parliament was also called more frequently: from 1509 to 1531 there were 11 sessions; from 1532 to 1540 there were ten. More significantly still, reform of the law became frequent, accelerating after 1540 and signalling a shift from change instigated by judges to change by legislative enactment. The last 12 parliamentary sessions produced upwards of 500 bills that received the royal assent, and many others that did not. This is not to say that Parliament was encroaching upon royal prerogative; rather, it was the supreme expression of royal power, and Henry VIII treated it as such, as only Parliament could really enforce his will by the 1530s. Many historians, including Ives (2007), have attributed the shift towards legislative enactment to the influence of Thomas Cromwell. For example, statutes passed in the 1536 session legislated on fishing, leather, enclosures, manufacture of cloth and town improvements, issues not at the forefront of Henry's mind. Perhaps because of Cromwellian legislation, Parliament became for Englishmen the accepted mechanism through which change nationally and locally could be achieved. This said, Henry was still heavily involved in government and ultimately he maintained his royal prerogative throughout his reign.

Privy Chamber

Henry VII had established a court system, which allowed the king to calculate public appearances and limit the number of people who had access to him to only six, in the Privy Chamber. Henry VIII desired friends and companions around him, and believed that menial service was acceptable for a gentleman. In consequence, by 1519 the staff of the Privy Chamber had been elevated socially and by 1546 increased in number to 20. It was the gentlemen of the Privy Chamber who would bring documents to the king to secure his signature. They were advantageously placed to talk up merits or blight the hopes of would-be beneficiaries. Being a member of the Privy Chamber was a lucrative affair as the example of William Brereton, Groom of the Privy Chamber, demonstrates: he enjoyed 30 royal grants, which brought him £1000 per year until his execution in 1536 (see the section on Anne Boleyn). Ives (1995) and Starkey (1985) agree that the Privy Chamber assumed even more importance in Henry VIII's final years, when he had grown tired of signing documents. Henry arranged that his signature could be officially forged by one of the chief gentlemen of the chamber, Anthony Denny. The unique position staff held in this chamber also meant Henry could rely upon them to go abroad as ambassadors on his behalf. As a consequence the men of the Privy Chamber were enormously experienced in diplomatic relations. The most important men of the Privy Chamber during Henry's reign were the Grooms of the Stool, a post held by William Compton, Henry Norris and, latterly, Denny. The groom had influence over who was admitted to see the king and was in charge of the privy purse. In the first year of Henry VIII's reign Compton received £2328 to spend and in the space of four years this had reached £17 517. This made the groom extremely important to the monarch.

Voices from the past

Thomas Wolsey

Thomas Wolsey was born in 1472, the son of a butcher, in Ipswich. He graduated from Magdalen College, Oxford and was ordained in to the priesthood in 1498. He was taken under the wing of Richard Fox and made a royal almoner under Henry VII. He joined the Royal Council in 1510 and quickly gained favour due to his willingness to please the king, particularly over the issue of war with France.

In 1514 he was promoted to Archbishop of York, but never held the see of Canterbury, which remained a disappointment to him. He was England's only cardinal in 1515 and became Lord Chancellor the same year; by 1518 he was a **papal legate** (a personal representative of the Pope to foreign nations). Historians widely agree that his power in government was unsurpassed while he was in the king's favour.

Council

Henry VIII kept most of his father's councillors and old methods were largely retained as individuals took on responsibility for specific areas of governance. Ives (1995) suggests that these councillors encouraged Henry VIII's passion for the trappings of kingship as they increasingly took on policy decisions as well as administration. Henry allowed his Council far more freedom than Henry VII to initiate policy, though it was always within the limits of Henry's trust and confidence. This form of conciliar leadership saw court attendance decline, allowing the king to become entrenched in the Privy Chamber with his closest friends. It was left to Richard Fox, Bishop of Winchester and Lord Privy Seal, to liaise with the king on behalf of the Council. Conciliar leadership could not last, however, given Henry's dislike of opposition, and the key issue came just two years after he acceded to the throne: whether or not to invade France. Henry VII's old councillors strongly opposed the newer generation of courtiers who sought influence with the king and one royal almoner in particular (Wolsey), was willing to do almost anything to please the king.

Ministers

Henry's ministers advised him and controlled the implementation of Crown policy. However, as Guy (in MacCulloch, 1995) asserts, the king might intervene or change his mind at will, making ministerial positions rather volatile. Although Henry VIII kept many of the ministers who had served his father, he was quick to promote men who were willing to serve at his pleasure, rather than those who were the most talented. One of those who rose to prominence was Sir Henry Marney. He had served the young prince and became a favourite, and when Henry became king, Marney was appointed Captain of the Guard and Vice Chamberlain. He was later given the Chancellorship of the Duchy of Lancaster, formerly held by the disgraced Empson and unanimously voted into the Order of the Garter in May 1509. It was an extraordinary accumulation of positions, turning Marney into one of the richest office holders under the Crown.

Key term

papal legates: an authorised representative of the Pope. Legates were frequently commissioned to carry out foreign diplomacy on the Pope's behalf.

Thomas Wolsey

In many ways, Cardinal John Morton prefigures Thomas Wolsey in his general management of the king's secular and ecclesiastical affairs. However, arguably no minister enjoyed greater freedom in the whole Tudor period than Thomas Wolsey. He rose to prominence quickly after graduating from Oxford, through the patronage of the Marquess of Dorset, who gave him access to the centre of political power in England, the King's Court. After 1501 Wolsey was appointed chaplain for Sir Richard Nanfan, Deputy of Calais. Nanfan recommended him to Henry VIII in 1507, and he became a royal chaplain who took part in diplomatic missions to Scotland and Flanders. By 1509 Wolsey was dean of both Lincoln and Hereford cathedrals and almoner to Henry VIII. Under the mentorship of Richard Fox, within five months of serving Henry VIII, Wolsey had acquired the position of registrar of the Order of the Garter and gained his seat on the Royal Council.

It was while serving on the Council that Wolsey achieved what Scarisbrick called his 'primacy'[9] superseding his mentor, Richard Fox, who resigned in 1513, and trampling on others, such as the Earl of Surrey to acquire the ear of the king. There has been a temptation for historians such as Elton (1955) to follow the accounts of Polydore Vergil, an Italian diplomat at the court of Henry VIII, in painting Wolsey as a man devoted only to self-glorification and promotion. Gwyn (1990) convincingly argues, however, that Wolsey maintained a positive relationship with Fox and regularly sought his advice, even after his resignation. Gwyn's Wolsey was a man of vast ability, unstoppable determination and vigilance and who was utterly devoted to Henry VIII. Guy (1988) argues that Wolsey was a man of 'no guiding principles'[10] who was a flexible opportunist. He happily counselled Henry VIII to indulge in pleasure and not to worry about attending council meetings, for he could take care of business. However, to assume that Wolsey manipulated Henry VIII is to underestimate the power of the king, for he was never really managed. Wolsey ascended to the heights of royal government because Henry VIII thought he should.

Figure 2.2: Cardinal Thomas Wolsey.

Wolsey established his prominence during the war against the French in 1514 (see the section on Relations with foreign powers). His organisational skills provided Henry with a well-equipped, well-disciplined army and he was rewarded handsomely, with the Bishoprics of Tournai and Lincoln in 1513. By 1514 he had assumed the Archbishopric of York and the following year became Lord Chancellor. For the next 15 years Henry VIII and Wolsey worked closely together on discussing diplomacy and military plans. This was an area the king was directly involved in, even down to the minute details. Gwyn (1990) argues that Wolsey was not much concerned about war per se; what was important was to dominate affairs and bring glory to his master and himself.

Wolsey also demonstrated little concern or aptitude for institutional reform as Loades (1999) argues, and operated highly personal methods of governance, based on managing men rather than creating machinery. He showed little regard for Parliament, only visiting the House once in his 14 years as Chancellor, in 1523. Even this was only to bully members into granting a subsidy of four shillings in the pound, which directly interfered with the established practice of the House to debate matters freely. Parliament was reluctant to grant subsidies given that Henry VIII had been living beyond his means for almost ten years, largely due to a foreign policy that necessitated constant extraordinary revenues. Wolsey had no sense of financial limitations – money was simply a way of gratifying the king – so he regarded Parliament as simply an obstacle that delayed his work. Historians such as Starkey (1985) have argued that Wolsey attempted to rid himself of rivals in court who might interfere with his work under the guise of the Eltham Ordinances in 1526. In essence, the Ordinances were an attempt to reform the royal household to increase cost efficiency. One consequence was the thinning down of the Privy Chamber from 22 to 15. Gwyn (1990) argues that Wolsey's practice was to conciliate and that he was far too intelligent to try and remove people the king favoured.

Wolsey's downfall has been much debated by historians. The traditional view has it that Wolsey had alienated significant members of the nobility, namely the Duke of Norfolk who, in his revenge, manipulated the king into getting rid of his favourite. This was supposedly done from 1527 onwards through encouraging the king to marry Norfolk's niece, Anne Boleyn. This view has more recently been significantly undermined. The Duke of Norfolk was undoubtedly the next most powerful man after Wolsey: he had become Lord Treasurer upon his father's resignation of the office in December 1522 thanks to his successful campaigns in Ireland and defending the northern borders against Scotland. Norfolk helped put down unrest in East Anglia following the Amicable Grant in 1525 and was on virtually every commission of the peace by 1529, a distinction shared only with Wolsey. Gwyn (1990) has suggested that far from being enemies, Norfolk and Wolsey were both loyal servants of the king and cooperated well together He goes further to suggest that there was no faction formed in 1527 to bring Wolsey down; on the contrary, the minister and the king had never been closer than in 1528 and expectations of Henry receiving an **annulment** of his marriage to Catherine of Aragon were high – Cardinal Campeggio was on his way to England from Rome to commission an investigation into the grounds for an annulment.

The annulment of his marriage to Catherine of Aragon, which Henry VIII sought, was extremely unpopular with the English people, as was the government that enabled him to pursue it. It is highly plausible that much of the people's blame was targeted at the king's chief minister, but crucially it was Henry VIII's confidence he lost. Wolsey had been made Papal Legate in England in 1518, which Henry had been happy with because he would expect in return that the Church would abide by his wishes, in matters close to his heart. By January 1529 Wolsey's attempts to secure a dispensation for an annulment by the Pope were in disarray and Henry was closer than ever to Sir Thomas Boleyn (Anne's father): as foreign ambassadors

 Key term

annulment: divorce was banned within the Catholic Church but an annulment was something the Pope could grant under special circumstances. It meant that a marriage was considered not to have been valid in the first place. Although Henry's seeking an annulment of his marriage to Catherine of Aragon is inextricably linked to the break with Rome, they were separate processes and it is important to note that his initial desire for an annulment did not inevitably lead to the abolition of papal authority in England.

note he was in constant attendance to the king. Wolsey faced enormous odds persuading Pope Clement to grant an annulment, which was bound to offend Emperor Charles V, King of Spain (Catherine of Aragon's nephew) who happened to be in a strong position to affect the fortunes of the papacy. By June 1529 suspicion was lodged in Henry's mind that Wolsey was deceiving him and did have the power to convince the Pope of the annulment but was refusing to use it. In the summer of 1529 the work of the legatine court the Pope had allowed to consider the annulment in England came to a halt due to the tactics of Cardinal Campeggio, who co-adjudicated it with Wolsey. This immediately affected Wolsey's position and Stephen Gardiner was appointed royal secretary to carry out much of the daily business previously carried out by the cardinal. Wolsey was still in Henry's service in September, but his position was by then precarious, even though he had managed to waive a formal summons on Henry to Rome and the financial penalties accrued by having the case heard in front of the Pope. However, Henry wanted to send a clear signal to the Pope that he would not give in, so he chose a method employed by kings during the 14th century. In October, two indictments of praemunire were brought against the cardinal and by 17 October he had surrendered the Great Seal, ceasing to be Lord Chancellor. Although officially pardoned in February 1530 and given a pension of £4000 per annum, by October Wolsey had been accused of treason. It is unlikely that the cardinal planned to overthrow the king, but he could not reconcile himself to exclusion from power and had been stoking support for himself in his Archbishopric of York, which provoked his enemies to action. It cannot be determined whether Henry really intended to execute Wolsey for his supposed crimes, for the cardinal died on 29 November 1530. Perhaps Wolsey's greatest error was that he failed fully to realise the lengths Henry would go to in order to secure his divorce, even if this meant **schism**, and with it the destruction of his most favoured minister.

Thomas Cromwell

The second of the ministers who dominated the royal court during the reign of Henry VIII has also caused great debate among historians, although undoubtedly his greatest biographer has been Geoffrey Elton, who first published his thesis on Cromwell in 1953. Elton (1955) rejected the view of Cromwell as an unscrupulous secularist interested in advancing his own position. Instead, he suggested that Cromwell transformed England by creating a national church, elevated the position of Parliament and recast the central administration, which replaced government by the king and recast it in the form of King-in-Parliament. This has been challenged by recent historians who play down the bureaucratic reforms made by Cromwell, and highlight Henry's personal methods of rule. Historians at least agree that Thomas Cromwell made an indelible impression on Thomas Wolsey when he joined the cardinal's service in 1516. He was no 'second Wolsey', however, not merely because of his holding fewer offices of power, but because Henry was much more engaged in decision making than he had been in previous years. Cromwell was in a different league from Wolsey when it came to 'political originality'[11] according to Ives (1995). Cromwell had to manage the inner ring of councillors who saw the king more than he did.

Key term

schism: a division or disunion within a church or religious body over a particular doctrinal difference. In the 1500s the great schism came within Christianity, between the Roman Catholic Church and a group of reformers calling themselves Protestants.

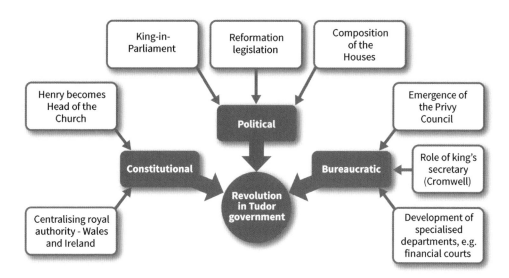

Figure 2.3: Illustrates the 'revolution' in government attributed to Cromwell by some historians, such as Elton (1955).

ACTIVITY 2.1

Figure 2.3 illustrated Elton's argument about the revolution in government that occurred under Cromwell. Can you find any evidence in your notes that might provide criticism of these claims?

Cromwell won the king's favour by rescuing him from the dilemma caused by the desire to annul his first marriage, showing the king how to use existing institutions and laws for the unprecedented task of repudiating papal authority. He was uninhibited by any sense of tradition, and therefore was able to make certain Henry's right to assert Royal Supremacy. He was appointed to the position of Master of the King's Jewels in April 1532. To this he added Clerk of the Hanaper (1532), Chancellor of the Exchequer (1533), Principal Secretary and Master of the Rolls (1534), Vice-regent in Spirituals (1536), and finally Lord Privy Seal (1536). These offices allowed him control over the administration of government, although his power, as with Wolsey, derived from the King's confidence. Loades (2013) argues that Cromwell had a vision of the state as a sovereign nation living under a law, which was controlled by Parliament. As such, Loades and Guy (in MacCulloch, 1995) attribute much of the changes that took place under Henry VIII's reign to the 'administrative genius' of Cromwell.[12]

Cromwell was not an intellectual like More, but read widely and deeply. He was a man who spent time seeking solutions to problems to ensure smooth transitions. Perhaps one of his greatest personal achievements was in his dealings with factions at court. There were two key factions: one in favour of Catherine and her daughter Mary, aptly named the Aragonese Faction, and the other, the Boleyns. Cromwell managed to manipulate both to create evidence that suggested Anne Boleyn had been unfaithful to Henry with Sir Henry Norris, Mark Smeaton, Lord Rochford, William Brereton and Francis Weston. All were convicted of treason and executed in May 1536, paving the way for Cromwell to become Lord Privy Seal and destroying the Boleyn faction at court. This coup left Cromwell's master free to marry Jane Seymour on 30 May 1536, less than a fortnight after the execution of Anne Boleyn. Following this, Cromwell convinced Mary to submit completely to her father, and therefore removed her as effective leader of the Aragonese faction at court.

Speak like a historian: King-in-Parliament

King-in-Parliament is a constitutional term used by Elton explaining the role of Henry VIII in relation to his Parliaments. Elton suggested that under Cromwell the king needed to work with Parliament more to substantiate the legitimacy of his reforms: this marks a shift from the medieval methods of kings passing laws on their own.

Perhaps Cromwell is most famed for his role in the dissolution of the monasteries, but the changes he made in his capacity as Vice-regent in Spirituals were arguably the most far-reaching. Cromwell ordered the clergy to defend the Royal Supremacy in sermons, to teach children according to a Protestant programme and to abandon pilgrimages. In 1538 he authorised the removal of idolatrous images from churches and in the same year gave the order for an English translation of the Bible to be made available to the public in every parish church. Historians have debated whether he was a true 'Protestant' or not. The truth is this label was not widely used at this time. Probably the most convincing argument made recently is by Coby (2009), who suggests that Cromwell's inclination towards Protestantism was as a result of '**Protestantism**'s tilt towards secular supremacy'.[13]

A key plank of Elton's argument for Cromwell revolutionising Tudor government is the importance he places on the emergent Privy Council. Historians mostly agree that Cromwell had a plan for the Council to be freed from the Star Chamber and to assume defined working practices, but events overtook him. It was the massive rebellion, the Pilgrimage of Grace, which caused political upheavals of such magnitude that he would hardly have had time to undertake such reform, and his correspondence reveals his silence on the matter. Elton's argument is also undermined by the membership of the reorganised Privy Council, who were largely religious conservatives opposed to his position. What was transformed, however, was the signing of letters on behalf of the Council from the minister of the day, towards a collective signature of the Council as a board. Only after Cromwell's execution in 1540 did the Privy Council gain its own registers and secretariat, arguably the hallmarks of bureaucracy. Cromwell thus witnessed, not masterminded, the birth of the Executive Council, which had assumed responsibility for Tudor government by Elizabeth I's reign.

Cromwell's downfall stemmed from politics, rather than any personal clashes with the king. Historians have debated the fall of the man whom Henry VIII lamented as his finest servant, after his execution in 1540. Scarisbrick (1997) claims that Cromwell was made to shoulder the blame for the failed marriage to Anne of Cleves. Hutchinson (2007) suggests that Henry VIII had already fallen for Catherine Howard and Cromwell delayed the Anne of Cleves annulment to prevent the Duke of Norfolk's niece being installed – in this way his fall would parallel Wolsey's. Guy (1988) claims it was his pro-Lutheran diplomacy and support for radical reformers and possibly even a clash with Henry VIII over financial objectives. The factors that brought about Cromwell's fall were many in truth, although it seems that religion lay at the heart of Henry's decisive change of mind, brought about by Stephen Gardiner as the critical agent.

Privy Council

The demise of the two chief executives, Wolsey and Cromwell, as well as the political crisis created by the Pilgrimage of Grace, a major rebellion that threatened the stability of the kingdom, (see the section on Pilgrimage of Grace) precipitated institutional change. Henry VIII needed the support of the nobility to regain control of the northern third of the country; he therefore defined the membership of his Council as a small, advisory, executive 'privy council' of senior politicians. This countered the Pilgrims' claims that Henry had been swayed by 'upstarts' who were not natural councillors. The period after 1540 saw royal favour and politics matter more than ever as the king increasingly used his Privy Council, and became ever more unpredictable in his policies. Cromwell's fall from grace had secured the centrality of the Privy Council, but it became a hotbed of political struggle. The Council struggled to operate within the court, particularly as Henry VIII continued to progress around the country. Once again Henry appointed a personal assistant, in the form of William Paget, the King's Secretary. From 1543 Paget effectively mediated between Henry and the councillors at court.

Factionalism

Competition to secure the ear of the ruler has characterised almost every personal monarchy since the Classical period. Henry VIII's was no exception. That Henry VIII had ultimate authority during his reign is beyond question, but he was not a victim of factionalism and was never weak on the throne. The role of his servants and advisers was to implement his expressed will, even when the king was reluctant to take responsibility for some decisions. Henry was amenable to pressure on the

> ### Key term
>
> **Protestantism:** a movement that originated in Germany from 1517 and questioned the traditional Catholic religion. Protestantism had certainly been discussed in some circles in England by 1530, particularly in coastal towns with ports, which had greater access to the Continent, such as Bristol and London. The most radical elements of Protestantism centred around personal devotion, Biblical study and the doctrine of justification by 'sola fide' (faith alone).

Voices from the past

Stephen Gardiner

Born in 1483, Stephen Gardiner served as a secretary to Wolsey and, after the latter's fall from grace, to the king. Despite supporting the Act of Royal Supremacy, Gardiner was a thorough opponent of the Reformation from a doctrinal point of view, and he was removed from his office as Bishop of Winchester under Edward VI. He regained the post under Queen Mary I and also served as her Lord Chancellor.

Gardiner felt so strongly about Erasmus's work that he wrote a letter to Henry VIII criticising it:

I have the booke with me; and so shall no manne saie that I mysreporte the boke. The words be theis: 'Render therefore unto Cesar, if anything appertain unto God: meaning that [it] is no hurte to godliness, if a man,

being dedicate to God, do give tribute to a propphane prince, although he ought it not.' Theis be the words in the booke ordered to be sett fourthe; wherein what needeth Erasmus to bring in doubte the dutie, when God putteth no doubte at all? Yt were to longe to write to your Grace everye faulte. This one I put for example, wher Erasmus doth corrupt Christes wordes with a condicion which Christ spake not.

Source: Gardiner S. In JA Muller (ed.) *The Letters of Stephen Gardiner*. Cambridge: CUP; 1933. p. 384.

Discussion points:

1. What is it that Gardiner seems to object to?
2. Why do you think he supported the Royal Supremacy if he had issues with reform in general?

Speak like a historian: contrasting views of Thomas Cromwell

Extract A

He played the leading part in subordinating the clergy to the crown; he orchestrated the press campaign in defence of the break with Rome. Above all, he enforced the Royal Supremacy by means of oaths of allegiance and extensions to the treason law. When Henry repudiated Anne Boleyn in the spring of 1536, Cromwell was deft enough to obtain the evidence needed to destroy Anne and her court allies in order that Henry might marry Jane Seymour. But he also took his opportunity to drive his own political opponents from court on the grounds that they had plotted to restore Princess Mary to the succession.

The *putsch* of mid-1536 gave Cromwell the pre-eminent ascendancy he had hitherto lacked. His power was real, but it was less secure than Wolsey's ...

Source: Guy J. 'Cromwell and the Reform of Government'. In D MacCulloch (ed.) *The Reign of Henry VIII, Politics, Policy and Piety*. London: Palgrave MacMillan; 1995.

Extract B

Certainly Henry VIII was a king willing to allow his ministers to rid him of the daily toils of government, and as several chapters have illustrated here, there were areas over which Cromwell had very real influence – even a measure of independence. With regard to the Crown lands, for example, on at least one occasion Henry refused to make a decision without first taking Cromwell's advice. He has also been shown promoting legislation in parliament of which the king had very little knowledge. But more often than not, Cromwell's independence was over the execution of policy, not its formulation. The significant point to emerge from many chapters here is that during the years 1531–1534, Cromwell was working for, and taking his lead from, his royal master.

Source: Everett M. *The Rise of Thomas Cromwell: Power and Politics in the Reign of Henry VIII*. New Haven: Yale University Press; 2015. p. 252.

Discussion points
1. What does Guy suggest were the strengths of Cromwell? What about Everett?
2. How does Everett differ from Guy?

right issues; however, it was undoubtedly the influence of faction that brought down Anne Boleyn, Wolsey, Cromwell, the Howards and Gardiner. Nevertheless, any full portrait of the monarch reveals a king who could dismiss Wolsey but miss him terribly, who was prepared to execute his closest friend when he would not admit to adultery with his wife, and who had his best servant executed. Occasionally, Henry VIII was persuaded to take decisions he might not have otherwise, but Henry always remained the ultimate source of power.

Domestic policies

Finance

Hoyle (in MacCulloch, 1995) explains the difficulty of evaluating Henrician finance due to original documentary losses, making precise figures elusive. However, historians have debated whether sources of revenue were adequate and the extent of the impact of Henry's policies.

Ordinary revenue

The Crown's ordinary revenue was largely inflexible and always more likely to fall than rise, because it was dependent upon Crown lands. The reversal of Henry VII's attainders cost Henry VIII around £15 000 from his landed income between 1509 and 1515. It is unlikely that Henry VIII's income from his estates ever exceeded his father's before 1536, even given the lands acquired after the fall of Wolsey and the attainders of the Duke of Buckingham and Marquess of Exeter. The overall trend for incomes derived from customs duties also followed a downward trend: in the early years from 1500 to 1520 the Crown could rely on approximately £41 000 annually, but this had fallen to £32 000 by the 1530s. Wolsey clearly saw the need to salvage income for the Crown, and the Act of Resumption passed in 1515 was part of a scheme of economies in government expenditure that included collecting debts, the abolition of the King's Spears, returning some lands to the Crown and reducing the garrison stationed at Tournai following the Battle of the Spurs (see the section on Relations with foreign powers). This probably raised up to £10 000 for the king's coffers, which was much needed given that royal income had sunk to approximately £25 000 per annum despite Wolsey's aggressive taxation policies. Cromwell's contribution to the development of finances was more in taxation philosophy than in the field of revenue collection. The Subsidy Act of 1534 was remarkable because it justified taxation on grounds of peace and not war and yielded £406 000 between 1535 and 1540.

The most significant augmentation of royal finance was taken from the Church. The Crown had always drawn some revenue from income of episcopal estates during vacancies and from the clerical subsidy. However, under Henry VIII, Church revenues were exploited as never before. The payment of a one-off tax to the Pope by newly elected clerics, known as **Annates** or First Fruits, was abolished in 1533 but revived the following year in the form of a payment to the Crown. This was coupled with 'Tenths', an annual tax charged at the rate of one tenth the value of the benefice. Together these taxes were oppressive. They brought in £42 000 annually but provoked clerical protests and so were amended slightly in 1536. Even more significant was the dissolution of the monasteries, which was instituted by statute in 1536. The Court of Augmentations was established to deal with this new revenue stream. The new income derived from smaller monastic houses in 1537 was around £38 000, after the deduction of expenses, officers' fees and pensions. Hoyle suggests that the dissolution might have been worth £50 000 annually in rents. However, Henry VIII sold off many of the monastic lands. In this respect Henry VIII threw away the major advantage the Crown had gained, for the monasteries could only be dissolved once and the longer-term income from rents would have provided more stability for the Crown. The middle-aged Henry VIII did have a much greater income than his father, drawn almost entirely from the

ACTIVITY 2.2

Draw a table with two columns and explain how and why Wolsey and Cromwell's roles in Henry VIII's government were similar, and how and why they were different.

Key term

Annates: taxes levied by the Pope on recently appointed clergy.

Church, clerical taxation and the monasteries, but he had undermined the future basis of royal finance.

Extraordinary income

Henry VIII levied taxes on his people to fund wars: between 1512 and 1517 this raised £260 000. However, it is estimated that Henry spent about £1 000 000 on war between 1512 and 1514 and there is no clear explanation from historians as to where these enormous sums were found, although many, such as Starkey (1985), suspect he spent what his father had managed to accumulate. It is certain that taxation was the main way in which Henry's wars were financed. Wolsey sought loans from the laity in 1523, having conducted extensive and unparalleled surveys of individual wealth and military capacity, raising £280 000. He then sought grants from Parliament in 1524 and 1525 that saw two shillings in the pound given over to the Crown. Wolsey had attempted to extract four shillings in the pound under the Amicable Grant, but public outcry forced a retreat. These were extraordinary achievements for the Chancellor by any standard, but it was insufficient to meet the costs of war. By September 1545 expenditure had reached new highs and the new Lord Chancellor, Thomas Wriothesley, was extremely concerned. Patterns of taxation exhibited earlier in the reign were repeated, except that the Amicable Grant was turned into the 'Benevolence' and was essentially a grant without parliamentary sanction. An extra subsidy was also placed on wealthier individuals in 1546, which required those who held lands worth more than £2 to pay a contribution of four pence in the pound for five months. Hoyle (1995) suggests this represented the heaviest taxation England had experienced since the 14th century. It is clear that Henry's foreign wars brought about short periods of heavy taxation, which often forced taxpayers to sell assets to pay the monies to the Crown. Hoyle suggests that the result may well have been unemployment for many and a contraction in the home market, which ate into accumulated capital. Henry VIII destroyed the future fortunes of the monarchy, and arguably undermined the fabric of society with his reckless wars undertaken in the 1540s.

Growth of Courts of Equity and the Star Chamber

On 22 December 1515 Archbishop Warham resigned as Lord Chancellor and the title fell to Wolsey. Within a few years, Wolsey's close attention towards the Star Chamber transformed it into a mainstream tribunal of law enforcement and impartial justice. Wolsey's ministerial sponsorship saw lawsuits initiated in the Chamber increase from 12 per annum under Henry VII to 120 per annum under Henry VIII. Star Chamber was crucial to Wolsey as his reputation here allowed him to exercise influence elsewhere. His first policy, unveiled in May 1516, planned to concentrate traditional enforcement jurisdiction into the Star Chamber. He aimed to improve law enforcement and deliver impartial justice, which included the investigation and prosecution of crime and corruption of justice. Wolsey investigated and attacked corrupt methods and abuses perpetrated by the king's own councillors, Justices of the Peace (JPs) and sheriffs. In doing so he made considerable enemies.

Wolsey also popularised the notion that justice was a right and therefore private parties could use the Star Chamber and Chancery if necessary. These plans backfired somewhat as the courts' machinery soon became clogged with civil actions. Part of Wolsey's notion of accessible justice led him to reconstitute a body that been founded in Richard III's reign, to hear the cases from those too poor for the other courts. In 1520 it was established as a tribunal sitting in the White Hall at Westminster and eventually became the Court of Requests in 1538. It rapidly lost its links with the Royal Council, because of the relatively trivial nature of the suits heard, and therefore was staffed with lesser judges. It played a specialised role in protecting tenancy rights for the peasantry. Wolsey had slightly less impact in the Chancery where the 500 or so petitions filed every year under Archbishops Morton and Warham were only slightly increased to 535 under Wolsey.

Enclosures

Wolsey launched a campaign against enclosures almost as soon as he was appointed Lord Chancellor. Tudor theorists believed enclosures brought about the decay of villages and unemployment. Enclosing had been attacked by statute in 1489 but new acts were introduced in 1514 and 1515 that forbade new enclosures and ordered demolished buildings to be reconstructed and land restored to tillage. Wolsey launched a national inquiry in 1516 to 1518, to discover the extent of the enclosures. The commissioners reported directly to the Chancery and as a result 264 landlords were prosecuted. One of these landowners was the renowned scholar, Thomas More. Many cases dragged on for many years, but 188 verdicts were reached, which was a high proportion by Tudor litigation standards. However, domestic programmes were entirely flexible under Wolsey as he suspended the enclosure policy for almost a year in 1523 as part of a deal in order to raise a subsidy worth £150 000. The programme was seen through, however, and by 1529 all unlawful enclosures were ordered to be destroyed.

Establishment of Royal Supremacy

Gunther and Shagan (2007)[14] have described Henry VIII's assertion of the Royal Supremacy over the Church as an 'epochal event in early modern history'. The Act of Royal Supremacy established in 1534 abolished papal authority in England and, in the process, created many socio-political-religious tensions that would shape developments until the Glorious Revolution of 1688, although it was not obvious to contemporaries what the implications of the legislation would be. In fact Henry VIII had no intention of passing such an act even 12 months before Parliament enacted it. It can scarcely be denied that had Pope Clement agreed to annul Henry's first marriage, the Act of Supremacy would not have been needed. However, the divorce alone cannot account for the **Reformation**, which occurred following the **break with Rome** (see the section on Reform of the Church).

In the autumn of 1529, following his failure to obtain an annulment for Henry, Wolsey was brought down on a charge of praemunire for a supposedly illegal exercise of his powers as papal legate. In the summer of 1530, 15 clerics and one layman were accused of complicity with Wolsey, and by January 1531 this charge had been extended to the whole of the clergy. Henry demanded a payment of £100 000 and recognition of his role as Supreme Head of the Church in England. Historians differ in their assessments of Henry's motives in demanding this payment, and it may at first have been based merely on a desire for short-term financial gain. However, in the wrangles that followed, Henry became increasingly infuriated by the clergy's defence of its liberties and determined to limit the

Key term

The Reformation: describes the movement that swept through Europe in the 16th century under the influence of Martin Luther, Huldrych Zwingli and John Calvin. The reformers aimed to rid the Church of abuses but ended by establishing separate 'reformed' Churches under the banner of Protestantism, free from the control of the Papacy. The Reformation took almost a century to develop and cannot be seen as one event, although historians disagree about the speed and extent of the reformation in England.

Key term

The break with Rome: represents the legislative changes to the status of the Church in England. The legislation removed the power of the papacy in England, but did not in itself bring about the end of Catholicism or Catholic practices.

Pope's authority. Bizarrely these charges were postponed and reignited again in January 1531, whereby the clergy were forced to give the title of 'Supreme head as far as the law of Christ allows' and a subsidy of £100 000 to Henry by way of settlement. Contradicting Scarisbrick (1997) this was a not a key manoeuvre by Cromwell as Guy (1982)[15] argues to reduce the clergy to 'impotent obedience to royal and parliamentary authority' enshrined in the Act of Appeals in 1533. Rather, he argues, this was an excuse to gain a subsidy for a potential war with Spain. By 1532 Cromwell had drawn up a document named the 'Supplication against the Ordinaries', which marks the beginning of the real attack on the liberties of the Church because it demanded that legislative independence of the clergy in Convocation be cancelled. Henry showed little interest at first until Stephen Gardiner drafted a response defending the traditional liberties of the Church, which angered the king a great deal. Two days later Henry demanded a submission from the clergy to the effect that Convocation could make no Church law that was contrary to the law of the land and which did not have royal assent. The 'Submission of the Clergy', as this became known, was reinforced by an Act of Parliament in 1534.

Parliament had also passed the Act in Conditional Restraint of Annates in the spring of 1532, which removed the right of the Pope to tax the clergy – clearly an attack on the privileges of the Pope fuelled by Henry's frustration. It was followed in 1533 with the Act in Restraint of Appeals, which is perhaps more renowned for its preamble than its provisions. The preamble introduced the concept of England as an empire, within which the Crown was supreme in Church and state; no appeal could be made to the Pope on religious or any other matters. Shortly after its enactment, Archbishop Cranmer annulled Henry's marriage to Catherine.

The Act of Supremacy was passed in the autumn of 1534. It not only confirmed the supreme headship of the Crown, but also gave the king specific powers within the Church. Henry was not merely the secular head of the clergy, he adopted the power of visitation, the right to discipline and correct preachers, the right to supervise canon law and doctrine and claimed the right to try heretics. Interestingly, only one of Henry's bishops, John Fisher, refused to acknowledge his claim. The Act in Restraint of Annates was passed in November 1534 and confirmed the previous legislation of 1532, abolishing appeals entirely. The right to grant dispensations was transferred from the Pope to the Archbishop of Canterbury, whose authority was subject to appeal to the Lord Chancellor. Parliament also removed the 'Peter's Pence', which was an annual tax of one pence per household paid to Rome. The legislation confirming the Royal Supremacy was completed with the Act of Succession, establishing the rights to the succession to the English throne of Henry and Anne Boleyn's heirs.

Treasons Act 1534

Elton (1955) called the Acts establishing the Royal Supremacy a 'conservative revolution',[16] which created constitutionalism. The final major piece of legislation to be implemented was the Treasons Act, adding new clauses that made calling the monarch a heretic or schismatic a treasonable offence. Moreover, it extended treason from intent expressed in deeds to intent expressed in malicious words. The ensuing executions have led some historians to describe the years 1534–40 as a period of terror, but in truth the Act only embodied in parliamentary legislation principles that had already been established in common law. Perhaps the most astonishing thing about the break from Rome is how few opponents it created, although those who did oppose it became martyrs to their cause. Following the careful repression of the bishops in 1531, only the adherents of the Nun of Kent, Sir Thomas More and a few monks felt strongly enough to take stands that made them fall foul of the treason legislation.

The Nun of Kent, as she came to be called, was a poor servant girl named Elizabeth Barton who was afflicted with epilepsy, but her trances and visions began to attract attention from 1525. A monk, Edward Bocking, stage-managed her episodes to rebel against the king's policy. Together, Barton and Bocking created a prophecy against the king's second marriage, and she even forced her way into the king's presence to tell him so. She and her accomplices were arrested in 1533 and executed the following April. Perhaps the most dangerous thing about Barton was that she was supported by the humanist bishop, John Fisher. Henry VIII grew intolerant of opposition from his own subjects extremely quickly, and was determined to ensure that particularly high-profile individuals should pledge their allegiance to him. The requirement to take an oath in support of the Act of Succession proved a crucial turning point in the fortunes of Sir Thomas More and John Fisher. The oath required not only adherence to the Act of Succession, but a condemnation of the first marriage and repudiation of papal supremacy. While they were prepared to acknowledge the first, More and Fisher refused to compromise their consciences on the second. Both Cranmer and Cromwell tried hard to save More, but the differences were fundamental. Both men were kept in the Tower until the Treasons Act was passed. Fisher, who had been elevated to the rank of cardinal by the Pope in May, was executed in June 1535, and More followed in July. Another eight clerics followed them to the scaffold. Most historians agree that these executions represented the implacable cruelty of the king.

 Voices from the past

Sir Thomas More

Sir Thomas More was born on 7 February 1478 in the City of London. Although he qualified as a lawyer, he contemplated taking holy orders as a monk. After entering the king's service, he rose to become one of Henry VIII's most effective and trusted servants, serving him as secretary, diplomat and adviser.

More was famed as a scholar and was a close friend of the Humanist theologian Erasmus. His most celebrated work is *Utopia*, published in 1516. A passionate defender of Catholic orthodoxy, he wrote polemics against Luther and other Protestant reformers and took personal charge of interrogating heretics.

More was appointed Lord Chancellor in 1529, after the fall of Wolsey, but resigned over the issue of Henry's appointing himself Supreme Head of the Church in England. In 1534 he was arrested after refusing to swear the oath of succession, which repudiated the Pope and accepted the annulment of Henry's marriage. He was tried for treason and executed on Tower Hill on 6 July 1535. Historians who have praised Wolsey have often criticised More, and vice versa. More is traditionally seen to be less ambitious and more highly principled than Wolsey.

Figure 2.4: *The Arrest and Supplication of Sir Thomas More* by the French painter Antoine Caron. This image was probably painted in 1591.

Discussion points:

1. Do you think this painting is sympathetic towards More? If so, what makes you think this?
2. Why was More's execution so controversial?

Relationships with Scotland and other foreign powers

Henry VIII had been educated with tales of Henry V's successes at the Battle of Agincourt in 1415. This was clearly an influence on the young Henry, as is shown by his more aggressive stance towards foreign policy than his father's. By the end of 1509 Henry had reinforced Calais, commissioned new artillery and initiated an expansion programme for the navy. In 1509 France was still the old enemy and many were jealous of her successes. Affairs were dominated by the Italian wars, where France had participated in the successes of the League of Cambrai against Venice in 1509. However, in 1511 Pope Julius revived the alliance as the Holy League, this time against the French, drawing in Ferdinand of Aragon and the Venetians. Henry VIII needed little convincing to join the war against France. In fact he was to spend about a quarter of his reign in open war against that country.

The First French War

Catherine of Aragon saw it as a duty to lobby her husband on behalf of her father, Ferdinand of Aragon. She did just this in 1511 to convince Henry VIII, as if he needed it, to enter into the Holy League and assist Ferdinand in Spain. Henry VIII may have couched war with France in terms of adhering to papal policy, but in reality the king himself was the decisive factor in England's waging war on the French in February 1512. He was in search of glory and was not pursuing the genuine interests of his nation. Parliament was summoned in 1512 and supplied the necessary grants, even though they were fully aware that war with France would also provide instability along the border with Scotland. Ferdinand convinced Henry to join him in attempting to conquer Guyenne. The Spaniards made no secret of the fact that the English force was only a pawn in a Spanish game and the English troops were used as a decoy for Ferdinand to capture Navarre. The Marquess of Dorset and his men, who had been sent by Henry, were ill looked after and many died from dysentery. Failure and disgrace only seemed to spur Henry VIII on to further action. Wolsey coordinated the next strike in 1513, with Maximilian I as his ally. Henry VIII took 25 000 men into Northern France, where he personally led a cavalry charge against the French. The latter were reputed to have retreated so quickly that nothing could be seen but the glinting of their spurs, and this Battle was later called the 'Battle of the Spurs'. The attack resulted in the occupation of Thérouanne and Tournai, and although these were of little strategic significance, Henry was thrilled.

Henry VIII was forced to follow war with diplomacy, for Maximilian and Ferdinand had already made their peace with France in August 1514. Wolsey negotiated the treaty whereby Henry and Louis XII promised peace until their deaths. Henry recovered arrears on the indemnity agreed under the Treaty of Étaples (1492), which was worth approximately £450 000 to the Crown, and Henry's younger sister Mary was betrothed to the lecherous Louis XII. Elton (1955) argues this treaty was the making of Wolsey, for he learnt quickly how to conduct diplomacy and that England was not half as powerful as King Henry liked to think.

The death of Louis XII on 31 December 1514 ended the brief entente between England and France. His successor, Francis I, won spectacular victories over the Swiss at Marignano, arousing the jealousy of Henry VIII. This prompted Henry to pursue an anti-French coalition, forcing Wolsey to agree with Maximilian I to fight with him in Milan against the old enemy. The death of Ferdinand of Aragon in January 1516 provided severe setbacks for the English. Both his successor, Charles I, and Maximilian sought separate peace treaties with France, leaving England diplomatically isolated. Wolsey was left with little choice but to repair relations with France. Anglo-French negotiations began in 1517 and resolved existing maritime disputes, as well as English differences with Scotland, for the time being.

Speak like a historian: The League of Cambrai

The War of the League of Cambrai, or War of the Holy League, was one of a succession of wars in Italy. Pope Julius II created an alliance with Louis XII of France, Maximilian I and Ferdinand of Aragon to curb Venetian power. However, after his victories against Venice, Louis XII of France started to become too powerful, and threatened to dominate Europe, causing Pope Julius to ally with Venice in a new Holy League against France in 1510.

The Treaty of London

Meanwhile, Pope Leo X sought to establish a general European peace. He dispatched legates to England, France and Spain to arrange a five-year peace among Christian princes and a crusade against the Turks. Cardinal Campeggio was named legate for England. Wolsey saw his opportunity for Anglo-papal cooperation, which would undoubtedly bring prestige to the Crown. Henry VIII denied Campeggio admission to England unless Wolsey was given the legatine commission, something the Pope had been refusing for four years. The Pope conceded and made Wolsey co-legate with Campeggio. Again Wolsey seized the initiative and transformed the intended papal truce into an international treaty under his presidency. The Treaty of London was signed in October 1518, by over 20 rulers, who pledged to keep the peace and act together against any transgressors. It was a diplomatic triumph. Two days later Henry concluded another treaty with France that ceded Tournai to France (it was an expensive outpost for the king so this was no great loss) and Henry's two-year-old daughter, Mary, was promised to the Dauphin.

Field of the Cloth of Gold

Maximilian I died in 1519, prompting elections for a new Holy Roman Emperor. Both Charles I of Spain and Francis I of France put themselves forward, as did Henry VIII. Charles I was victorious and became the most powerful ruler in Europe – making him Charles V, Holy Roman Emperor. War between him and Francis loomed and, as a result, both leaders sought to reach agreements with Henry VIII. Wolsey rightly wanted to demonstrate evenhandedness towards both monarchs, so a complex series of personal meetings was arranged between Henry VIII, Charles V and Francis I. The meeting with Francis I at the Field of Cloth of Gold in June 1520 was heralded as a chivalric display of diplomacy that was much to Henry VIII's taste. In reality it was no more than a two-week long jousting tournament that cost a year's revenue and required 6000 people to attend to the king.

Figure 2.5: Painted in c. 1545 this celebrates the Field of the Cloth of Gold and demonstrates the extravagance of the occasion.

Figure 2.6: The kingdoms of Europe, showing power distribution in 1510.

Discussion points:

1. Who were the two biggest powers in Europe at this time?
2. Why was this a problem for Henry VIII?
3. Who might Henry's natural allies be?

Diplomacy 1520–21

After the Field of the Cloth of Gold, Henry VIII arranged to meet Emperor Charles V, which produced a treaty in 1520. This committed Henry to very little and simply meant that both monarchs undertook to avoid making any alliances with Francis I for two years. Charles V had hoped to win Henry over to invading France, but it was not worth the risk to abandon the Treaty of London so soon. Within a year, relations between Charles and Francis had broken down and war looked certain. Henry VIII offered to arbitrate between them, and a conference was called at Calais. Yet secretly Henry VIII entered into an imperial alliance with Charles V, promising Henry's daughter Mary to Charles instead of the Dauphin. Historians have debated why Henry VIII took the risk in allying with Charles V: Wernham (1966) suggests that it was fuelled by Henry's concerns about his succession. Perhaps a more convincing argument is that Henry was concerned about his prestige on the European stage. If he could not maintain the peace between France and Spain, the Treaty of London would be redundant and he would become a pawn in their game. Wilkie (1974) argues that it was Wolsey who was influenced by the Pope in allying with the Holy Roman Emperor, in the hope of securing a permanent legateship. However, Gwyn (1990) convincingly argues that an imperial alliance might have provided opportunities for gaining new conquests and this was probably the most important motive for Henry VIII at the time.

The Second French War

War was declared on France on 29 May 1522 when the Earl of Surrey led 15 000 men into Picardy. Owing to a lack of support from Emperor Charles V, the invasion amounted to nothing more than aimless raids, making any English incursion limited in scope. Members of the Royal Council urged Henry to withdraw from the 'Grand Enterprise' against France and turn instead to a conquest of Scotland. Henry oscillated between pursuing negotiations for peace and further invasion. However, in 1523 the Duke of Bourbon, one of the most powerful noblemen in France, took up arms against Francis I. Ever opportunistic, Wolsey hastily arranged for the Duke of Suffolk to enter France with 11 000 men after signing a new treaty with Charles V, agreeing to immediate invasion. Bourbon failed to deliver a serious revolt, however, and Henry's support from Spain and the Netherlands never materialised. Suffolk's army returned in disarray, many suffering from frostbite and the failed battles had cost the king £400 000.

Return to diplomacy

On 24 February 1525, Emperor Charles V routed Francis I's forces at the Battle of Pavia, with the death of some ten thousand French soldiers. On hearing news of the battle, Henry implored the Council to renew war with France. Wolsey was tasked with levying a non-refundable contribution to the royal war effort, called the Amicable Grant. However, Charles V refused to ally with Henry in the total dismemberment of France and the Amicable Grant provoked such opposition in England that Henry VIII was forced to abandon his plans. By the end of August he had concluded five treaties with France known collectively as the Treaty of the More, in which he agreed to relinquish some territorial claims in France in return for an annual indemnity. By 1526 English diplomacy had encouraged the formation of the anti-imperial League of Cognac, which made Henry its 'protector'.

This was followed in 1527 by the Treaty of Westminster, which arranged a marriage match for Princess Mary and agreed a perpetual peace between France and England. At the Agreement of Amiens, France and England were brought closer together still when Henry VIII agreed to pay part of the costs of a French invasion of Italy, which ended in a costly disaster. The Treaty of Cambrai, signed in August 1529 between France, the Holy Roman Emperor Charles V and the Pope, left Henry VIII completely isolated at a moment when he needed papal favour. The failure of Wolsey's foreign policy to secure England's place at the negotiating table did a great deal to bring about his downfall in October 1529.

Scotland

For much of the 16th century, Scotland was a client state of France, and the English had fully expected an invasion from the North following action in France. Henry VIII returned from France in September 1513 to discover that the Earl of Surrey had won considerably more substantial gains and defeated the Scots, who were in league with Louis XII of France, at the battle of Flodden. James IV had declared war in July 1513 and crossed England's northern borders in August. The Scottish army was larger than the English when they met at Flodden Edge, but Surrey had forced them into action on disadvantageous terms. The battle was a glorious success, wiping out the elite of Scotland, including the king, three bishops, 11 earls and 15 lords; over ten thousand men were slain. Despite this apparent success, Henry VIII still found it difficult to exercise political authority in the lowlands of Scotland.

James V succeeded to the throne aged one in 1513, leaving Scotland at the mercy of the European powers. When James entered into personal rule at the age of 18, the Lutheran reformation was sweeping through Europe. This and Henry's later break with Rome divided the Scottish nobility and caused James V many problems. The accession of James, son of Henry's sister Margaret, should have ended the danger from Scotland for the majority of Henry's reign. However, he was keen to maintain Catholicism in Scotland and Henry VIII feared encirclement from Roman Catholic powers – he was after all a heretic and despoiler of the Church (see the section on Reform of the Church). Henry VIII invited James to a meeting in York to reach an agreement in September 1541, but the Scottish Privy Council managed to dissuade James from attending. In his anger, Henry VIII ordered the northern armies to cross the border in a vicious campaign of looting and pillaging.

By November 1542 the Scots had been defeated and James V died on 14 December the same year. James V's daughter, Mary, was now Queen of the Scots at one week old. Henry VIII began negotiations for her marriage with his son Edward VI, then aged five, but these were at first prevented by the Catholic Cardinal Beaton in Scotland. A treaty was struck at Greenwich in 1543 by which the kingdoms of England and Scotland would have been united and Edward and Mary married, but this was rejected by the Scottish Parliament on 11 December 1543. For the following eight years, England fought Scotland in a war now known ironically as the 'Rough Wooing'. Mary was dispatched to France for safety, where she remained until she was 19. English raids continued well into 1547 when France offered 50 captains and a force of 6000 men to support their ally. Following this, the Scottish Parliament assented to the marriage of Mary to Francis, the Dauphin of France, in July 1548.

Securing the succession

From 1529 onwards Henry VIII's foreign policy was completely tied up with his 'Great Matter', obtaining an annulment from his marriage to Catherine of Aragon. He was desperate for a son to provide a clear line of succession for the Tudor dynasty and after bearing him a daughter, Mary, and suffering several miscarriages, it looked as though Catherine would not be able to produce an heir. The context Henry VIII was operating in was important here. Charles V, the Holy Roman Emperor, had sacked Rome and kept Pope Clement VII as an effective prisoner in the Holy City throughout 1527. Charles V was also nephew of Catherine of Aragon and was completely opposed to the annulment. The Pope still relied on Charles V even after his release and the imperial stranglehold on Rome would have dire consequences for Henry VIII seeking annulment. From 1529 to 1532 Henry VIII sought evidence to prove that the Pope had no jurisdictional rights over England, to avoid Clement having to hear the divorce case.

Some historians have argued that in 1532 Henry had already decided to break with Rome to secure a divorce from Catherine, having been exasperated with the refusal of Pope Clement VII to acquiesce to the annulment. This was his apparent motivation for seeking agreements with Francis I, coupled with the encouragement provided by Henry's new love interest, Anne Boleyn, who did much to encourage cultural exchanges between the two countries. Francis I had his own agenda, however, and sought to encourage Henry to marry Anne secretly before gaining the Pope's consent afterwards. The two kings did co-operate throughout 1530–32 and successfully concluded a defensive alliance, meeting at Boulogne in France. Using his influence, Francis arranged for two French cardinals to be dispatched to Rome to lobby on Henry's behalf, and although some headway was made, it was too slow for Henry. In January 1533 he discovered Anne Boleyn was pregnant and swiftly married her, declaring her queen. In the short term, the impact of the breach with Rome severed links between England and the Habsburgs, forcing Henry VIII to seek alliances elsewhere. In many ways it was lucky that the German Protestants (see the section on Religion) and Ottoman Turks were occupying Charles V, for he could have used force to defend his religion and his aunt's rights. Considerable diplomatic activity followed at the behest of Henry to find Protestant allies. Little was achieved except an ill-conceived treaty with the government of Lübeck in 1534. The Protestant princes did not trust Henry's motives and the king was unwilling to make any doctrinal concessions, therefore by 1536 negotiations had reached an impasse. Foreign policy seemed less important over the next few years as dynastic interests took precedence. By 12 October 1537, Henry VIII could rest easy in the knowledge that, at last, he had a son by his third wife, Jane Seymour.

Final years

In January 1539 under the Pact of Toledo, Charles V and Francis I severed links with England and withdrew their ambassadors from the court of Henry VIII. Pope Paul III simultaneously published a bull deposing Henry and requesting James V of Scotland and Francis I to rouse support for a Catholic crusade against England. Although there was perhaps nothing to worry about given other events distracting the kings in Europe, Henry reacted quickly to improve England's defences, at enormous cost. At the same time Henry VIII extended overtures to the King of

Denmark, the Princes of the Schmalkaldic League and anyone else who might be hostile to Charles V. In 1538–39 Henry's attempt to find a fourth wife were again prompted by his desire to end England's isolation. His subsequent marriage to Anne of Cleves, sister of Duke William of Cleves, the most powerful of the German princes, was to engineer a Protestant alliance. By 1540 relations with Francis I had much improved and England no longer needed to worry about French invasion. The Anne of Cleves affair was an embarrassment to Henry VIII and he quickly sought to extricate himself from it. Politically this was embarrassing to Cromwell too as he had engineered the match. The marriage was to have adverse affects for Thomas Cromwell, as Catherine Howard had caught the eye of Henry VIII, creating rivals at court for the minister.

Just as the opening of the conflict between the Spanish Habsburgs and the French Valois facilitated conditions that led to England declaring war on France in 1522, so they did again in 1543. Again Henry VIII opted to ally himself with Emperor Charles V, and pledged to invade France within two years. Henry VIII was delayed by events in Scotland, but a major campaign was planned for June 1544, when over 40 000 men left for Calais. Henry VIII failed to define his objectives until they arrived in Calais and therefore the campaign was disorganised. The plan was that Charles V and Henry VIII would meet at Paris, but Henry appeared to abandon his agreement in search of his own territorial gains and split his forces: the Duke of Norfolk attacked Montreuil and Henry besieged Boulogne and successfully acquired it in September 1544. However, Henry's abandonment of Charles V backfired when the latter suddenly reached a settlement with Francis I at Crépy on the same day that Boulogne surrendered to the English. Francis I was now free to enact revenge, and Henry VIII was isolated. Scarisbrick (1997) suggests this was the greatest threat England had faced for generations. What's more, Henry's coffers were empty.

Luckily, the French invasion mounted in September 1545 came to little. Henry VIII took personal control of the naval campaign from Portsmouth, which sadly saw the sinking of the *Mary Rose*, and loss of perhaps 500 men on board. However, Henry was remarkably successful at blocking Francis' attempts to invade via Scotland or across the Channel. In June 1546 the Treaty of Ardres was signed, and Henry VIII managed to retain Boulogne. In addition, France was to pay England all the financial arrears from the former treaties, but it failed to bring more amicable relations between the two countries. The treaty was only signed because neither side could continue to fight.

Conclusion

The final wars cost Henry dearly: it is estimated that he spent almost £2 million on them. MacCulloch (1995) suggests that Henry had unwittingly engineered a mid-Tudor crisis because of the debts he had accumulated to fight these costly and unrewarding wars. In total it is estimated Henry VIII spent £3 437 765 on war with France. In comparison, his father had spent £108 000 in the Perkin Warbeck campaign of 1492–99, demonstrating the differences between the two monarchs. Even though Henry VIII was hampered by economic concerns, he could never have enjoyed the successes of Francis I or Charles V, as he was king of a nation that was simply less powerful. Therefore Henry VIII's achievements must be seen in light of the limitations he faced.

Speak like a historian: The Schmalkaldic League

The Schmalkaldic League were a group of Protestant princes who formed a religious defensive league within the Holy Roman Empire in 1531. Originally just a pledge to defend each other against Charles V, it developed so that conditions about accepting Lutheran principles were implemented. The movement developed into a territorial political movement, to provide economic advantages for those who broke from the Catholic Church.

ACTIVITY 2.3

Go back through your notes and chart how successful Henry was in implementing his foreign policy. Complete your own copy of the graph shown in Figure 2.7. Mark the main events against the correct date and at the correct height to show how successful you think each was for Henry. Join up the points to create a line graph.

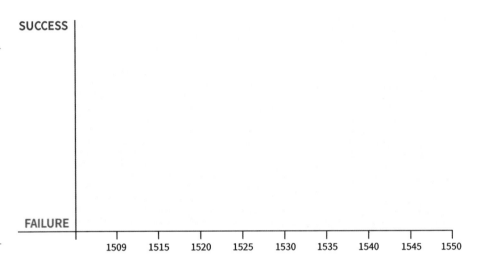

Figure 2.7: Henry's foreign policy.

Society

Elites and commoners

Elton (1955) argues that the Tudor age was the age of the gentry. The reasons for this are many, although the restoration of stability under the Tudors must be considered an essential condition. Both Wolsey and Cromwell sought to 'swear in' landowners as servants to the king on a supernumerary (stand-by) basis, by 1535 there were 263 of these. Another obvious factor was that the gentry relied for its existence on land, and the 16th century witnessed land transfer on an enormous scale, provoked of course by the dissolution of the monasteries. When the great monastic estates were sold, many men could acquire land for the first time, or augment their existing holdings. The great inflation (see the section on Prosperity and depression) provided desire for investment, thus 1540 saw the beginning of the spread of the gentry.

Cromwell attempted reform of county government by attacking territorial franchises or 'liberties' that thwarted the full operation of royal justice. The Act for Recontinuing of Certain Liberties and Franchises (1536) drastically curtailed local anomalies. It prevented ecclesiastical or feudal officials from interfering with sheriffs or JPs performing their legal duties within their jurisdictions. However, the balance of power at county level remained with the landowners who served as sheriffs and JPs. Guy (1988) suggests that in this respect, the Henrician 'revolution' in government changed nothing.

Not until Thomas Cromwell became Henry's unofficial chief minister was any effort made to tackle the major socio-economic problems of the realm. Intellectual circles were applying pressure for 'commonwealth' measures, that is, measures that would provide social and economic justice for all of the King's subjects. Morris (1998) argues that Cromwell seems to have had some sympathy with 'commonwealth' ideas and promoted many of the bills before Parliament containing them. In 1531 and 1532, acts were passed to fix the prices of certain foodstuffs at a reasonable level and another act in 1533 attempted to create machinery for determining fair food prices. These were largely impossible to enforce and were eventually repealed in 1542.

Vagabonds

In the early days of his influence, Cromwell created what became known as the first Tudor Poor Law, 'the Vagabonds Act' in 1531. From his house alms and foodstuffs were distributed to the London poor; sources suggest up to 200 people came every day for the support Cromwell offered, so it is perhaps not surprising it was he who implemented these changes. A clear distinction was made between those unable to work and those deemed to be unwilling. The former were to be licensed to beg, under certain restrictions, rather than simply expelled, and the latter were punished in the traditional manner. The burden of administering this system, and issuing begging licences, was placed firmly on the JPs. However, no provision was made for those who were unable to work: they still had to rely on alms from churches or charity from generous merchants. In 1536 Cromwell strengthened the Act, making significant improvements. The new principle in this Act made it a legal obligation for parishes to care for their poor. This Act effectively ordered JPs and sheriffs to carry out alms collections for the poor, to provide charity for the weak and helpless, but also provide material for the idle and able-bodied to work, so that they could make their own living. Every parish was to appoint two overseers of the poor to administer and collect the money contributed, then ensure that those who received it would not resort to begging, which carried harsh punishments. The overseers were given the additional, onerous task of accounting for what they had received and distributed. All these measures bore the hand of Cromwell, who sought to minimise the social disruption caused by economic circumstances outside the government's control, such as the increase in population, which was gathering momentum in the 1530s.

Regional issues

Wales and the North

Law and order in the Welsh Marches was essential in order that the revolution in Church and state could occur between 1529 and 1536. Maintaining law in Wales had been a perennial problem for English monarchs since Edward IV. Thomas Cromwell was particularly active in restoring good governance in Wales, as demonstrated when all felons were prevented from crossing the River Severn to or from South Wales and the Forest of Dean. Other acts were passed to increase the likelihood of juries convicting defendants, as sheriffs had struggled in the past to persuade them to return verdicts of guilt. The Franchises Act of 1536 was an important constitutional amendment to bring the administration of the Welsh shires into line with England. It effectively abolished any rights that the semi-autonomous lords had held there before. Ives (2007) suggests that this is powerful evidence of a deliberate Crown policy to move towards a sovereign unitary state. This assertion is supported by Loades (2013), who argues Cromwell effectively merged Wales into England, reducing the Marcher Lordships into the counties of Denbigh, Montgomery, Radnor, Brecknock and Monmouth.

Following the Pilgrimage of Grace (see the section on Rebellion) in 1536, Cromwell reconstructed the Council of the North. Its remit was altered so that it was more directly dependent upon the King's Council in London. The effect of this was that by 1540 England was more centralised than it had ever been, and represented much of Cromwell's vision of state. The reorganisation of the Council also meant that 29 seats were added to the House of Commons, predominantly from Wales.

Ireland

The ninth Earl of Kildare had to suffer more direct interference from Henry VIII than his father had ever received from Henry VII. This was largely due to Henry VIII using Irish offices as rewards for his courtiers, such as the appointment of John Kite as Archbishop of Armagh in 1513 and the admission to court of Sir Thomas Boleyn. The Boleyn family laid claims to the Ormonde inheritance, making them serious rivals to the Kildares, who had served as Lords Lieutenant on behalf of the king for generations. Thomas Boleyn rose ever higher due to the interest Henry VIII held for his daughters, Mary and Anne – the latter to become queen and mother to Princess Elizabeth. Henry VIII replaced the Earl of Kildare in 1519 with an English nobleman, Thomas Howard, Earl of Surrey, the future Duke of Norfolk. Ellis (1985) argues that Surrey's arrival in Ireland in 1520 with an army effectively restored royal authority over the whole island and represented a fit of reforming energy on the part of the King. Surrey's expedition cost approximately £13 000 and served to break the power of the Kildares. Piers Butler, Earl of Ormonde, succeeded Surrey in 1522, shifting the reliance of the Crown onto Kildare's rivals, the Ormonde family. It was cheaper for Henry VIII to rely on them as they could draw on Irish resources to maintain law and order for the Crown.

After several rebellions, changes in personnel and still no satisfactory solution to the governance of Ireland, Thomas Cromwell began interfering in Irish administration to ensure officials who were appointed were loyal to him rather than the Kildares. This coincided with Henry's efforts to gain a divorce from Catherine of Aragon. The Earl of Kildare was arrested after making clear he would not permit any reformation of the Church to take place in Ireland, and died in the Tower of London in 1534. Rebellion spread throughout Ireland, led by Kildare's son, Silken Thomas. Henry VIII ordered a military response and William 'Gunner' Skeffington was put in charge of besieging Maynooth Castle, the headquarters of the Kildare's military power. By February 1537 Silken and five of his uncles were executed at Tyburn and Ireland had surrendered to the king. By 1539 the legal reformation of the Irish Church was complete with the dissolution of the monasteries. Many Gaelic leaders took English titles in submission to the king under a policy named 'Surrender and Re-grant' where they could receive their ancestral lands back and pass them on to their eldest sons, as happened in

England. However, many Irish lands belonged to the kin and not the person elected head of the family, and efforts to assimilate the two countries were limited.

In June 1541, under the new Lord Deputy, Sir Anthony St Leger, a new direction in Irish policy was established. An Act of the Irish Parliament saw the ancient medieval lordship of Ireland constitutionally changed by declaring Henry VIII King of Ireland. One of the reasons for this was that the title 'Lord of Ireland' had been granted to Henry II by the papacy in the 12th century. One of the arguments of Kildare's sons during the rebellion of 1534 was that by rejecting the papacy Henry VIII had forfeited his claims to Ireland. This Act was therefore significant in establishing the English monarchy's independent right to lands in Ireland.

The social impact of religious upheaval

Although historians have accurately charted dates for the political decisions that were taken, it has been much harder to describe the enforcement and particularly acceptance of new ideas. Therefore it is not surprising that the Reformation has been extensively debated between historians. The seminal text on this matter was written by AG Dickens (1964) who saw the Reformation 'from below', stressing that the links between anti-clericalism and Lollardy created a climate for swift and easy changes. Dickens has since been criticised for relying too heavily on Yorkshire, Essex and Bristol as examples of heretical Protestant activism. Elton (1955) saw the English Reformation as one aspect of a greater reform programme that was implemented from above, largely by Thomas Cromwell in the 1530s. In this respect Elton sees the Reformation as a political act, which 'nationalised' the Church and was accepted at the centre and imposed on the localities. To challenge this view, historians including Duffy (2005) have argued that Catholicism still retained the firm support of the English people, and therefore that the Reformation was slow to take effect and met considerable opposition. For Haigh (1995),[17] many specific studies support a view of the Reformation as 'a struggle to achieve political victory at the centre and a struggle to achieve secure enforcement in the localities' where at many points 'events could have developed in dramatically different ways'. There are many more historians developing theories about the Reformation as new studies of localities take place.

For the majority of the population it was not the diplomatic or constitutional consequences of the break from Rome that mattered. The concerns of the people were associated with their local parish churches, local shrines and religious houses and, most importantly, the provision of the 'rites of passage' from baptism to marriage and burial. The progress of the Reformation therefore varied from place to place although, broadly speaking, the south and eastern counties, with their proximity to the universities, the capital and the court, were more susceptible to Protestant ideas. Even here generalisations are difficult to make, however, given that it seems Catholicism survived among the Sussex and Norfolk gentry well into the 1570s. Perhaps even more important were the evangelistic efforts of the preachers. For example, Hugh Latimer launched a preaching campaign in Bristol; similarly Matthew Price disseminated Protestant ideas in the Severn Valley and evidence suggests their ideas took hold.

Rebellion

Henry VIII's government was never subject to the dynastic rebellions faced by his father, although he was vulnerable to a certain kind of pressure that Loades (1999) calls the 'quasi-rebellion'[18]. One example of this followed the introduction of the 'Amicable Grant' in 1525. A revolt in Suffolk threatened to spread across East Anglia. Luckily for Henry VIII, the Dukes of Norfolk and Suffolk were able to negotiate the surrender of 10 000 rebels at Lavenham, in Suffolk. This quasi-rebellion did not intend to bring the Crown into jeopardy, but was formed to instigate a change in policy. The court had to make the distinction between whether these demonstrations constituted treason or simply political pressure. Over 500 men were subsequently indicted for riot and unlawful assembly, but charges were never pressed. What was so dangerous for the monarchy was that this form of opposition could hardly have been more successful, as it resulted in an immediate retreat from the proposed levy and no serious punishments followed. Making the distinction between opposition and treason was something future Tudors would have to grapple with.

Pilgrimage of Grace

The most prominent cause of rebellions before the Reformation had been taxation, and perhaps what marks the Pilgrimage of Grace out from other rebellions is not only the scale of it, but the causes. In early 1536, Parliament had passed an act dissolving all smaller monasteries worth less than £200 and rumours circulated of further destruction of all parish churches. Set against this backdrop of abrupt religious change, householders were being assessed for the payment of new taxes. This seemed to confirm to many that central government was illegitimately interfering in everyday life, prompting widespread anger. In October 1536, a group of men in Lincolnshire, led by 'Captain Cobbler' (a shoemaker whose real name was Nicholas Melton) and other prominent villagers, formed an armed demonstration against these policies. The rebels marched behind banners bearing the '**Five Wounds of Christ**', proclaiming their loyalty to traditional religion. The Bishop of Lincoln was murdered and the city stormed by 10 000 armed rebels who drew up a list of complaints and submitted them to the king.

The Duke of Suffolk led a substantial force north under the express orders not to negotiate with armed rebels. The Lincolnshire gentry, faced with the unyielding royal forces, capitulated. However, news of the Lincolnshire rebels' demands had spread to Yorkshire, where people had already pledged to defend their traditional beliefs. A much larger, coordinated rising of the counties of Yorkshire, Westmorland, Cumberland and Lancashire was inspired, co-opting up to 35 000 men to their cause. By late October the rebels had reached Doncaster, to face royal forces led by the Duke of Norfolk. Like the Lincolnshire rebels, these men presented themselves as pilgrims, seeking their monarch's grace to maintain their religion, although their demands were as much about taxation and social change. They maintained their allegiance to the king, but demanded the removal of the king's advisers, particularly Cromwell, who was seen to be responsible for the dissolution of the monasteries. Robert Aske, a talented lawyer, emerged as a key figurehead for the rebels in drawing out negotiations with Norfolk. Fletcher and MacCulloch (2008) suggest that the northern gentry and nobility cooperated to contain and channel the anger of the rebels.

Speak like a historian: The Exeter Plot

The Exeter Plot is the name given to a vague mass of suspicions and accusations made during the period 1538 to 1541 that resulted in the execution of Geoffrey Pole and members of the Courtenay family, as well as Sir Edward Neville and Sir Nicholas Carew, together with various servants and retainers of the men involved. The feverish atmosphere of the time, and the threat of foreign invasion from France or Spain, provoked genuine fear. Loades (2013) argues that Cromwell ought to be commended for thoroughly investigating their treason.

After protracted negotiations, which forced Henry to promise a pardon and allow Parliament to hear their complaints, the rebels finally dissolved in December. An embittered minority of northern leaders carried out small uprisings thereafter, prompting Henry VIII to refuse to honour his commitments and launch what Fletcher and MacCulloch have referred to as 'a systematic policy of punishment'.[19] Aske was executed along with 215 others comprising knights, abbots, monks and several lords including Sir Thomas Percy. The combination of protest from a wide geographical and social spectrum made this particular rebellion potentially fatal for Henry's government and was certainly the most dangerous Henry VIII ever faced.

As Lipscomb (2009) points out, apart from the leaders of the Exeter Plot and the Pilgrimage of Grace, most of the high-status individuals executed for treason after 1536 did not see due process of law; they were 'convicted and executed on the basis of parliamentary attainder – that is, an act passed through Parliament that declared the accused guilty and condemned them to death without recourse to a common law trial'. [20]

ACTIVITY 2.4

Go back through your notes for this chapter and look at the threats Henry VIII faced through opposition, then create and complete a table using the following four headings:

Opponent
Why did they oppose Henry VIII?
How did they demonstrate their opposition?
How serious a threat do you think this posed?

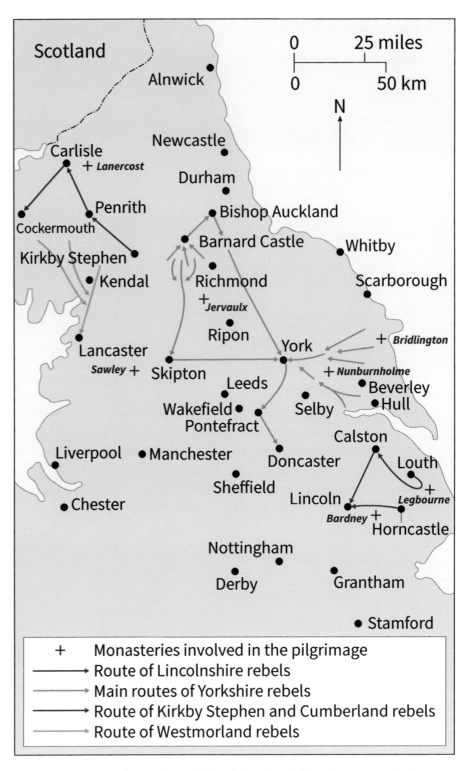

Figure 2.8: The most threatening rebellion during Henry VIII's reign was the Pilgrimage of Grace, which spread across five counties in the North and was a direct response to the dissolution of the monasteries.

Economic development

Trade and exploration

Elton (1955) argues that while prices rose, the export of cloth from London increased threefold between 1500 and 1550, creating mounting prosperity in some circles from the merchants down to the sheep herders. The Hanseatic League no longer had to compete aggressively with merchants as it had under Henry VII, as there was enough trade for all. The increasing trade with Spain, brought about by Spanish exploitation of the Americas, drove up prices in the rest of Europe. England remained in an advantageous position because merchants could buy cheaper goods at home and sell them at higher prices on the continent. In this way the debasement of coinage actually helped merchants to prosper further, even though it endangered the domestic economy of England.

Henry VIII expanded upon his father's imperial ambitions. He invested heavily in the navy, increasing its size from seven to 53 ships, and established Deptford and Woolwich as the Royal Dockyards. Henry was interested in exploration and colonisation, but failed to capitalise on his father's overseas initiatives as few of the ventures he supported were successful. A projected voyage by Sebastian Cabot and Thomas Spert to Newfoundland in 1516 came to nothing, as did another planned for Cabot in 1521. Several voyages were made to the coast of West Africa, bringing back cargoes of pepper and ivory: this served to reignite Henry's interest in exploration and so he decided to finance John Rut's transatlantic voyage in 1531. By the end of Henry's reign the English were regularly fishing off the coast of Newfoundland and had established trade with Brazil, the West Indies, Guinea, the Canaries and the Azores, the Baltic States, Italy and much of the rest of Europe. If he had achieved little in building an empire, what Henry did achieve, albeit through Cromwell's reforms, was the capacity to support commercial and oversees ventures. This resulted in the commercial and military enterprises that marked the reigns of his children.

Prosperity and depression

Elton (1955) attributes the Tudor economic crises of the 1530s to a steady, although not always linear, rise in prices that had been climbing since the turn of the century. This was no particular monarch's fault, given that the effect of money supply on prices was not understood until at least the 1570s. However, the first serious English inflation was due to Henry VIII's foreign policy, which increased government spending and used up the treasure amassed by Henry VII. An effect of this was to encourage Wolsey and Henry to undertake debasement of coinage. Reduction of the precious metal content of coins, resulting in inflation, which enabled the monarch to pay off or repudiate government debts, was a high-risk method of raising revenue that had been employed by medieval kings. Edward IV had carried out profitable debasement in 1464, but Henry VIII was more reckless than previous kings, particularly in his later years. He had begun debasing Irish coinage in the 1530s, but did not return to the practice in England until 1544 when smaller coins were released with lower silver content. It was a dangerous practice because once started, it was difficult to find alternative ways to draw silver in to the mints, without losing profits. Before 1542 the silver content of an English coin was 92%, but by 1546 it was just 33%, a debasement which, combined with an increase in volume, caused inflation to soar and induced unhealthy slumps in the cloth trade. Bad harvests in 1530 also caused grain prices to rise rapidly, and this hit peasants hard for the next decade.

Religion

Renaissance ideas

Historians have debated the extent to which the 15th-century Lollardy (see Chapter 1 section on Religion) movement influenced the '**evangelical**' movement, which was gathering pace at the turn of the 16th century. A key similarity between Lollards and evangelical groups includes the emphasis on the transformative power on the word of God. The two most important evangelicals were Martin Luther, from Saxony and Huldrych Zwingli from Zurich. What was new about their evangelism was the insistence on justification in the eyes of God, which came through faith alone, formed by reading and hearing the scriptures. The implications of this view were to lead them to reject other cornerstones of the Catholic faith, and to argue that masses, saints, pilgrimages and the elaborate hierarchy of the Church were all a distraction from true faith. The evangelicals went much further than the humanist, Erasmus, who was highly critical of certain practices of the Roman Catholic Church – such as pilgrimages and the veneration of saints – but still believed in papal supremacy and Catholic doctrine. The evangelicals were theological dissenters.

Henry was extremely interested in theology and had read Martin Luther's *Babylonian Captivity of the Church*, which attacked papal power and Church indulgences, and claimed that hardly any of the sacraments had been instituted by Christ. Henry VIII was personally affronted by Luther's text and in response, wrote a pamphlet entitled *Declaration of the Seven Sacraments Against Martin Luther*, which challenged Martin Luther's criticism of the Catholic Church. Henry's pamphlet went through 20 editions across England and Europe and as a result of it, Henry was made '**Defender of the Faith**' or 'Fidei Defensor' by Pope Leo X in 1521 as a reward for his efforts. Henry VIII enlisted the help of Thomas More in preparing his pamphlet. Interestingly, More had warned Henry about his unqualified defence of papal power, in case he had reason to quarrel with the Pope in the future, but Henry would not listen. The title was revoked by Pope Paul III in 1536, following the break with Rome and Henry was later excommunicated. However, Henry VIII made Parliament confer the title on him in 1544, for he was now a defender of the Anglican faith.

Key term

evangelical: refers to members of a loose movement, united by an emphasis on the transformative power of the word of God. Opponents referred to them in a disparaging way as those who promoted the 'new learning' – though some of their ideas had long been discussed among Lollards.

'Defender of the Faith': one of a number of similar titles bestowed upon monarchs of Europe who had provided protection for Rome or had promoted Catholicism in some way. Henry VIII was given this title in 1521 by Pope Leo X.

Figure 2.9: This image shows Henry VIII delighting in his Christian evangelism. He is shown holding a text from Mark 16, which translated into English reads 'go out in to the world and preach the gospel to every creature'.

Reform of the Church

Christopher Haigh (1993) helpfully explains the English Reformation as a long and complex process, rather than a specific event. The Reformation in this context includes 'a break from Roman obedience, an assertion of secular control over the Church, suppression of Catholic institutions such as monasteries and a shift in doctrine towards Protestantism'.[21] Starkey's (1985) clear account of the Reformation during the Tudor period demonstrates that Henry VIII's desire to produce a male heir, the rise of Anne Boleyn and growing opposition to Wolsey split the court and made religious principle a polarising issue during 1529. Henry VIII's divorce project was not the beginning of the Reformation, however,

Key term

Lutheran: denotes a follower of Protestant Christianity who subscribes to the teachings of Martin Luther. The main way in which Luther differed from the Catholic tradition was his belief in justification by faith alone: that is, only God can grant passage into heaven and forgive sins.

as Marshall (2012) asserts. In the years when Henry VIII was still the 'Defender of the Faith', small but increasing numbers of men and women began working for a transformation of the Church (See the section on Renaissance ideas). Among those who advocated evangelical reforms was Thomas Cranmer, who, under the patronage of the Boleyns, found himself in the position of Archbishop of Canterbury in 1532. He was to remain in that position for over 20 years. Other significant promotions to the episcopal benches were Hugh Latimer, Edward Foxe and Nicholas Shaxton, all of whom provided Cranmer with a counterweight to conservative factions at court. Henry did not necessarily agree with their beliefs, but his main concern following the Act of Supremacy in 1534 was the threat of papists, rather than Protestant-leaning heretics.

In these circumstances the evangelicals made significant gains in the 1530s. One notable success was in the Henrician Church's first official statement, the 'Ten Articles' of 1536. Haigh (1993) argues that the articles were distinctly **Lutheran**, for example only three of the seven sacraments were discussed (penance, the Eucharist and baptism) and some justification by faith was mentioned as well as criticism of abuses connected with saints and idols. Even more positive was persuading the King to issue Royal injunctions that sanctioned the order for an English Bible to be placed in every Church in 1538. Allowing the word of God to be translated into the vernacular was a crucial part of evangelical doctrine. Bernard (2007), who has been influential in recent debates about the Reformation, suggests that Henry was taken with some aspects of the 'humanist' reform programme, and could even be described as 'Erasmian', that is, influenced by Erasmus (see Chapter 1, the section on Humanism). Perhaps the view of Rex (2006) reflects Henry's thinking that allowing the people to read an English Bible might foster obedience to the supremacy. Nevertheless, the Bibles that found their way into English churches from 1539, largely based on the translations of the renowned evangelical scholar William Tyndale, were markedly different from any that had come before.

Figure 2.10: Holbein's title page to the 'Great Bible', published in 1539. Henry VIII is shown seated in majesty, handing out Bibles.

Dissolution of the monasteries

Monasteries played a significant role in village life as places of shelter, sanctuary, charity, education and medicine. However, by the 16th century, they were in decline and many had become critical of the relative wealth of abbots and abbesses. The second major triumph for the evangelicals was the dissolution of the monasteries. Dissolution was a two-stage process: the smaller monasteries were closed by statute in 1536 and the larger houses occupying land worth more than £200 were forced to surrender in 1537 and 1540. The actions have been described as state vandalism and a symbolic demonstration of royal supremacy. Cromwell had arranged a visitation of the monasteries during the winter of 1535. His agents were hand picked and the reports they compiled painted a negative picture of sexually corrupt monks possessing suspect relics, promoting superstition. These visits have been labelled a sham, and undoubtedly the visitors were looking to find fault, although some monasteries, such as Durham, received favourable reports. The act of dissolving the smaller houses was presented as a necessary reform, not an attack on monasticism itself. This was probably to ensure that the abbots who sat in the Lords would accept it because it referred back to a policy instigated by Wolsey in the 1520s. Only 243 of 419 houses assessed at £200 were actually closed: those that were exempted had made payments to the king, or transferred monks, nuns and friars to larger houses.

Henry was keen on associating his actions with religious reform, and he sought to show that monastic wealth might be assigned to other religious and charitable uses. Six new dioceses were founded in Bristol, Chester, Gloucester, Oxford, Peterborough and Westminster. This was on a small scale relative to the amount raised from the dissolution, however. The second dissolution act was passed in 1539, and within one year all the monasteries were gone, largely due to the 'voluntary' surrender of larger houses.

The dissolution of the monasteries was a revolution in land ownership second only to that which took place after the Norman Conquest. It has generated debate among historians who have been concerned with the extent to which the policy was driven by Henry, or his radical advisors, and whether the policy formed a part of a wider ecclesiastical reform programme or was a result of financial opportunism. Earlier historians saw monastic communities providing a political threat to Henry VIII as remnants of papal supremacy. Therefore the sale of monastic lands, at a fraction of the real market value, provided a political masterstroke in creating a vested interest among the laity in dissolving these institutions. More recent research has significantly undermined this view. Haigh (1993) suggests that the dissolution of the monasteries was a case of avarice cloaked in the language of spiritual reform. That is to suggest that the motives behind dissolution were financial and not borne out of a perceived threat; in any case, only a handful of members of the Holy Orders were executed for opposition to Henry's supremacy. Contrary to this view, more recent accounts focus on the ideological motivation Henry may have possessed, for the majority of opposition came from religious orders and the association of monasticism with treason was only reinforced by the Pilgrimage of Grace in 1537. Marshall (2012) suggests that Henry was flattered by the idea of reforming the Catholic Church of abuses and was never pushed further than he was willing to go. This is supported by evidence that Cranmer and Cromwell failed in moving Henry to abolish Mass, for example.

Later years
The twin scares of the Pilgrimage of Grace in 1537 and threat of Franco-Imperial invasion in 1538 made Henry VIII anxious to demonstrate his Catholic credentials. Haigh (1993) argues that the king 'stopped the Reformation dead'.[22] While this is an exaggerated claim, the scares certainly provoked a conservative reaction,

with proclamations defending traditional ceremonies and the trial of the **sacramentarian** John Lambert as a heretic. In 1539 the Duke of Norfolk and his new ally in court, Cuthbert Tunstall, the Bishop of Durham, engineered the Act of the Six Articles, which reaffirmed confession, transubstantiation, private masses and clerical celibacy, all of which evangelicals had campaigned against. The conservatives at court won further gains when Thomas Cromwell was sent to the scaffold in July 1540, removing perhaps the most formidable of the reformers at court. A week after Cromwell, three leading evangelicals were burnt for heresy, although to display even-handedness, Henry also burnt three papist supporters of Catherine of Aragon at the same time. A King's Book was issued to replace the 1537 Bishops' Book, transubstantiation was asserted and justification by faith alone was decisively rejected. Stephen Gardiner pressed Henry to abandon the English Bible, which he argued was encouraging dissent. The king decided to issue an Act for the Advancement of True Religion, which forbade members of the lower orders and all women below the gentry to read scripture. It is tempting to see these measures as a 'swing' back to Catholicism. It is important to note that monasteries and shrines were never restored, the reformers such as Cranmer were able to maintain their positions at court and Henry was certainly not going to abandon his supremacy over the Church. In this way, Henry's role must be seen as crucial in the developments of the Reformation; for all his devotion to the mass, he was deeply

Key term

sacramentarians: evangelicals who denied transubstantiation (that the bread and wine taken at Eucharist would transform into the body and blood of Christ once consumed).

Voices from the past

Thomas Cranmer

Thomas Cranmer became Archbishop of Canterbury in 1532, probably thanks to his support for Anne Boleyn. He pronounced the annulment of Henry VIII's marriage to Catherine of Aragon in 1533 and with Thomas Cromwell established the early doctrinal and liturgical changes in the Church of England, including the first officially approved service in English. Under Edward VI he was responsible for more radical reforms, which led to his being burnt at the stake under Mary I for his refusal to accept the authority of the Pope and the validity of the Mass.

This extract is taken from a letter Cranmer wrote to Cromwell recommending Tyndale's Bible:

And as for the translation, so far as I have read thereof, I like it better than any other translation heretofore made; yet not doubting but that there may and will be found some fault therein, as you know no man ever did or can do so well, but it may be from time to time amended.

And forasmuch as the book is dedicated unto the King's Grace, and also great pains and labour taken in setting forth of the same, I pray you, my lord, that you will exhibit the book unto the King's Highness, and to obtain of his Grace, if you can, a license that the same may be sold and read of every person, without danger of any act, proclamation, or ordinance heretofore granted to the contrary, until such time that we the bishops shall set forth a better translation, which I think will not be till a day after doomsday. And if you continue to take such pains for the setting forth of God's word, as you do, although in the mean season you suffer some snubs, and many slanders, lies, and reproaches for the same, yet one day He will requite altogether. And the same word (as St. John saith) which shall judge every man at the last day, must needs show favour to them that now do favour it. Thus, my lord, right heartily fare you well. At Forde, the ivth day of August. [1537.]

Source: www.luminarium.org/renlit/cranmercromwell2.htm (Accessed 13. 10. 2015).

Discussion points:
1. What sort of relationship do you think Cranmer had with Cromwell?
2. What does Cranmer think of the new translated Bible?
3. Why would this Bible have appealed to Cranmer?

distrustful of clerical power and therefore the sort of Catholicism that developed was uniquely Henrician.

Timeline: events of the Reformation.

The narrative of the Reformation is complex. An excellent way of checking your understanding of the events is to create a chronological framework for your notes. Go back through notes you made on this chapter and use them to complete a timeline like this one, which has already been started for you.

Years	Domestic policy	Explanatory notes
1527	Henry decided on an annulment.	
1528	October: Cardinal Campeggio arrived in England to hear Henry's case for annulment.	
1529	October: November: Reformation Parliament was assembled.	
1530	Clergy are accused of praemunire.	
1531		
1532	January: First Act of Annates. March: Supplication of the Ordinaries. May: Submission of the Clergy – the clergy accepted Henry, not the Pope, as their lawmaker.	Banned the payment of Annates to Rome. Thomas More resigned the following day.
1533	January: Anne and Henry marry in secret. February: Act in restraint of Appeals to Rome.	Began the work in transferring papal powers to the king.
1534	January: Second Act of Annates. Act to stop Peter's Pence. March: Act for the Submission of the Clergy. First Act of Succession. November: December: Treason Act. Act for first Fruits and Tenths.	
1535	Cromwell commissioned Valor Ecclesiasticus.	A survey into the wealth and condition of the Church.

Years	Domestic policy	Explanatory notes
1536	February: Act for the Dissolution of Lesser Monasteries.	Those worth less than £200.
	May: Anne Boleyn beheaded – ten days later, Henry married Jane Seymour.	
	July: Act of Ten Articles.	A clear move towards Protestantism – the 'seven sacraments' of Catholic doctrine were rejected.
	August: Royal injunctions to the clergy issued by Cromwell.	
1537	July: *The Institution of a Christian Man*, also known as the Bishops' Book.	Further drift towards Protestant doctrine.
1538	September: Royal injunctions to the Clergy issued by Cromwell.	
	December: Henry excommunicated by Pope Paul III.	
1539	June: Act of Six Articles.	
	Act for the Dissolution of the Greater Monasteries.	
1540	January: Henry VIII marries Anne of Cleves.	
	July: Cromwell executed.	
	Henry marries Catherine Howard.	
1541		
1542	February: Catherine Howard executed.	
1543	May: Act for the Advancement of True Religion.	This book was written by Henry VIII himself and defended transubstantiation and the Six Articles.
	The Necessary Doctrine and Erudition of Christian Man.	
	July: Henry marries Catherine Parr.	
1544	May: English **Litany** introduced into churches.	
1545	December: Chantries Act passed.	
1546	July: Henry names mostly Protestant Council of Regency for his heir.	
1547		

Continuity and change by 1547

To a certain extent, Henry VIII brought dramatic changes to the Church, to government and the royal household and to controlling the nobility. Foreign policy had shifted into aggressive point-scoring on the continent, forcing the king to ask for taxes in peace time to pay for ever-more costly wars. Parliament had become a tool for the king in legitimising radical changes, although it rarely checked his authority. The Church was fragmented under its new supreme head, Henry VIII. Priests had to choose whether they were willing to engage with Protestantism or whether they should stay rigidly faithful to the Roman Catholic tradition. Increasingly, this meant choosing whether one was prepared to become a martyr for one's beliefs. How much this was noticed by an average peasant is difficult to assess, for most of the changes occurred at the political centre of the realm. Ordinary people in the shires may have noticed a rising population, the threat of increasing numbers of enclosures, inflation and increased government interference with the look or teachings of the Church, and JPs having greater powers. Perhaps the most significant changes were outside the control of Henry VIII. Religious debate was sweeping through Europe and Protestant centres had emerged in Germany and Switzerland. In England, the debates once reserved for the educated elites in the universities were beginning to encompass ordinary folk living in towns and particularly those near ports. London and the South-East could even be said to be much more Protestant leaning by 1547.

None the less, the vast majority of English people would still have referred to themselves as Catholics, would still have had poor literacy, and would still have little reason to leave their village. The governance of the realm was still dependent on the will of the monarch, but what a monarch Henry had been. Henry VIII had ruled for 38 years with little threat, he had brought true stability and reduced the power of the nobility further than his father had done, through sheer force of character if nothing else. There was no question that his son would become king as the Tudors had become a dynasty under Henry.

Henry's last will and testament

Few documents have more potential to cause trouble than a will. Henry VIII's was no exception: it was a cause of dissension from the first and still intrigues historians today. Elton (1977) and Guy (1988) have argued that the will was the product of factional struggles in the last weeks of the king's life and that the effect, far from embodying the king's dying wishes, reflected the political alignments in December 1546. The factional struggles must be seen in the context of many expecting the overweight king to die in his fifties and seeing the promise of controlling the country during the impending minority of the young Edward as a truly great prize. The significance of the will had been increased by the Henrician succession statutes, passed in 1536. Henry had declared that the Crown would pass to his children by Jane Seymour, or any subsequent lawful wife, but also allowed him to designate a successor should the legitimate children die. Crucially, the document suggested that if Henry's successor was a minor, he could by his will set up a council to fulfil the functions of a guardian. The following Act of 1544 seemed to retreat to a more conventional form whereby it was determined that if Henry and Edward were dead, the Crown would pass to Mary and then to Elizabeth.

The protagonists in the factional struggles that dominated the final days of Henry VIII's life were, on the one hand Thomas Howard, Duke of Norfolk, his heir, Henry Howard, the Earl of Surrey, and Stephen Gardiner, Bishop of Winchester, and on the other, Edward Seymour, Earl of Hertford and his close ally, Thomas Paget, the king's secretary, supported by John Dudley, Viscount Lisle and Anthony Denny, chief gentlemen of the Privy Chamber, and backed by the Queen, Catherine Parr, and Thomas Cranmer, Archbishop of Canterbury. The newer faction, the Seymours, began to conspire against the 'old' and by December 1546, Henry Howard found himself arrested and charged with high treason. Gardiner too fell out of favour with the king, securing the way for the Seymours, although they still had to create constitutional legitimacy for their dominance. Henry VIII was no fool though, and the final will ensured that the council he had chosen to lead the country following his death were bound by clauses that gave equality to all voices. No individual was to have any special independent status. Henry VIII could not, however, impose his will from beyond the grave, and it only took eight weeks for Edward Seymour to dismantle the 'ingenious constitutional provisions'[24] (Ives, 1992) that Henry VIII put in place in his final days.

ACTIVITY 2.5

Create an obituary for Henry VIII using one of the three following headings:
Vain and unpredictable
Pious and despotic
Effective and misdirected.

Practice essay questions

1. 'Anticlericalism was responsible for the development of the English Reformation in the years 1529 to 1547.' Explain why you agree or disagree with this view.
2. 'Administrative reform was the most significant development in government during Henry VIII's reign until 1547.' Assess the validity of this view.
3. Reread Extracts A and B in the section on Thomas Cromwell and decide which provides the more convincing interpretation of the effectiveness of Cromwell as the king's principal minister.
4. 'The foreign policy of Henry VIII failed to achieve its objectives in the years 1509 to 1547.' Assess the validity of this view.

Chapter summary

After studying this period, you should be able to:

- describe the impact of religious upheaval on society
- explain why Henry VIII's government developed differently to his father's
- evaluate the successes of Henry VIII's foreign policy
- assess how much change had occurred under Henry VIII.

Further reading

Undoubtedly a tome, but an absolutely phenomenal read is Peter Gwyn's *The King's Cardinal: The Rise and Fall of Thomas Wolsey*; 1990. Gwyn's masterful use of sources and the way he guides the reader through his argument is thoroughly engaging.

The most distinguished account of Sir Thomas More, which demonstrates a masterful use of sources, is *Thomas More: A Biography*, by Richard Marius; 1999.

Probably the best book written on the impact of the Reformation, not just in Henry VIII's reign, but throughout the later Tudors, is Eamon Duffy's *The Voices of Morebath: Reformation and Rebellion in an English Village*; 2003. Duffy uses the parish accounts to chart the drama of the Reformation through the eyes of the people who lived through it.

End notes

1   Quoted in Penn T. *The Winter King: The Dawn of Tudor England*. London; Penguin; 2012. p. 359.

2   Scarisbrick J. *Henry VIII*: New Haven: Yale University Press; 1997. p. 4.

3   Cited in Lipscomb S. *1536: The Year that Changed Henry VIII*. London: Lion Hudson; 2009. p. 61.

4   Lipscomb S. 'Who Was Henry VIII?' *History Today*. 59(4); April 2009. p. 32.

5   Smith LB. *Henry VIII: the Mask of Royalty*. London: Jonathan Cape; 1971. p. 328.

6   Scarisbrick JJ. *Henry VIII*. Yale: Yale University Press; 1997. p. 17.

7   Guy J. *Tudor England*. Oxford: OUP; 1988. p. 81.

8   Ives EW. 'Henry VIII's Will – A Forensic Conundrum.' *The Historical Journal*. 35(4); Dec. 1992. p. 779–804.

9   Scarisbrick JJ. *Henry VIII*. New Haven: Yale University Press. p. 35.

10 Guy J. *Tudor England*. Oxford: OUP. p. 5.

11 Ives EW. 'Henry VIII: The political perspective.' In D MacCulloch (ed.) *The Reign of Henry VIII: Politics, Policy and Piety*. London: Palgrave Macmillan. p. 27.

12 MacCulloch D. (ed.) *The Reign of Henry VIII: Politics, Policy and Piety*. London: Palgrave Macmillan; 1995. p. 42.

13 Coby P. *Thomas Cromwell: Machiavellian Statecraft and the English Reformation*. Lanham: Lexington Books; 2009. p. 196.

14 Gunther K and EH Shagan. 'Protestant Radicalism and Political thought in the Reign of Henry VIII.' *Past & Present*, 194; Feb 2007. p. 35–74.

15 Guy J. 'Henry VIII and the Praemunire Manoeuvres of 1530–1531.' *The English Historical Review*. 97(384); July 1982. p. 482.

16 Elton GR. *England under the Tudors*. London: Folio Society; 1955. p. 133.

17 Haigh C. 'The Recent Historiography of the English Reformation' In Todd M (ed.) *Reformation to Revolution*. London: Routledge; 1995. p. 13–32.

18 Loades DM. *Politics and Nation, England 1450–1660*. 5th edn. Oxford: OUP: 1999. p. 121.

19 Fletcher A and D MacCulloch. *Tudor Rebellions*. Harlow: Pearson. 2008.

20 Lipscomb S. 'Who Was Henry VIII?' *History Today*. 59(4); April 2009. p. 14–20.

21 Haigh C. *English Reformations: Religion, Politics and Society under the Tudors*. Oxford: OUP. p. 152.

22 Haigh C. *English Reformations: Religion, Politics and Society under the Tudors*. Oxford: OUP. p. 152.

23 Ives EW. 'Henry VIII's Will – A Forensic Conundrum.' *The Historical Journal*. 35(4); Dec. 1992. p. 804.

3 Instability and consolidation: 'the Mid-Tudor Crisis', 1547–1563

In this section we will consider the extent to which minority government, short reigns and religious turmoil resulted in an unstable kingdom, and how Elizabeth I had to try to reconcile polarised religious views when she came to the throne. We will examine:

- Edward VI, Somerset and Northumberland; royal authority; problems of succession; relations with foreign powers.
- The social impact of religious and economic changes under Edward VI; rebellion; intellectual developments; humanist and religious thought.
- Mary I and her ministers; royal authority; problems of succession; relations with foreign powers.
- The social impact of religious and economic changes under Mary I; rebellion; intellectual developments; humanist and religious thought.
- Elizabeth I: character and aims; consolidation of power, including the Act of Settlement and relations with foreign powers.
- The impact of economic, social and religious developments in the early years of Elizabeth's rule.

Introduction

The Mid-Tudors have been largely ignored by historians in the past. The towering personalities, and long reigns of Henry VII, Henry VIII and Elizabeth I have led some to view Edward VI and Mary as weak or insignificant by comparison. In fact recent research suggests that there was a remarkable amount of continuity between Henry VIII and his children, not least because of some of the long-serving personnel in the Privy Council. There were a number of crises; of the economy in 1551 and, perhaps more importantly, the bad harvests in 1551 and 1556. Yet the rebellions during this period were largely prompted by religious upheaval, although every Tudor had to face uprisings within the kingdom. By far the most serious crisis for the dynasty was the Duke of Northumberland's attempts to divert the succession to Lady Jane Grey, although even this was thwarted within a matter of weeks.

To some extent, any period of 11 years encompassing two whole reigns and the beginning of another will be bound to experience some turbulence, and with that, unpredictability too. Elizabeth I would inherit a Crown under serious financial strain, deep divisions between Catholics and Protestants, and foreign threats from France and Scotland. The young queen immediately showed remarkable skill in political diplomacy and managed to settle the religious question within the first year of her reign. Although she faced opposition to her settlement in the House of Lords and was humiliated by the realms of foreign policy through the loss of Calais, Elizabeth demonstrated keen political analysis and a strength that her siblings lacked. She is credited with stabilising the kingdom and creating the conditions that allowed it to flourish in the latter half of her reign.

Edward VI, Somerset and Northumberland

Henry VIII's will had made provision for a council of 16 to implement decisions on behalf of the young king, by a majority decision. Almost all of the executors were drawn from Henry's existing Privy Council. However, before Henry's final will was revealed to the rest of the Privy Council, Sir William Paget, chief secretary, drafted a clause giving the regency council 'full power and authority' to undertake any action necessary for the government of the realm during Edward's minority. Controversially, and hotly debated among historians is the 'unfulfilled gifts clause', which may have been rewritten or added after Henry's death to award posthumously any grants made but not legally fulfilled by the king. The distribution of lands that followed (the Duke of Norfolk was attaindered and spent the entire reign in prison) seems highly suspicious in these circumstances, as Edward Seymour, the Earl of Hertford, and those loyal to him seemed to benefit the most. The news of Henry's death was kept a secret for three days to enable Hertford to build his position and ensure the Council's support. On 31 January the Regency Council elected Hertford Protector and governor of Edward's person. He promptly made himself the Duke of Somerset. Six days later, after promoting his closest men, he overthrew the will: obtaining letters granting him near-sovereign powers as Protector and enabling him to appoint anyone of his choosing to the Council. Jennifer Loach (2002) reminds us that the elevation of one man above others is not surprising: it was entirely the norm during the 16th century to organise government run by a sole leading hand.

Speak like a historian: minority kings

Minority kings have traditionally been seen as weak by historians. Edward V was sent to the Tower, never to be seen again, and deposed after 11 weeks. The other four, Henry III (1216), Edward III (1327), Richard II (1377) and Henry VI (1422), reached adulthood, but were seen as failures. Edward VI then was unique because he died just before he turned 16, so truly was a boy king.

The Somerset Protectorate

Few politicians have received more favourable treatment than Somerset. AF Pollard began the trend in the early 20th century, suggesting Somerset was an idealist, concerned primarily with reform of Church and state. However, Guy (1988) and Loach (2002) have done much to discredit this view. Loach suggests he was a military man who was not particularly religious or committed to reform. Guy goes further and suggests he was slow to reach decisions, authoritarian and obsessed with war against Scotland. Somerset's style of government was so personal that the Council's role was steadily undermined. He often settled state business in his own household, where he relied on his own men like William Cecil and Sir Michael Stanhope, none of whom were Privy Councillors. Somerset's arrogance aroused resentment. Memoranda addressed to him equated the king's business with his personal affairs; some complained letters had not been so princely written since Wolsey. Somerset also kept the 'dry stamp' of Edward's signature – enabling him to warrant financial business and raise troops. This effectively made him a quasi-king and alerted the Council to his increasing autocracy. His attitudes, as well as his policies can be said to have provoked a coup by the Earl of Warwick in 1549.

Factionalism surrounded Somerset at court, led by the scheming Earl of Warwick. Warwick managed to convince Thomas Seymour (Somerset's brother) to plot against the Protector, because he had not been named a member of the Regency Council, despite also being an uncle of Edward VI. Seymour was charged with 33 counts of high treason and was executed on 20 March 1549. For these reasons Williams (1995) argues it is perhaps understandable that Somerset sought to avoid the Council, although his failure to take heed of them or reward them with patronage was highly risky and cost him dear. Elton (1955) has criticised Somerset for employing a more authoritarian style of government, revealed by his use of proclamations, which were commands usually issued by the personal authority of the monarch, validated by the Great Seal. Somerset used proclamations no less than 76 times in under two years, the highest rate at any time during the 16th century.

Somerset's political authority was severely damaged with the execution of his brother, but the rebellions of 1549 were catastrophic and it was only a matter of time before he was usurped. Warwick initiated matters, by gathering the support of the Earls of Arundel and Southampton and attempting to enlist Princess Mary's support. Mary refused to be drawn into the conspiracy, but Warwick continued regardless and by October he was ready to strike, having gained the support of Paget and Archbishop Cranmer. Cranmer convinced Edward VI and reorganised the staffing of the Privy Chamber and Warwick mustered several thousand troops

Speak like a historian: peerage titles

Many peers took different titles as they gained more influence with the king, which means they are sometimes referred to by different names.

Edward Seymour (Jane Seymour's brother and therefore Edward's uncle) was made Earl of Hertford in 1537. He made himself Duke of Somerset in February 1547. From 31 January 1547 until 31 October 1549 Somerset ruled as Lord Protector.

John Dudley was Viscount Lisle until he was made Earl of Warwick in February 1547. He made himself Duke of Northumberland on 11 October 1551. On 21 February 1550, Northumberland was appointed Lord President of the Council, and held this position until Edward's death.

in London. Somerset's support melted away and he was taken to the Tower on 14 October 1549.

Northumberland's regency

Warwick's transition to Lord President of the Council was not as smooth as Somerset's had been. Thomas Wriothesley, the Earl of Southampton, was not interested in taking second place in the government, and quickly sought Princess Mary's support against him. However, Warwick had men in the Privy Chamber, his brother Sir Andrew Dudley and Sir John Gates, both of whom had a great deal of access to the king. Warwick was astute enough to see that executing Somerset would discredit his own authority, therefore he released the ex-Protector and allowed him back onto the Council. Southampton died several months later, ending a contest that could have erupted into civil war. Yet Somerset sought to involve himself in plots almost as soon as he was released from the Tower. He was tried by his peers and beheaded on 22 January 1552.

Northumberland (as he was self-titled from October 1551 onwards) was well placed to dominate central government. He appointed William Cecil as Secretary to liaise between him, the Council and the royal household. About 20 councillors met regularly and controlled policy and administration. The Duke appreciated that Somerset's neglect of the Council had led to his downfall, and therefore he set out to improve its efficiency. He allowed Paget to draw up routines for conducting business and added 12 new councillors of his choosing, taking the number up to 33. Northumberland used proclamations much less than his predecessor and on the occasions he used them he was cautious to found them on parliamentary statute. His government was unfortunate that it presided over terrible harvests during 1549–51, forcing the price of wheat up 100% in just a year. Sweating sickness also befell London, leading many to suggest God was sending punishments for failing to implement the Reformation fully. The uprisings of 1549 (see the section on Rebellion) also left Northumberland with the enormous task of restoring stability to the kingdom. These immense difficulties were compounded in 1551 with the collapse of the cloth trade, the country's main industry, and soaring grain prices. The Council took harsh measures to suppress unrest, passing statutes against unlawful assembly and reimposing censorship laws that had been relaxed under Somerset. The duke also formed the 'gendarmes', armed guards who protected London and were the first form of standing army, but they had to be disbanded in 1552 due to financial constraints. Some of the social policies implemented (see the section on The social impact of religious and economic changes under Edward VI) demonstrated more concern for social justice than Somerset and were largely more effective. The religious settlement Northumberland promulgated provided a clean break from previous compromises. Historians still debate his motivations for pushing England towards Protestantism, for he himself was never very religious. Smith (1997) and Williams (1995) argue that he had to lean on Cranmer for his influence over Edward, and the settlement was his reward (see the section on Humanist and religious thought under Edward VI).

Traditionally seen as the scheming, ambitious duke who altered the succession in favour of his own family, Northumberland has undergone something of a rehabilitation by recent historians. He inherited a most unenviable position, as Smith (1997) asserts. Given that he was never Lord Protector, merely Lord President of the Council, he had to take advice and work with others far more than Somerset had. Loach (2007) suggests that the main differences between Northumberland and Somerset were in their methods of rule, rather than character or policy, as they were both ambitious and greedy.

 Voices from the past

William Paget

William Paget first served as a Member of Parliament, then, through his friendship with Stephen Gardiner, was chosen for several diplomatic missions for Henry VIII. He became a member of Henry's Privy Council in 1543. Paget vigorously supported Somerset's Protectorate, until Warwick's coup, and was made Comptroller of the King's Household as well as obtaining extensive land grants. He was committed to the Tower along with Somerset in 1551, but was restored to favour in 1553. Although involved in Edward's settlement of the Crown on Lady Jane Grey, he made his peace with Mary and served on her Privy Council too. He retired when Elizabeth I acceded to the throne.

Paget wrote to Somerset in July 1549, just after Kett's Rebellion:

I told your Grace the truth, and was not believed: well, now your Grace should see it, what does your Grace see? The King's subjects out of all discipline and all obedience, and care neither for you nor the King. What is the cause? Your softness, your wish to be good to the poor. It is a pity that your gentle approach should cause such evil as the rebels now threaten. A society is maintained by religion and law. Look carefully to see whether you have either law or religion, and I fear you shall find neither. I know that in the matter of your treatment of the common people every man in the Council dislikes your proceedings and wishes it were otherwise.

Source: Cited in Skidmore C. *Edward VI: The Lost King of England*: London: Phoenix; 2007. p. 208.

Discussion points:

1. What is Paget's message to Somerset?
2. Why might this have been a galling letter to receive from Paget particularly?
3. What is Paget's criticism of Somerset? Is there evidence to suggest this was fair criticism?

Royal authority

Edward VI was the sole legitimate heir of Henry VIII; in fact, he was the only Tudor to be born expecting to rule. However, Edward VI was only nine years old when he became king. Therefore the history of his reign must be the history of those who ruled in his name. Edward's minority provided both an opportunity for others to exert their influence, but a serious problem too, as royal minorities had been disastrous in the past. There has been much debate among historians about whether Edward's reign constituted a 'crisis' of monarchy. Most historians, thanks to revisionists like Loach (2002) have rejected this view, now highlighting aspects of his reign such as Parliament. Edward's parliaments were extremely active, passing 164 acts in just two sessions. However, Edward's minority did result in a decline of the Crown's legislative authority: some of the Henrician Acts, such as the statute which allowed the king to use his prerogative in order to repeal all legislation passed in 1533, was itself repealed in 1547. The Edwardian Reformation Acts rested on the 'authority of Parliament', no doubt because the Council felt the need to gain consent of the governing classes to implement such changes. Most importantly, the Treasons Act was repealed, demolishing the structure of punitive and deterrent laws erected under Cromwell's stewardship. This was a shortsighted move as the Act stripped the regency of necessary deterrents and coercive weapons.

Royal authority in Ireland

Cromwellian reforms in the 1530s had seen the subjection of Dublin to London; never again would a Kildare rule Ireland in the King's name. Yet royal control had not been established beyond **'The Pale'**. Following several rebellions in 1546 and 1548 by Irish gentry, provoked by the Lord Deputy, Anthony St Leger, the Protector Somerset changed tactic. He appointed the bellicose Sir Edward Bellingham who embarked on a policy of protecting the Pale by fortification and colonisation. Forts were built across several counties and English settlers were placed on the lands of the rebels.

Key term

'The Pale': the region of Ireland directly controlled by England – the area this encompassed varied across time but it always centred on Dublin.

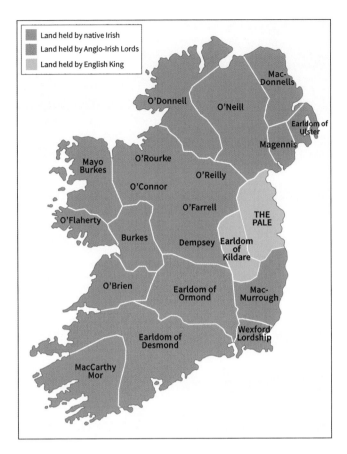

Figure 3.1: The lordships of Tudor Ireland in 1547.

Northumberland's approach to Ireland was little different from Somerset's, except that his religious policy made firm action necessary. Sir James Croft was provided with 2000 soldiers and £24 000 to pay for his army. With this force he was able to make some progress with the establishment of English colonies (known as 'plantations') in Leix and Offaly. Edward's religious reforms bred further mistrust, however. A state Church was established in Ireland, but it was less readily accepted there and liturgical reform was very slow to filter through. Croft managed to prevent revolt, but at huge cost – £250 000 was spent on Ireland during Edward VI's reign.

Problems of succession

Edward's health collapsed in the spring of 1553, when he was not yet 16 years old. Doctors diagnosed a 'suppurating tumour', which was probably tuberculosis. Historians have debated Edward's strength as a monarch, but it seems that on the succession he was resolute: Mary should be excluded from the throne. Edward began work on a 'Device for the Succession' to override the terms of Henry VIII's Third Act of Succession and ensure that the next king would be Protestant. The initial plan was to divert the succession towards a prospective male descendant of Henry VIII's younger sister, Mary. However, no such descendants had yet been born, and so when Edward's condition worsened, Mary's eldest granddaughter, Lady Jane Grey, was named as heir. Lady Jane, the daughter of the Duke of Suffolk, was married to Northumberland's eldest son in May 1553 so that the Duke could maintain his position of influence. On 21 June 1553 letters were issued declaring Princesses Mary and Elizabeth illegitimate and Parliament was summoned to turn the 'Device' into legislation. Edward died earlier than expected on 6 July, leaving Northumberland somewhat unprepared. It was four days before Lady Jane Grey was announced as Queen, during which time Princess Mary fled to Norfolk to muster forces at Framlingham and prepare her attack. Many people supported her. Guy (1988) argues that her supporters were not religiously motivated; if anything they expected her to uphold the religious policy set out by Edward VI. The people supported her because they respected her legitimacy as next in line to the throne and they hated Northumberland and his men for their treatment of rebels who had revolted in 1549 (see the section on Rebellion).

Northumberland rallied his guards and marched north, on 18 July the Council in London recognised Mary as Queen. Mary entered London on 3 August 1553 as Queen of England, and Northumberland and his associates were thrown into the Tower. In some respects the succession crisis supports the view that the Tudor monarchy was strong, as the people of England would not countenance an illegitimate heir and Mary had genuine popular support in East Anglia.

Discussion points:

1. What was the nature of Lady Jane Grey's claim to the throne?
2. Another person had a claim to the throne other than Lady Jane Grey. Who was this, and why were they not considered as an alternative to Mary?

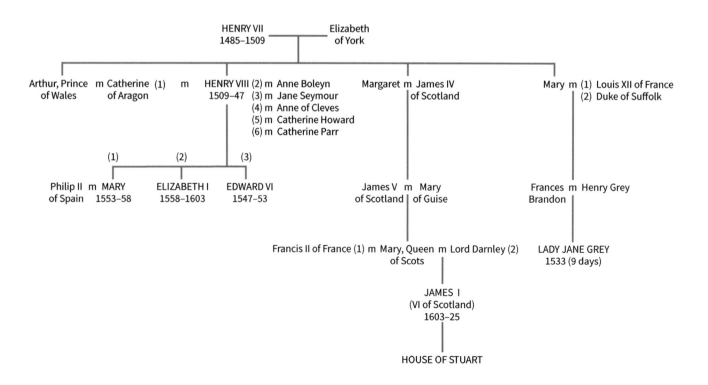

Figure 3.2: The Tudor family tree.

Relations with foreign powers

Nowhere is continuity between Henry VIII and his children more marked than in foreign policy. The decade after his death was dominated by tensions with France, and this had some significant consequences. Primarily it pushed England into a number of alliances with the Habsburgs of Spain, who sought to counter-balance French power. Hostility towards France also made conflict with Scotland more likely. Perhaps the most significant impact of foreign policy between 1547 and 1558 was the cost: wars were desperately expensive and prompted Edward VI and, later, Mary constantly to seek new revenues of income.

Scotland

Henry VIII's death brought about a change of emphasis in policy rather than a change of direction. Somerset aimed at dynastic union of England and Scotland through the marriage of Edward to Mary Stuart. Jordan (1968) suggests that Somerset genuinely sought peace with Scotland in these negotiations, although this has been contested by Bush (1975), who has suggested that these were half-hearted attempts and the duke really wanted to continue Henry's wars. The policy failed and, like Henry, Somerset resorted to military action, which was partly successful at the Battle of Pinkie in 1547. However, as Somerset had been responsible for executing raids on Scotland under Henry VIII, he knew of their ineffectiveness, and therefore sought a different strategy from that of the previous king. Somerset attempted to place permanent military garrisons along the Scottish border as a means to enforce his policy and sought peace with France to give him a free hand to do so. English garrisons were also set up from Dundee to islands in the Firth of Forth by 1548. This was intended to apply pressure to the Scottish government to agree to the marriage of Mary and Edward VI. It was a costly venture: Somerset spent £580 000 on garrisons in two years (almost double the cost of Henry VIII's five-year campaign). Although they proved strong enough to rebuff the French, the garrisons could never defeat them and resentment towards the English grew among the Scottish people. At the same time English-language Bibles were distributed to try to persuade the Scots to the Protestant and English cause, although this had little impact.

France

In March 1547 Francis I signed a defensive Treaty with Somerset, although he died shortly after, leaving his son, the bellicose Henry II, King of France. Henry II saw a treaty with England as weak and repudiated the treaty immediately, demanding that England return Boulogne and Calais to France. By June 1548 Henry II had assumed the status of 'Protector of Scotland' and sent 10 000 troops to Edinburgh. Meanwhile Mary was carried off to marry the Dauphin in France. French hostilities soon spilled over into territorial claims against the English and Henry II became more confident that England was weak, due to rebellions that had broken out in 1549. Although they failed to recapture Boulogne, the French had made it clear they were willing to throw military weight behind their claims.

The fall of the Somerset protectorate in 1549 and rise of the Earl of Warwick (later Duke of Northumberland), saw a more conciliatory approach to foreign policy. In November 1549 Warwick embarked on the sale of Boulogne to the French, supported by members of the Council. The Treaty of Boulogne, signed in 1550 was

A good way of revising is to try to summarise information succinctly in your own words. You could go through your foreign policy notes and make a table with the four headings France, Scotland, Spain and Ireland. Try to sum up in ten words the relationship Edward VI and Mary I had with the countries listed.

described by Pollard as 'the most ignominious treaty signed by England during the century'[1] although Guy (1988) suggests that there were advantages to both sides and, in any case, retrenchment depended on it. Although the English were offered inadequate indemnity for Boulogne (400 000 crowns – still more than Henry II wanted to pay) it cut down the cost of military commitments in France to £25 000 per annum for the defence of Calais. Further rapprochement culminated in the Treaty of Angers of 1551, which envisaged the marriage of Edward to a daughter of Henry II, compensating somewhat for the betrothal of Mary Stuart and the Dauphin. These concessions were motivated by a desperate need to restore the Crown's finances and secure stability and peace at home, following Kett's Rebellion (see the section on Rebellion). In these circumstances, Warwick's actions can be considered an act of statesmanship.

Spain

Somerset was wise enough to realise that the Habsburg ruler, Charles V, was a useful ally to maintain, particularly as tensions rose with Scotland and France. As such, Somerset presented himself to the Spanish king as a religious conservative and delayed the introduction of religious reform in England to keep relations friendly. Charles V agreed that French ships would not be able to use ports in the Netherlands if they were engaged in supporting the Scots. The amity between England and the Habsburg emperor deterred Henry II from declaring war on England for some time. Warwick was not on such good terms with Charles V, who in March 1551 threatened war if Mary Tudor was forced to conform to the anti-Catholic provisions of the Act of Uniformity, but conflict was averted due to the renewal of Habsburg–Valois hostilities. Northumberland secured England's position by the Treaty of Angers, whereupon Edward VI was matched with Henry II's daughter.

The social impact of religious and economic changes under Edward VI

Religious change

Catherine Davies (2002) suggests that Edward VI's reformation overturned religious practice at all levels in society and became repressive by 1549. It was a revolution from the top, as the extent of the Act of Supremacy was fully realised under Edward as no other monarch had dared to go further than him. The **liturgy** and doctrine of the Church were systematically transformed and its assets were stripped, and its legal system only survived due to Edward's untimely death. By 1553 the Church had lost 60% of its income, devastating Church resources and causing severe damage to pastoral provision. The calendar was transformed and all but the major festivals were abolished. There is much evidence to suggest that Edward might have continued to use the Royal Supremacy to reform the Church had he reached independent kingship. There is a good deal of discussion about the extent to which hearts and minds were changed during this period, but what is certain is that nobody was unaffected by such wholesale religious change.

The final years of Henry VIII's reign had not been primarily concerned with spiritual issues, but the leadership of the Church had been seriously divided between the orthodox conservatives like Gardiner and reformers led by Cranmer. In London

Key term

liturgy: the customary form or pattern of public worship carried out by congregations.

particularly, the death of Henry was followed by popular agitation for reform. Yet the drivers for reform under Somerset came from the government, not popular or clerical pressure. The first step was taken shortly after Henry's death in July 1547 when injunctions were issued and a general visitation ordered for the whole Church. These were not so radical, as they ordered the clergy to perform their spiritual duties, but they indicated a shift towards Protestantism. The superstitious worship of images was condemned, sprinkling of holy water was forbidden and processions were banned. 'Homilies' (sermons) were to be read in churches and set out the doctrine of justification by faith alone in unequivocal terms, thereby aligning the English Church with the reformed churches of Europe. Stephen Gardiner and Edmund Bonner, who protested against these, were imprisoned, and the latter subsequently deprived of his position as Bishop of London.

Edward VI's first Parliament pushed the Protestant programme further. The Heresy Acts and the Henrician Act of Six Articles were repealed, and an outpouring of literature followed. Over 400 books were published under the Protectorate, about 160 of which were radical religious texts. The dissolution of the **chantries** put into effect a statute which had been prepared in 1545. The original motivations then had been fiscal, but the Edwardian act condemned the superstition inherent in the chantries' existence. Unlike the dissolution of the monasteries, there were no physical remnants of the destruction of the chantries and **fraternities**, but they had been part of the fabric of communal life of the time, and their wealth, amounting to £600 000 was considerable. Parliamentary statutes were followed in 1548 by proclamations that sanctioned the destruction of sculptures, rood screens and altars. Along with this went the abolition of Candlemas, Ash Wednesday, Palm Sunday and Good Friday, devastating the visual symbolism of the English Church.

The most significant religious measure of Somerset's regime was the introduction of the Book of Common Prayer in 1549, which was enforced by the First Act of Uniformity. Cranmer led the committee to work on the new liturgy. In many ways the book was fairly conservative, merely providing services in English, not necessarily Protestant. What gave it a Protestant character were the omissions – the rubrics of Communion for example. Debates ensued in the House of Lords over the **Eucharist**, but Cranmer and the Bishop of Rochester had already accepted the Protestant view. Eight bishops voted against the Prayer Book and it upset just as many radicals as conservatives, which meant that it would not survive long unaltered. In the same session, statutes were passed allowing priests to marry: the Lords tried to oppose this measure, but were unsuccessful.

Most historians agree that by far the most influential measures of Somerset's Protectorate were the changes in religion. The changes were by no means uniformly imposed, but all over the country traditionalists watched in horror as images, lights and ceremonies were stripped away. By late April 1548 the Royal Council were alarmed by disturbances breaking out in Cornwall, spurred on, they assumed, by priests. Therefore licences had to be issued by Cranmer to be able to preach, apparently protecting parishes from itinerant preachers. The Western Rising in 1549 (see the section on Rebellion) was so brutally put down that it discouraged others from emulating similar revolts. However, as Duffy (2005) argues, 'oblique resistance was widespread'[2] as judges and the local gentry

Key term

chantries: a form of trust fund that paid for priests to sing hymns and say prayers, for the benefit of the soul of a specified deceased person, usually the donor. It was believed such masses would speed the deceased's soul through **Purgatory** and onwards to eternal rest in Heaven.

Key term

fraternities: lay organisations allied to the Catholic Church. They provided opportunities for people to become involved in the work of the Church and offered support for the poor within the congregation.

Key term

Eucharist: rite considered by most Christian churches to be a sacrament. During the Last Supper, Jesus gave his disciples bread and wine and said they should eat and drink in his memory. Catholics believe in transubstantiation, that is, the bread and wine is changed into the blood and body of Christ, whereas Protestants believe they are symbolic.

Key term

Church plate: the name given to Church objects made of precious metal.

refused to enforce edicts from Parliament. When rumours of Somerset's arrest spread, many assumed the Henrician settlement would be reimposed and Mass was even revived in Oxford.

The liberal nature of the earlier Protectorate changed with the coming of Warwick as the Council brought a swift end to any hopes traditionalists may have had and in January 1550 enshrined in law the defacing of images and abolition of old service books. There was a concerted effort to drive England towards Protestantism. In March 1551 commissioners ordered all remaining **Church plate** to be called in and disposed of. Parishes all over the country sold off their Church plate and other treasures to prevent confiscation, the proceeds set aside for use of the parish. Commissioners found very little to confiscate by the time they made their visitations. For historians like Dickens (1964), convinced of the bankruptcy of Catholicism, the astonishing degree of conformity achieved across thousands of communities is not surprising. Of course there was a growing number of people who would call themselves Protestants by the 1540s, particularly in London, Bristol and even Hull, but even then they were not in a numerical majority. Duffy (2005) suggests the flood of sales of images, treasures and stripping of altars that took place does not represent a swing to reform, but a 'panic-stricken stampede to avoid theft by the Crown'.[3] The religious changes implemented by the government required massive spending for small parishes on constructing pulpits and communion tables and whitewashing walls, and many were forced to sell off chalices and other valuable items to pay for the new requirements. Corresponding with the disposal of valuable religious wares was a dramatic increase in theft from churches, lining the pockets of people from all levels of society.

The religious settlement promulgated by Northumberland marked a real break from the compromise of 1549, committing England unequivocally to the Protestant cause. The Second Act of Uniformity was a significant piece of

Voices from the past

Robert Parkyn

Robert Parkyn was a Yorkshire priest who served through Henry VIII's to Elizabeth's reign. He kept a chronicle charting the changes made to liturgy and doctrine and how he felt about those changes.

In many places of this realm (but specially in the South parts, as Suffolk, Norfolk, Kent and Wales etc.) neither bread nor water was sanctified or distributed among Christian people on Sundays, but clearly omitted as things tending to idolatry. Yea, and also the pyxes hanging over the altars (wherein was remaining Christ's blessed body under form of bread) was spitefully cast away as things most abominable, and did not pass of the blessed hosts therein contained, but villainously despised them, uttering such words thereby as it did

abhor true Christian ears for to hear; but only that Christ's mercy is so much, it was marvel that the earth did not open and swallow up such villainous persons, as it did Dathan and Abiram.

Source: Dickens AG (ed.) 'Robert Parkyn's Narrative of the Reformation'. *English Historical Review*, 62(242); 1947. p. 64–82.

Discussion points:
1. Which of the reforms during Somerset's Protectorate does Parkyn refer to in this passage?
2. Which of the reforms does he dislike the most?
3. Why is Parkyn a really useful source for historians to use in assessing the impact of the Reformation?

legislation that required every person living in England, Wales and Calais to attend Church on Sundays. It replaced the First Book of Common Prayer with a second, and instructed judges to enforce its use under penalty of life imprisonment for third time offenders. The Prayer Book was radical, and although only opposed by two bishops and three lay peers in the Lords, it was deeply controversial. The lack of opposition to the new Prayer Book can be explained by the few remaining traditionalist bishops who had been allowed to keep their position. Bonner, Gardiner and Tunstall had all been swapped for more radical thinkers by 1552.

The last planned reforms were not authorised before Edward's death; however, Cranmer drafted 42 articles of faith, 39 of which Elizabeth would adopt in her religious settlement. Cranmer and others had also tried to reform canon law, but this was defeated in the Lords in 1553. Peers who had just about managed to swallow reforms in rites and doctrine would simply not accept the reformation of discipline too. Martin Bucer, a contemporary German Protestant reformer who had

Figure 3.3: This is an allegorical painting (supposed to tell a story, rather than reflect events accurately). It represents Edward VI being handed power by his ailing father, Henry VIII. On the ribbons of the Pope's tiara is written 'idolatory' and 'superstition'.

Discussion points:

1. What do you think is happening in the right-hand corner of the picture?
2. Why is the Pope slumped forward at the front?
3. Who might the men on the right-hand side of Edward be?
4. What do you think the message of the painting is?

been exiled to England, noted that the English Reformation was too negative; it was imposed by removing the instruments of the old 'superstition' but little effort was made to substitute it with a new faith, particularly outside of London. This might explain why so many Tudor men and women welcomed the accession of a Catholic Queen.

Economic changes

Economic malaise gripped the country in the 1540s and 1550s: inflation, depression in the cloth industry, rising incidences of poverty and unemployment characterised the decade. Military expenditure under Edward VI was a staggering £1 386 687, of which Somerset spent £580 393 on the Scottish campaign alone. He had to spend this huge sum to pay for the mercenaries he hired to serve in Scotland, as little had been done since Wolsey, to address England's military recruitment problems. The disastrous policy of coinage debasement, started under Henry VIII, continued. The government made £537 000 from this in 1547–51, but it had a devastating impact in the form of inflation. More money was raised during the dissolution of chantries and colleges, totalling £110 486 by the end of 1548. Parliamentary taxation yielded £335 988 in Edward's reign, but this could not cover the costs of war and defence. A novel 'Sheep Tax' was implemented on sheep, wool and cloth to raise extra funds, but this yielded even less than customary taxes, so the balance had to be met by borrowing and selling off Crown lands.

The political and religious drama of Somerset's Protectorate was played out during a time of social distress. Population increases put enormous pressure on the land and many were left homeless. The Vagrancy Act of 1547 was perhaps the clearest demonstration of Somerset's lack of humanitarianism; it certainly shows the increasing concern for public order early on in the Protectorate. The Act was a savage attack on vagrants looking for work as the new law suggested that anyone out of work for three days was to be branded with a 'V' and sold into slavery for two years. Even children could be taken from their parents and set to work as apprentices in useful occupations. The new law was widely unpopular and many counties simply refused to enforce it.

Coupled with population pressure was an agrarian struggle, between breeding sheep for wool and cattle for milk, butter and cheese. There was no shortage of corn and harvests were good under Somerset, but there were serious shortages of dairy foodstuffs, which were essential elements in the diet of the poor. Enclosure of common land for parks and overstocking of commons by sheep owners were common grievances and provoked sporadic rioting throughout the 1540s. Enclosure commissions were launched in 1548–49 to investigate the extent of the problem. These commissions were extremely unpopular with landlords, particularly under John Hales who used critical rhetoric in his inquiries. A proclamation was issued against enclosures in April 1549, which triggered a wave of revolts. The government met the challenge by offering pardons and using trusted noblemen of the shires to pacify landlords. The calm was short-lived (see the section on Rebellion).

Northumberland's primary concern was the restoration of the Crown's finances. The Council decided upon a period of **retrenchment** and Sir Walter Mildmay (long-serving surveyor of the Court of Augmentations) and Sir William Cecil, who acted as Northumberland's personal and private secretary, were asked to find the means to achieve this. The far-sighted Mildmay understood the need to reform administration and create a single exchequer to replace the many revenue-gathering institutions typical of earlier reigns. Northumberland raised revenue through selling Crown lands and confiscated lead, coining bullion melted from Church plate, seizing more Church lands and securing taxation. Borrowing was initially extended from Flanders, but thanks to the manipulation of foreign exchanges by Sir Thomas Gresham, £132 372 was repaid by 1553. Northumberland knew that debasement was a liability, but could not resist it one more time, netting £114 500 for the Crown before implementing remedial action on October 1551. Northumberland correctly assessed that the success of retrenchment depended on ending Somerset's wars, which he did in 1550 with the Treaty of Boulogne. Northumberland's subsequent deflationary policy was successful, and prices finally started to fall. However, recoinage drained the treasuries of bullion and the Crown was bankrupt by 1552, prompting 20 financial commissions in that year to investigate new revenue streams. The reports they delivered to the Council made a host of suggestions, some considered too radical for the conservative Lord Treasurer, the Marquess of Winchester. Edward died before any changes could be implemented, and it was therefore left to Mary to accomplish the Crown's financial reforms.

Despite Northumberland's efforts, some of the most significant factors affecting the economy were out of his control. Population was still rising, making work more difficult to find and decreasing living standards for the majority of the people. This was compounded by an unexpected drop in cloth exports, which created widespread unemployment within the textile working communities in East Anglia and the West Country. There were several poor harvests in 1550–52 pushing grain prices up. To combat some of these problems, Northumberland's council pushed through anti-enclosure legislation, which aimed to protect arable farmers, and the unpopular enclosure commissions were ended. A new poor law was passed in 1552, which made parishes responsible for supporting the 'deserving poor' (the aged, infirm or disabled).

Rebellion

Western Rebellion

The first demonstration of deep-seated discontent with the Edwardian Reformation took place in Cornwall. William Body, an archdeacon who was carrying out a visitation to check that church images had been removed was murdered in Helston. Ten of the ringleaders of this outbreak of violence were hanged, and for a while, calm was restored. Fletcher and MacCulloch (2008) argue that it was the new liturgy in the Prayer Book of 1549 that turned Cornish opposition into full-scale rebellion. It should be noted that other factors such as the Sheep Tax (aimed to discourage enclosure) would have hit Devonian farmers hard, as Devon had been an enclosed county for many years. The rebels argued that religion should be left alone until at least Edward came of age at

Key term

retrenchment: an act of reduction, particularly in the realm of public expenditure.

24. Humphrey Arundell, a gentleman with extensive estates in the area, led the rebels from Bodmin, where they set up camp. By June a considerable force had gathered as the rising spread to Devon. Sir Peter Carew, a committed evangelical, tried to pacify the situation, but instead exacerbated the anger of the rebels when one of his men set fire to their defences. The hapless Carew was replaced by Lord Russell shortly afterwards. Somerset, beset by enclosure riots in the Midlands and South East, did little to support Russell who had scant option but to try and enlist forces in Wiltshire and advance slowly, for fear of being outnumbered. The rebels, numbering 2000 people, marched to Exeter on 10 July and besieged the city. Russell eventually gathered enough forces of 8000 men and relieved Exeter by 14 August. He then marched west to tackle Cornwall before suppressing more rebels in Devon and Somerset. Some 4000 inhabitants of the West Country may have been killed in the campaign.

Kett's rebellion and the rebellions of the Commonwealth

The risings in the South and East Anglia in many ways echoed the Western Rebellion. Beginning in May 1548, rebels attacked the property of Sir William Cavendish in Northaw (who had attempted to enclose extensive common land) and set up camps on it. Very little was done to the participants in this rising, apart from fines levied in the Star Chamber. The rising prompted Somerset to launch commissions for investigating illegal enclosure in the Midlands the same summer and he even established a court of requests in his own household to give justice to the poor. The risings that followed were blamed on Somerset for spearheading concessions to the people. Arguably, the 'Good' duke's actions set the scene for further risings the next year, encouraged by the muted consequences for the Northaw rioters. Peace collapsed in July 1549 when spontaneous outbreaks of violence occurred in Essex and Norfolk, where villagers tore down hedges of enclosed land. Robert Kett, a tanner by trade but also a substantial tenant farmer in Wymondham, was an inspirational leader to local villagers, and he vowed to support them until they had obtained their rights. Kett and the rebels' demands stated that feudal taxes should be restricted to the gentry and priests should be barred as landowners. They made it clear that they eschewed violence, and respected good governance. Defence of the common land also emerged as a crucial issue in the rebels' manifesto. As Loach (1993) argues, it was the prosperous tenant farmers like Kett who were disgruntled that wealthier farmers were keeping too many sheep. This rebellion was dangerous because it was a massive demonstration against the local governing class. It was no peasants' revolt and was most alarming because the leaders were drawn from just outside of the magisterial class and were highly effective.

Kett marched the villagers to Norwich where he gained considerable support and set up camp on Mousehold Heath with 16 000 rioters in tow. With astonishing speed uprisings had swept through the Thames Valley, the Home Counties, the Midlands and much of East Anglia. Camps sprang up in Downham Market, Ipswich, Great Yarmouth, Canterbury and Maidstone to name but a few. Somerset vacillated, not wanting to abandon his Scottish campaign, but finally sent the Marquess of Northampton with an expeditionary force to quell Norfolk. Some 300 died in a bloody battle for the city of Norwich and what might have stayed a vast popular demonstration turned into full-scale rebellion. The Earl of Warwick replaced Northampton, and along with 12 000 men entered Norwich and hanged some of the rebels. From there they cut off the camp's supply lines and killed as many as 3000 of the rebels. Kett panicked and fled, and on news of this rebel resistance crumbled. Kett was hanged at Norwich Castle on 7 December 1549 and 49 others were executed with him. Popular unrest did not end here though. The Privy Council register reveals commotions in 1550 in Nottinghamshire, Kent and elsewhere. In August 1551 insurrection began in Leicestershire, Northamptonshire and Rutland.

Intellectual developments under Edward VI

Edward VI's education is revealing of the intellectual developments taking place in England at the time. He was tutored by John Cheke, one of the brightest Classical scholars of the time, who challenged the establishment by suggesting new ways of pronouncing Ancient Greek, apparently just as it would have been spoken at the time. His godfather was Archbishop Thomas Cranmer, therefore his religious education was almost certainly of the new Protestant variety. Edward VI kept a 'chronicle', which reveals much about his education and the values that were being instilled in him. He wrote that he often thought of Cicero, who had said that the wise man alone was rich. The study of the Classical denotes Erasmian influence. Erasmus, founder of the Humanist tradition, had long argued that the best kind of ruler was virtuous, educated and enlightened, and valued knowledge and wisdom over possessions. The best-known humanist scholars and idealists, who advocated Christian justice within the state, were so called 'Commonwealth Men'. These men, of whom John Hales, Sir John Cheke and Robert Crowley are the best known, were not social revolutionaries, because they believed firmly in the subordination of the Commons to the aristocracy. Nor were they a united party. However, as individuals they were concerned that the aristocracy felt no sense of responsibility towards their inferiors and issued thundering criticisms of enclosures. Hales led the enclosure commissions that took place in 1548 and managed to alienate landlords with his high-handed rhetoric in front of juries.

Although Humanism had become a firm addition to English intellectual thinking, Jennifer Loach (1993) suggests that the continuing presence of military skills and chivalric notions was still prevalent under Edward VI and Mary I. She attributes this to the continuing wars with France and Scotland. Despite a great deal of humanist writing about the virtue of meritocracy and the value of learning, the Court remained imbued with notions of military prowess and honour. The figures that dominated court under both Edward VI and Mary I were those who had proven themselves on the field of battle. This is true of both Somerset and Northumberland.

Humanist and religious thought under Edward VI

Humanism had taken root in the University of Cambridge and parts of London as early as Henry VII's reign, when scholars such as John Colet fostered the work of Erasmus and shared his views on education. It is highly likely that William Tyndale, who was to become a leading figure in Protestant reform during the reign of Henry VIII, was attracted to Cambridge because of the teaching of the great scholar there, and some historians suggest that the focus on biblical translation during

Speak like a historian: ML Bush

Extract A

The bulk of the stirs tended to embarrass the government by seeking to implement rather than resist its policy. The government at no point fought for its life. No rising in 1549 threatened the government physically in the manner of those of 1381, 1450 and 1497 with a sustained march on London. Nor did the rebels plan to release the king from the grip of evil ministers. If anything, the aim was to aid the government against the aristocracy, or to make it change the religious policy. Also to the government's relief, the 1549 risings stand out for their lack of aristocratic participation and leadership

Source: Bush ML. *The Government Policy of Protector Somerset.* London: Edward Arnold; 1975. p. 85.

Discussion points:

1. How serious does Bush think the rebellion was? What reasons does he give?
2. How convincing do you find this interpretation given what you know about Kett's Rebellion?

the English Reformation was in large part due to Erasmus's influence. However, Erasmus was never interested in leading religious reformation: he criticised abuses of the Church but intended the papacy to instigate reform. Conservatives such as Stephen Gardiner and Thomas More had been committed Humanists, but the younger scholars who followed his teachings were more radically inclined.

Thomas Cranmer had established links with Protestant reformers across Europe. Many distinguished continental theologians therefore came to England to spread a whole variety of ideas, including those of Calvin and Zwingli. The Italian Peter Martyr was appointed to a chair at Oxford in 1548, and the following year Martin Bucer, one of the most prominent Protestant scholars of Germany, was made Regius Professor at Cambridge. Cranmer was Bucer's patron and they both continued to search for truth, moving from a **Lutheran** to a Zwinglian position by the end of their lives. The influence of these thinkers is difficult to assess outside of the universities in which they worked. Their arrival certainly established England as a European centre for theological debate.

Mary I and her ministers

Mary I has traditionally been vilified, by historians, for the burning of Protestants at the stake. Even Elton (1955) who recast the earlier Tudors in a new light said of Mary 'positive achievements there were none'.[4] Modern historians such as Doran and Freeman (2011) have tried to rehabilitate her reputation, but, as John Guy (1988) asserts 'Mary I will never appear creative'.[5] This assessment of Mary may have much to do with her character and position. When she acceded the throne Mary was 37 years old and toughened by her experiences. She was pious and unmarried, and had been bastardised, slimming her prospects of matrimonial proposals. The first Queen **Regnant** of England, Mary sought a husband to attend to matters of state and took the advice of her cousin, Charles V of Spain, to marry Philip, his sole heir. In this decision she seemed intellectually limited, apparently having little regard for the domestic political implications this would bring. A more astute politician might have noticed the anti-papal and anti-Spanish xenophobia that had swelled under her father's reign. But Mary's dominant aim, when she attained the Crown, was to end the schism with the papacy and make England once more part of Catholic Christendom. On this, she was inflexible.

Historians have traditionally devoted more consideration to Mary's religious policy than to other aspects of her reign, perhaps because it is seen in contrast to Edward's. Nevertheless, in secular matters it seems there was remarkable continuity. Mary's government was concerned with the same problems as Edward's had been – crucially, money, but also maintaining law and order. Many of the solutions were the same as they had been under Edward too. This is not surprising given the continuity of personnel at most levels of government. Mary was wise to recognise that jettisoning experience acquired during the previous reign would be foolish. At Court, however, Mary surrounded herself with devotees instead of experienced advisers. Mary brought almost all of her existing servants to the Privy Chamber, which facilitated insularity and increased factionalism.

Most of Edward's principal officers were ousted, although Sir Thomas Cheney and Sir William Paget were retained. The Earl of Arundel became Master of the Household in 1553; the Earl of Oxford became Lord Chamberlain and Sir Henry Jerningham replaced Gates as captain of the guard. It was these men, along with those who had supported her at Framlingham, who made up the Privy Council. Although Mary tried to build a broad government, her Court was dominated by imperial envoys, such as Simon Renard from Spain and reactionary conservatives. She never really trusted Gardiner and Paget, whom she inherited from the reigns of her father and brother. Although the Privy Council was at its largest under Mary (it was twice the size of Henry VIII's Council) its efficiency was enhanced. A system was established to create 12 subcommittees, which were set up in 1554 and each provided with a specific administrative function, for example, the administration of the navy. Mary also retained the most able law officers, regardless of their religious persuasion. However, her reintroduction of the Heresy Laws led to the burning of many Protestants at the stake. In 1553 a codification for treason was introduced, which has been described by Tittler (1983) as 'one of the major treason statutes of the century'.[6] Mary's government was also successful in refurbishing the English navy, which had been laid to waste since Henry VIII's reign. Six new ships were built and an annual peacetime appropriation of £14 000 was provided.

Royal authority

Much has been made of Mary's health and state of mind as factors affecting her security. Of course the rejection by her father as a bastard from his marriage to Catherine of Aragon and her living in fear through at least part of her brother's reign must have taken its toll. Physically, she had a weak heart, extreme headaches and, it is said, oedema (an observable swelling in body tissues caused by fluid). Most discussed has been the recurrent amenorrhoea, which drove her

Key term

Regnant: a Queen Regnant reigns in her own right, not through marriage to a king.

to alternating phases of despair and euphoria during her phantom pregnancies. When matters of the succession were raised, her ailments may have been a troublesome factor, but were probably no more intrusive than Edward's illness in the final year of his life. In fact, except for matters of conscience, Mary showed herself to be flexible and in matters close to her heart (return of Catholicism, marriage to Philip of Spain and war with France), she achieved what she wanted, so could hardly be viewed as a monarch without power.

Parliaments

Mary's five parliaments passed 104 acts in five sessions, so compared with her siblings, this was not a particularly productive record. Guy (1988) suggests this was mostly due to a lack of leadership in the House of Lords and the nature of Marian Parliaments. The sessions were characterised by brief sessions, inferior standards of record keeping and absenteeism, some of which was politically motivated. This is despite the fact that Mary had remodelled Parliament to a large extent. She replaced radical bishops, created four new peerages and 19 new Commons seats, intervened in elections and dispensed patronage to her supporters. It is therefore somewhat shocking that Mary failed to obtain constructive unified leadership in Parliament.

Opposition to Crown policy in Parliament was uncommon. Tensions ran highest over issues of property, such as the restoration of the Bishopric of Durham, which was only carried through the Commons by 201 votes to 120. The return of **First Fruits and Tenths** to the Church was accomplished in 1555, but it was a close run thing of 193 votes for and 126 votes against. The second Parliament of the reign reopened in April 1554, and was by far the most dramatic as the tension between Gardiner and Paget was palpable. Gardiner was determined to press on with the suppression of heresy, and he hoped to exclude Elizabeth from the throne. Paget feared that Gardiner would attack property obtained through the dissolution of the monasteries. Such was his fear that Paget prevented treason laws applying to Philip and heresy laws being passed, which was unforgivable in Mary's eyes. Paget really showed Mary that the Crown could achieve its objectives only if they were accepted by the Council. Parliament was relatively compliant in other religious policy, aside from maintaining ex-religious property rights (see the section on Religious change), although absenteeism was conspicuous when it came to dealing with the reconciliation with Rome. Royal authority was maintained in Parliament because the interests of the Crown and members were largely the same: positive relationships were probably maintained because of a shared fear of social revolution, following Kett's Rebellion of 1549.

Key term

First Fruits and Tenths: the clergy were obliged to pay a portion of their first year's revenue from their benefice and a tenth of their income every year thereafter.

Voices from the past

Simon Renard

Renard came to England in June 1553 as one of Charles V's envoys. Trained in the law, he was highly ambitious and vain. He quickly won Mary's confidence and operated at the centre of English affairs. He was a persuasive diplomat and historians have relied on his records as evidence for judging Mary's reign, although Renard was quick to disparage English councillors and his work must be seen in this light.

Ireland

Ireland reverted to Catholic worship and papal authority without waiting for formal enactments on Mary's succession to the throne. Yet although the religious policies of Edward were immediately reversed, secular policy remained constant. Anthony St Ledger was appointed Lord Deputy again just before Edward's death with instructions to reduce the garrison and run Ireland more economically. He was replaced in 1556 by the Earl of Sussex who took a more aggressive line. He stepped up plantation policies in Leix and Offaly, now renamed Queen's County and King's County. Sussex created forts, to the west and north of the Pale, funding them from the expropriated Irish lands. The authoritarian government of Sussex won him few friends and many enemies. He managed to unite magnates, churchmen and Anglo-Irish Lords and men of the Pale in hostility to English rule.

Problems of succession

In her will dated 30 March 1558, Mary named the unborn child she believed herself to be pregnant with as her heir. She made Cardinal Pole her leading executor and left £1000 as alms for the poor. By October she was seriously ill, and after considerable pressure from the Council, she added a codicil accepting Elizabeth I as her successor, although she could not bring herself to name her half-sister. Philip was completely supportive of Elizabeth's succession. Mary requested that Elizabeth should pay her (Mary's) debts and ensure that the English Church remained Catholic. Clearly Elizabeth's assurances on this matter were insincere. When Mary died there was none of the secrecy there had been on the death of her father or brother. Her coronation ring was taken swiftly to Elizabeth at Hatfield House to indicate beyond doubt that the Queen was dead, and Parliament were informed within hours. In England at least, there was no doubt that the throne would pass to Elizabeth: the Tudor dynasty was still strong. France, however, had declared Mary, Queen of Scots the Queen of England, which would provide the new regime with inherent difficulties.

Relations with foreign powers

Mary's foreign policy has perhaps been the most heavily criticised aspect of her reign. Her reign is significant in that it marks the last time in the 16th century that foreign policy was embarked on in pursuit of dynastic interests. Doran (1996) suggests Mary's marriage to Philip of Spain was ill-judged and even resulted in parliamentary protests, a major rebellion and factionalism. Both Habsburg and Valois kings competed for influence at the Marian court until her marriage, when the French began to conspire with her enemies.

Spain

Mary's decision to marry Philip lay at the heart of her foreign policy. Although with hindsight it is easy to criticise, there were few eligible Catholic candidates for her to choose from. Edward Courtenay, Earl of Devon and of Yorkist descent and the Archduke Philip, eldest son of Charles V, were two of the strongest. Although Courtenay was favoured by the anti-Habsburgs, historians generally agree he was a man of little worth. Philip, on the other hand, offered the prospect of a Habsburg alliance, which would be useful protection against Henry II, who still coveted Calais and was strongly allied to Scotland. Mary was also emotionally attached to Charles V, who had protected her during the reigns of her father and brother, and was happy to heed his advice. Mary excluded the Council from marriage negotiations, leading to fears that she would listen to Spanish advisers in future instead of deserving Englishmen. The weight of opinion against the marriage, led by Gardiner, influenced lesser figures at court – men such as Croftes, Throgmorton, Carew and Wyatt who became prepared to revolt against the marriage in hopes of thwarting it (see the section on Rebellion). Mary has been praised for managing to channel opposition to the marriage into constructively devising safeguards in the marriage treaty, building in protections for the realm against a foreign king.

Philip came to England and married Mary on 25 July 1554. At first, the marriage had no visible impact on foreign policy: Mary and her councillors were united in their wish to avoid war. When tensions rose between France and Spain, Mary sent Paget and Gardiner to La Marque to arrange a general peace in May 1555. Although this mediation failed, France and Spain signed their own treaty, which depleted Henry II's enthusiasm for supporting the plots of Dudley and others (see the section on Rebellion). The truce was short-lived, however, as war broke out in Italy, which inevitably dragged France and Spain into conflict again in 1557. This time, Philip called for English aid. The vast majority of Mary's Council were against any intervention, not least because of the financial implications. It was only a raid on Scarborough Castle in April by Sir Thomas Stafford and French exiles that convinced the Council to change its mind. Wernham (1966) suggests England was never so little prepared for war. Troops were difficult to muster due to the famine of 1555 and only £109 000 was collected by a forced loan. It should, however, be noted that many of the ex-conspirators against Mary fought for her in August 1557, including the Duke of Northumberland's three sons.

By October 1557 the campaign seemed to be over as the Pope was willing to accept Spanish peace terms, following English successes in the siege of St Quentin, under Pembroke. Shrewsbury had also managed to hold back the Scots along the borders, despite Henry II calling on them to mount a full-scale invasion. However, a spell of dry weather inspired Henry II to attack Calais. Neither the Council nor Philip sent aid in time, and it took Henry just eight days to take the English fortress. This was a great and demoralising loss.

The English continued to fight the French, despite deep reservations held by many on the Council about Philip's support in other areas, but no attempt was made to retake Calais. Reluctantly, the English led a large-scale attack on Brest in the summer of 1558, but it failed dismally. By October settlements were being drawn up which would leave Calais in French hands, but Mary died just before terms were finalised. This left the problem of relinquishing Calais to her sister, Elizabeth.

The social impact of religious and economic changes under Mary I

Religious change

Mary's government faced a complex set of ecclesiastical problems, because the Queen herself wanted to repeal all of the religious reforms made under her father and brother. Duffy (2005) suggests that the so-called 'Marian reaction' to undo Edwardian reforms is a misguided term. Duffy suggests that much of the Marian programmes of reform were constructive and sought to incorporate whatever they saw as positive from the Edwardian and Henrician reforms. There is also considerable evidence, as Haigh (1993) suggests, that the restoration of Catholicism was met with a great deal of enthusiasm, even inside London, which was traditionally considered the most Protestant of places.

Mary was resolute in restoring the authority of the papacy. Yet certain statutes made it difficult to separate doctrine from questions of authority. Holders of monastic lands particularly feared a return to Rome would threaten their property. Despite these fears, a return to doctrinal and liturgical orthodoxy was fairly easily achieved. The statute passed in December 1553 authorised services to be said as they had been under Henry VIII, effectively repealing all Edwardian religious legislation. Particularly remarked upon was the clause that forced clergy to relinquish their positions, if they wished to remain married. Approximately 20% of the priesthood had decided to marry under Edward VI: some put their wives aside to continue their career, but many left the Church. The legislation was followed by injunctions to every diocese requiring the removal of married priests, the restoration of the old services and the preaching of Catholic doctrine.

Once Mary's marriage had been settled in July 1554, she felt able to pursue the reconciliation with Rome. Pope Julius III chose Cardinal Reginald Pole, an exiled English Catholic, as his legate to England. The Pope had been persuaded by Charles V and Philip that it would be impractical to attempt a recovery of Church land, but the question of whether the dispensation he would grant would recognise the rights of the new owners caused problems. A first Statute of Repeal had been passed in October 1553 abolishing the religious legislation passed under Edward VI. In November 1554 Mary's third Parliament had the task of repealing the legislation passed under Henry. Pole was reluctant to recognise the validity of the new owners of Church land, which led to much wrangling during December. However, in January 1555, a second Statute of Repeal was passed, abolishing all the legislation limiting the power of the Pope in England passed under Henry VIII, but also confirming the holders of former monastic lands in their titles. Significantly, this Act was accompanied by a statute reviving the heresy laws, originally devised to fight the Lollards in the 14th century.

Following the third Parliament's dissolution on 16 January 1555, Bishop Gardiner summoned 80 imprisoned preachers to his house and urged them to recant their religious beliefs. Only two complied. This marked the beginning of the heresy

Voices from the past

Cardinal Pole

Reginald Pole was born in England but spent most of his adult life on the Continent at various universities. He was made a cardinal in 1537 and assisted the rebels during the Pilgrimage of Grace rebellion in for which a flood of Protestant books and writings, 1537, his family were harshly punished by Henry VIII. He returned to England during Mary's reign as Papal Legate and was ordained as Archbishop of Canterbury – the last Catholic ever to hold this position. He was Mary's chief minister and adviser, which caused resentment among other councillors.

trials, and on 4 February 1555 John Rogers was the first, to be burnt at the stake. The burnings were intended to persuade the people of God's true way and limit the spread of heresy. Gardiner seemed to favour them at the start, but realised they were ineffective at intimidating Protestants and withdrew from an active role. Renard was hostile to the burnings and feared revolt, Pole was sceptical of this violence as a way of countering private expressions of doubt, but Philip neither opposed nor encouraged the burnings. Therefore it is likely that Mary felt it was necessary to carry out the persecution, albeit without rashness and directed only against learned men who might lead others. The first of the 'martyrs' were clerics, including Rogers, John Hooper, Bishop of Gloucester and Worcester, and Rowland Taylor, a minister in Suffolk but of the more than 287 who went to the stake, most were humble folk who were not at all learned. The most celebrated victims were the Oxford martyrs – all three had been educated at Cambridge but they were tried and executed in Oxford because it had fewer Protestant sympathisers. Accusations of heresy were laid against Nicholas Ridley, who had been deprived of his office as Bishop of London in 1553, Hugh Latimer, chaplain to the Duchess of Suffolk, and Archbishop Thomas Cranmer. Ridley and Latimer were burnt at the stake in October 1555. Cranmer, who was kept alive a few more months, initially repudiated his Protestant faith, only to surprise his captors by reasserting it on the day of his execution. History has not forgiven Mary these bloody executions.

Figure 3.4: This sketch was presented in John Foxe's *Book of Martyrs* (1563). It illustrates the martyrdom of Thomas Cranmer. Foxe's book sought to highlight the cruelty of the Catholic Church and the bravery of Protestants. It helped to shape the views of many English people about the Catholic Church in the following century.

Yet Pole genuinely wanted to rebuild the Catholic Church in England, and a thorough visitation process was instigated at his request. Altars were restored along with Church plate and service books, although images and the cult of saints remained obsolete. Recruitment to the clergy increased and money was restored to the Church. In March 1557 Pole's legatine commission was revoked by the new Pope, Paul IV. Paul IV had long been hostile to Pole, considering him a heretic for accepting justification by faith alone. This greatly damaged the reconstruction of Catholicism in England, although Williams (1998) argues that on Mary's death there can be little doubt that England was still largely Catholic.

Social and economic change

Perhaps the most damaging problems that occurred during Mary's reign were completely out of her control. In 1555–56 heavy rain caused the worst harvest failures of the century, which resulted in unprecedented rises in the price of grain and widespread famine. This was compounded by typhus and influenza epidemics, which spread throughout the country in 1556–58. One in ten people were killed by these deadly diseases and the death rate rose by more than double. Population increase had been a feature of the previous decades, but the epidemics were so serious that the population fell as much as 5% between 1556 and 1561. As a result, in the 1550s the real wages of rural labourers fell to levels some 40% below those of the early years of the century. These figures reveal only some of the real hardship that the people of England had to endure, but there was little Mary or her government could do.

Northumberland's policy of retrenchment was continued under Mary, although some innovation occurred in the administration of finance. The Exchequer was expanded as the Commissions of 1552 had recommended, which in the main increased efficiency. Mary inherited debts of £185 000, which swelled to £300 000 due to involvement in war with France. In order to balance the books, Mary sold Crown lands worth £5000 per annum in 1554 and another £8000 per annum in 1557. Customs duties increased substantially from £29 000 to £83 000. Responsible for reforms in finance was, according to Elton (1955), William Paulet, Marquess of Winchester, although Smith (1997) credits Mary for allowing him to pursue changes without the consent of Parliament. Davies (1977) even suggests that Mary's administration was more successful in the realm of finance than Henry VII or Edward VI, 'but a good part of this reform came too late to help Mary's government … It was Elizabeth, not Mary, who benefited from the financial reforms.'[7]

Mary's benevolence towards the Church reduced her income by £29 000 per annum and restoring lands to the Percies, Howards and Nevilles by a further £9385 per annum. This was somewhat compensated for by attainders against the Duke of Northumberland, Sir Thomas Wyatt and various of their associates, which brought in £20 000 per annum and at least £18 000 in cash and plate. At the same time, base coinage still created nagging and consistent problems under Mary, who failed to put plans into action on this issue. Expenditure at court rose steeply at first, but was then curtailed and by 1557 regular revenues in the Exchequer remained in modest surplus. Yet it had become clear that government could no longer function

ACTIVITY 3.2

The religious upheaval under the Tudors has been much written about, but can be confusing. Go back through your notes and summarise where each monarch stood on these key issues:

- Bible
- Mass
- Eucharist/Communion
- Clerical marriage
- Ornaments

adequately without new sources of revenue or periodic taxation to meet the costs of normal administration.

Rebellion

Wyatt's Rebellion

When, in November 1553, the House of Commons petitioned Mary to marry within her realm, she thought it most odd that they should interfere in such a personal matter. But many were afraid of a Spanish marriage alliance and the restoration of the 'tyranny of papacy'. Sir Thomas Wyatt, Sir Peter Carew and Sir James Croft conspired to persuade Princess Elizabeth to marry Edward Courtenay and depose Mary. Their back-up plan was to restore Lady Jane Grey to the throne if Elizabeth refused. Plans were made for a national and popular rising on Palm Sunday, before Philip of Spain arrived. The French were willing to lend their support in the Channel, Wyatt would hold the South-East, Croft would lead Hertfordshire, Carew would lead Devon, the Duke of Suffolk would lead Leicester and all would converge on London. The success of the rising depended on the energy and enthusiasm the gentry could inspire among commoners. It was winter, there were no economic crises and prices were stabilising. However, the rising was also dependent on the element of surprise, which they failed to achieve as news of the conspiracy was leaked, almost certainly by Courtenay himself. Abortive risings followed in the Midlands and the conspirators found little enthusiasm for their cause. Only Wyatt, who managed to raise 2000 supporters, had any success and managed to reach Blackheath by February 1554.

Mary kept her nerve and rallied Londoners with a flattering speech, which cast her enemies as heretics. By the time Wyatt arrived at Southwark on 3 February, London Bridge was heavily defended. Although he managed to lead his rebels across the Thames at Kingston, they suffered losses before they reached the City. With his force greatly reduced and none of the support he had expected materialising, Wyatt surrendered soon after. Princess Elizabeth was held in the Tower for several weeks, but Paget urged leniency. Mary pardoned over 400 of those who took part in the rising. The evidence against Elizabeth was extremely weak and as Paget rightly argued, the fallout of executing her could have been politically disastrous. It was perhaps inevitable that Lady Jane Grey, Wyatt and the Duke of Suffolk would be executed.

Intellectual developments under Mary I

Many works of anti-Marian propaganda were written by Protestant exiles between 1553–58. These often had an immediate polemical purpose, but several authors, including Christopher Goodman, John Knox and John Ponet, produced what can be regarded as political theory.

John Knox was a Scottish clergyman who had served under Edward VI as Royal Chaplain. He was forced to resign under Mary I and fled to Frankfurt for his own safety when it became clear Protestant clergy would be persecuted. On 20 July 1554, he published the pamphlet *A Faithful Admonition unto the Professors of God's Truth in England* attacking Mary Tudor and the bishops who had brought her to the throne. Knox condoned violence in resisting idolatry and irreligion, although it was his tracts in *First Blast of the Trumpet against the Monstrous Regiment of Women* that provoked the most reaction. Knox argued that a woman ruling over men went against nature, and used the book of Genesis to justify his views. Knox had to clarify his views when Elizabeth I came to the throne, arguing that because she was unmarried and had not usurped the throne, she was rightful sovereign.

Knox was good friends with Christopher Goodman and they wrote to each other frequently. Knox persuaded Goodman to join him when he returned to Scotland and they both served on the Scottish Council. Goodman thought Mary I had usurped the throne and praised individuals like Sir Thomas Wyatt for leading a rebellion against her. In many ways Knox and Goodman are similar, in as much as both used examples from the Bible to justify their ideas on resistance and both suggested that private individuals could take up arms against a tyrannical monarch who had imposed the old religion.

John Ponet was one of Archbishop Cranmer's advisers and became Bishop of Winchester in 1551. He fled to Strasbourg when Mary acceded to the throne and his position as bishop was invalidated due to his being married. Not much is known about his life abroad, except that he used literary methods to battle against Mary, publishing works such as *A Short Treatise on Political Power, and of the True Obedience which Subjects owe to Kings and Civil Governors* in 1556. Ponet's purpose was to prove that Mary's subjects had a right to resist her unlawful rule. He argued that men should have inalienable rights that the secular ruler should uphold, including equality before the law and the right to private ownership. There is little doubt that his tracts on private property were provoked by Mary's wish to restore Church lands that had been sold off under the dissolution of the monasteries in 1536. Ownership of property was, for Ponet, derived from the natural law, which bound ruler and ruled alike. He placed emphasis on the doctrine of limited obedience and upheld the right to conscience in both the religious and the political. His emphasis on conscience and his call for death to tyrants were similar to those of Goodman and Knox. All three agreed that resistance to a tyrant was lawful, although their reasoning differed considerably. Knox and Goodman also went further than Ponet, as they both maintained that introducing false religion was grounds for tyrannicide. Ponet, Goodman and Knox were all writing during the years when Protestantism was being suppressed by Mary. Thus, in some ways the exiles' tracts can be read as political theories about governance and in some ways as sedition.

Humanist and religious thought under Mary I

Mary removed Bishops appointed under Edward and replaced those he had dismissed. Upon their deaths she replaced them largely with theologians educated in the Humanist mode who adhered to the Catholic doctrine. Many of these new bishops were scholars of note: Baynes of Coventry had been a Professor of Hebrew at the University of Paris, and Aldrich of Carlisle had been a student of Erasmus. Pole was the leading light among this group. He was a committed Humanist and ardent church reformer who had presided over the **Council of Trent** from 1545 to 1547. The new bishops were not merely academics but men of energy and decision: they influenced the printing of collections of catechesis, sermons and devotions, particularly in 1553–54. The publication of books built on the Protestant tradition established under Henry VIII, but Loach (1993) suggests that

Key term

Council of Trent: a council of the Catholic church that was organised in response to the Protestant Reformation. The Council issued key statements and clarifications on Catholic doctrine and teachings, addressing a wide range of subjects. It is said to have begun the 'Counter-Reformation', a period of Catholic revival across Europe.

Speak like a historian: Fletcher and MacCulloch

Extract B

The foundation of Tudor authority was the dynasty's hold on the confidence of London and the south-east. The Londoners' attitude at Rochester shows that Mary had temporarily lost it. Wyatt came closer than any other Tudor rebel to toppling a monarch from the throne, yet in the political development of the century the rebellion's significance is that it failed. This demonstrated the bankruptcy of rebellion as a way of solving this kind of political crisis. The critical issue posed by the Spanish marriage and the succession of a Catholic queen was the question as to who should rule. It appeared that the only sanction, if Mary changed national religion or Philip and Mary broke the terms of the marriage treaty, was rebellion. This was a weapon that, after the social disorders of 1549, few were prepared to risk using. So the gentry learned to channel their opposition through parliament.

Source: Fletcher A and D MacCulloch. *Tudor Rebellions.* Harlow: Pearson; 2008. p. 101.

Discussion points:
1. What are these historians arguing here?
2. How convincing do you find their arguments?
3. Can you find anything in your notes that might support or refute their argument?

the Marians put greater emphasis on instructing the laity by the clergy, rather than self-education.

The return to doctrinal and **liturgical** orthodoxy were, in principle, achieved in the statutes that suppressed the Book of Common Prayer, ordered the restoration of altars and banned the marriage of priests. These bills were discussed against the background of protracted theological discussions in **Convocation**. In many ways the learned debates were futile, for neither side was likely to alter its opinion. Further religious debate was somewhat hindered by the appointments of Catholics to replace theological scholars at both Oxford and Cambridge, and in this way Mary's reign had a more significant impact on the universities than Edward's reign. Cardinal Pole saw the need for the education of the clergy, whose numbers had been depleted substantially during the upheavals of the previous 20 years. His legatine **synod**, held in London in 1555, provided for the establishment of diocesan seminaries for the education of the clergy. This pioneering step was later taken up by the Council of Trent as a means of improving the quality of the Catholic clergy. However, it required many years to train priests and Pole's scheme died with him, in England at least, limiting its impact.

The lay leaders of Protestantism, of which there were approximately 800, largely fled to the Continent during Mary's reign. These were men like Sir Anthony Cooke, Sir Francis Knollys, later a distinguished Elizabethan Councillor, as well as Edmund Grindal, who would become a bishop under Elizabeth I. The exiles often quarrelled among themselves over points of liturgy and doctrine, but they were united in

Key terms

liturgical: liturgy is the customary form or pattern of worship carried out by congregations.

Convocation: held either at Canterbury or York, these were large gatherings where representatives from the Church (mostly bishops) would meet to discuss and decide on Church policy.

synod: traditionally denotes a council meeting of a church, designed to determine a doctrine, for example.

wanting to see the restoration of Protestantism in England. Together they financed a flood of Protestant books and writings, which Mary's government failed to keep out of England.

Elizabeth I

Character and aims

It would be easy to assume, given that Elizabeth I reigned for 44 years, that she had all the qualities needed to be a successful monarch and received excellent preparation for her role as queen. Indeed it is difficult to find much criticism of Elizabeth, in either sources at the time or from historians since, perhaps because her reign is compared with the instability of the Stuarts that followed. However, she was, as her learned tutor Roger Ascham remarked, academically intelligent with an excellent command of Latin, Greek, French and Italian. In rather condescending terms, her male tutors suggested she had none of the weaknesses of women and was similar in character to her father. Yet she had spent most of her youth in country houses, away from the Court. She had no dealings with ambassadors or foreign princes and very few meetings with courtiers and administrators. She had lived a precarious existence under her sister's reign. Wyatt and other rebels called on her to launch a rebellion, but Elizabeth had continued to profess her loyalty to Mary. This was a useful apprenticeship in the art of politics: she managed to avoid the scaffold when she was taken to the Tower and made to profess her Catholic faith. She developed a strategy of caution, revealing very little of her emotions and being patient to let events unfold. These lessons would serve her well. As Williams (1995) points out, there were two other qualities within her, which became apparent early on in her reign and would allow her to be a successful monarch, 'the ability to choose first-rate advisers and a remarkable gift for winning the devotion of the public'.[8]

At the age of 25 Elizabeth inherited a throne under considerable strain from bad harvests, coinage debasement and the disruption of ancient traditions caused by religious upheaval. She was also under threat from the French, who disputed her legitimacy as ruler of England. Yet the throne Elizabeth inherited was supported by a firm administrative and legal foundation, and for the people of England, she was the rightful heir to the throne. The young queen would have to find her way to heal the religious divisions that threatened the domestic security of the kingdom. It was also expected that she would marry and produce an heir to retain its stability. However, even before she became queen there were signs that finding a suitor might not be so straightforward. The Spanish Ambassador, Feria, said of Elizabeth that she was determined to be governed by no one. This might help her overcome faction, but would cause her ministers grave concerns when she procrastinated over the question of marriage.

Consolidation of power

Privy Council
Perhaps the most pressing task facing Elizabeth upon hearing the news of her sister's death, was choosing a Privy Council. She would have to retain some of those members who served Mary, but ensure that the majority were loyal to her.

Speak like a historian: NL Jones

The historian Norman L Jones has written about the first year of Elizabeth's reign and her beliefs about monarchy.

Elizabeth Tudor was a very conservative woman with well-developed ideas about her place in the world. At twenty-five she had already learned hard political and personal lessons, and they had shaped her vision of herself as monarch, blending naturally with political ideas derived from her humanist education and the traditions of English kingship. With a temper as fiery as her red hair, her personality led her to be cautious and stubborn, sure of her authority and petulant in the face of change. In a land and time when the personal rule of the monarch was very real, these traits had a profound impact on the course of English history from 17 November 1558, when she acceded the throne.

To understand what happened when she took the nation's helm, it is important to realise that Elizabeth believed Bracton's famous dictum that the king is under God and the law … This belief, however, imposed great responsibilities on a ruler. Responsible before God for her people, she was careful never to let them challenge her right to that responsibility. Politics and theology taught her that, when the people overreached themselves in religion or government, revolt and bloodshed were likely to follow. Stability, she believed, was what God wanted and would be the best for her beloved people, as well as what pleased her cautious, conservative personality, so she devoted herself to maintaining the status quo, showing great reluctance to innovate.

Source: Jones NL 'Elizabeth's First Year: The conception and birth of the Elizabethan political world.' In C Haigh (ed.) *The Reign of Elizabeth I:* Macmillan; 1984. p. 27–28.

Discussion points:
1. Sum up Jones's argument in no more than 50 words.
2. Is Jones criticising Elizabeth or praising her?
3. What are the 'hard political lessons' Jones refers to in relation to Elizabeth's education?
4. Jones suggests that Elizabeth had a humanist education. Look back at your notes from previous chapters and summarise humanist ideas in relation to political leadership.

The chosen members would send strong signals to the nation about the kind of religious settlement Elizabeth would seek, which meant this was not a simple or straightforward task. Without hesitation she appointed Sir William Cecil as Secretary of State: not only was he experienced because he had served under Edward's government, but he had worked with Elizabeth at Hatfield House during Mary's reign, and they had an excellent working relationship. Cecil was politically astute and religiously adaptable, therefore he was not a controversial choice. Elizabeth dismissed two-thirds of Mary's Council, almost all of them her personal retainers or staunch Catholics. Only ten of the former Queen's Council remained, including the great regional magnates of the North, Derby and Shrewsbury and experienced politicians Arundel, Winchester and Pembroke. The new councillors were a mixture of blood relations on the Boleyn side, Protestant peers and members of her own household. Her Council was small compared with Mary's, but the balance was held in favour of men with specific experience or training. It was a body designed for administrative efficiency and knowledgeable counsel. The return of the Edwardians was obvious and strong indications that Elizabeth would seek to undo her sister's religious reforms were made clear.

Coronation

The coronation was the first opportunity for Elizabeth's public to receive her in a procession from the Tower to Westminster. An enormous £16 000 (8% of the royal income) was spent on the coronation, an exorbitant amount for a cash-strapped Crown. She was given a Bible in English and welcomed as 'Deborah – the judge and restorer of Israel', but the Mass was held in private to avoid any visual statements of faith. Elizabeth made the most of the opportunity with the public. She stopped off in her carriage to hear prepared oration and received small bunches of flowers from even the humblest of subjects, which she kept in her carriage until she reached Westminster. She was met with cheers and cries of delight. Elizabeth would use similar processions throughout her reign to make herself an 'accessible' monarch.

Act of Settlement

The coronation had left many questions about the religious direction Elizabeth would take. Elizabeth's own religious views have been debated. Guy (1988) suggests she was a moderate reformer who almost certainly rejected the papacy, but kept candles on the altar and continued to employ Catholic organists such as Thomas Tallis and William Byrd. Elizabeth probably had more pressing concerns on her mind in any case. England was not only at war with France and Scotland when Elizabeth acceded the throne, but she was effectively at war with the anti-Habsburg Pope, Paul IV too. In Catholic canon law, Elizabeth was the bastard daughter of an adulterous king, and would need a dispensation from Rome if she were to be seen as a legitimate Catholic queen. There was a danger that the Pope might push for Mary Stuart to be queen, therefore it was far too risky for Elizabeth to attempt to continue her sister's policies. It was much safer for her to pursue Protestantism and continue to fight for Calais (see the section on Relations with foreign powers). However, the delicate political situation on the Continent, as well as the warm reception the restoration of Catholicism had received in England during Mary's reign, forced Elizabeth to err on the side of caution.

The principal lines of the religious settlement of 1559 were laid down in two Acts, which were passed in the first of Elizabeth's parliaments. The first was the Act of Supremacy, which once again rejected papal authority and gave Elizabeth the new title 'Supreme Governor of the Church' – some felt that her father's title of Supreme Head was unsuitable for a woman, while the title of 'governor' may have been more mollifying for Catholics. All clergymen, magistrates and royal officials had to swear an oath of allegiance to Elizabeth under this Act, but the penalty for refusing to do so was only a loss of office. This Act also repealed the heresy laws that had formed the basis of Marian persecution. These provisions meant that even if the Lords rejected the rest of the religious settlement, Protestants could

Figure 3.5: This allegorical portrait of Henry VIII and his family was painted during the reign of Elizabeth. Henry's attention is on his Protestant successors, as he hands a sword to his son Edward, and gazes approvingly towards Elizabeth. His Catholic daughter Mary and her husband Philip hover in the background, dressed in dark robes and accompanied by War. Elizabeth, in the foreground, is attended by figures depicting Peace and Prosperity. Attributed to Lucas de Heere (1534–84).

not be prosecuted in the meantime. There were no other organisational changes to the Church: the Archbishoprics of Canterbury and York would remain and there was no move towards Calvinism or Lutheranism in this sense.

The Act of Uniformity reintroduced the Book of Common Prayer, which had been banned under Mary, but with some alterations that gave it a less radical Protestant character than the 1552 version. The first of these changes followed the 1549 Prayer Book in mandating more traditional church ornaments and vestments. The words of the communion were also altered in a way that suggested Christ was present in some spiritual sense. This mollified conservatives but still denied transubstantiation. The Catholic Mass could no longer legally be celebrated and those who ignored the Act risked imprisonment. Absenteeism from Church would be punished through fines of one shilling per week.

The other two statutes concerned Church property. One restored First Fruits and Tenths to the Crown, thereby reversing Marian policy. The other, 'The Act of Exchange', was debated at length in Parliament since it involved questions of property. It allowed the Crown to lease out vacant episcopal sees and acquire the temporal revenues. It was an example of the Crown encroaching on ecclesiastical possessions as it meant Elizabeth could seize property belonging to bishops and force them to rent land to her. Interestingly she declined to authorise clerical marriage by statute. Williams (1995) argues this was more because it would raise the social status of more women by marrying bishops, which threatened the social hierarchy. The Acts were followed up by Royal Injunctions of 1559, which were drafted by Cecil. The injunctions ordered the clergy to condemn images, miracles and relics; preach against the papacy and superstition; report recusants to JPs and marry only with the permission of their bishop and two JPs. Over 125 commissioners were appointed to carry out visitations throughout the country, enforcing the oath of supremacy, which resulted in a great deal of destruction of Church ornaments.

The religious settlement perhaps seems like a compromise that both Catholics and reformers could have agreed to. Yet the acts were fought over vociferously in Parliament. The Commons, it seems, was on the side of the Crown, but the Lords most definitely wanted to retain as much of the Marian settlement as possible. Elizabeth was lucky that when the Act of Uniformity reached the Lords, Bishops White and Watson were in prison and two others missed the vote, allowing an extremely narrow victory for the queen. When it came to taking the oath as stipulated under the Act of Supremacy, all the bishops, except one, refused. In comparison, the clergy, of whom there were approximately 8000, seemed to accept the new settlement and no more than 400 refused to take the oath. Elizabeth had to find a new senior Church hierarchy, and she sought Matthew Parker as her Archbishop of Canterbury. This was a wise choice because, as Somerset (1991) argues, he was 'the very embodiment of the moderate spirit of the Anglican religious settlement'.[9] It was less easy to fill other vacancies without resorting to some of the more radical priests who had been in exile under Mary, and more than half had to be filled by exiles. However, by 1561 only Oxford and Bristol were left without a bishop.

The traditional view of Elizabeth's religious settlement, written by one of her great biographers JE Neale (1950) suggests that Elizabeth did not want a Protestant prayer book, she merely wanted to restore the Royal Supremacy and was pressured by reformers in the House of Commons to impose a more Protestant settlement. This analysis of events sees a defeat for the queen in establishing the religious direction of the country, and a success for the more radical Marian exiles who spearheaded a campaign for a radical settlement. The main challenge to this view (supported by others) has been from NL Jones (1984), who suggests that the settlement of 1559 was essentially what Elizabeth I wanted, based on the Edwardian reforms that had been carried out in 1552, because as the daughter of Anne Boleyn it was in her interests to have a Protestant Church. Perhaps what is most important about the Act of Settlement is that the Lords, Commons and Crown did agree to the Acts of Uniformity and Supremacy, the basis of which still forms part of the Church of England today.

Thirty-Nine Articles 1563

The Canterbury Convocation met in 1563 amidst a flurry of opposition to the injunctions imposed as a result of the religious settlement. The new bishops objected to religious symbols such as the use of the sign of the cross, kneeling during Communion and the wearing of the surplice by priests. However, the group did give its approval to the Thirty-Nine Articles, which were a statement of doctrine for the new Church of England. The articles were based on Cranmer's Forty-Two Articles of 1552. In most respects, the text was unchanged, reaffirming the Protestant nature of the new Church.

Relations with foreign powers

Elizabeth inherited a country still technically at war with France, which had troops in Scotland, while Mary Stuart, Queen of Scotland but resident in France where she was married to the Dauphin, had declared herself to be the legitimate Catholic claimant to the English throne. The Pope had declared Elizabeth a bastard, leaving the young queen dependent on an alliance with Spain as a means of protection. Luckily, Philip saw no benefit in Mary Stuart establishing enlarged French territory in England and so was willing to support Elizabeth in the peace negotiations with France, which commenced in 1559 at Cateau-Cambrésis. The main issue for Elizabeth was Calais, as she could not afford to take it back and Henry II was in no mood to surrender it. She negotiated directly with Henry II to bring about an acceptable compromise: the French would retain Calais for eight years and would then either return it to England or pay a form of compensation. The French also conceded one of their fortresses on the Scottish borders.

Neale (1953) suggests the treaty with France freed Elizabeth to implement a full reformation of her own making, because she did not have to appear conservative to maintain the Spanish alliance. Doran (1996), however, suggests that the treaty had little impact on relations with Spain as Philip was interested in a marriage alliance with Elizabeth. The treaty hardly improved relations with France either. Henry II continued to uphold Mary's claim to the English throne, which might have worried the Council more had Scottish Protestant nobles not rebelled in 1559 against the pro-Catholic policies of Mary's mother, Mary of Guise, the Regent of Scotland. William Cecil advocated sending help to the Protestant rebels, but Elizabeth would not countenance supporting subjects in removing their 'natural prince'.

The death of Henry II in July 1559 brought Mary Stuart to the French throne as wife of Francis II, forcing Elizabeth's hand. Determined to stamp out the rebellion in Scotland, the French king had sent 2000 French soldiers there and prepared another 8000 men to go. The Scots appealed to Elizabeth for aid. Cecil, Pembroke and Howard supported military action to support the Protestant lords, but Nicholas Bacon led a group in the Council very much opposed to this, and Thomas Howard, the fourth Duke of Norfolk (who had succeeded his father in 1554), even argued a marriage to the Archduke of Austria to counter Scotland. Elizabeth was reluctant to support such radical Protestants, but news that French troops had reached Leith and Cecil's threatening resignation if she failed to act, forced Elizabeth to agree to send Norfolk to Newcastle to command an army. Elizabeth agreed at the Treaty of Berwick (1560) that she would give the Scottish lords protection, and sent Lord Grey to lead English troops into Scotland. Luckily the French decided to negotiate because Mary of Guise had died on 11 June 1560. This was fortuitous because Grey's campaign was poor. On 6 July 1560 the Treaty of

Edinburgh was signed, providing for the withdrawal of English and French troops from Scotland. This forced Mary to renounce her right to claim the English throne, and also left Protestant lords governing Scotland.

Elizabeth's caution had been successful. Delaying military intervention until such time that the French were weakened by their own domestic problems with the **Huguenots** paid dividends. When civil war broke out in France in 1562 and the Huguenots pleaded for Elizabeth's aid, she showed little hesitation in sending them loans and dispatching soldiers. Perhaps this time the recovery of Calais, fear for security or religious motivations were factors in her decision. The war went badly for England, losing Rouen and Dieppe to the Catholics within the first year. The leader of the Huguenots was captured and decided to support Catherine de' Medici in expelling the English. On 29 June 1563 the French captured Le Havre, the last English garrison. This marked the end of Elizabeth's ambitions for Calais and forged a new view of foreign policy. From now on, she would be extremely cautious in undertaking continental adventure, and Cecil supported her views.

The impact of economic, social and religious developments in the early years of Elizabeth's rule

Social developments

The wretched harvests of 1556 and the epidemics of influenza in 1557 as well as fighting expensive wars with France had combined to present Elizabeth's government with pressing social and financial problems that were inflicting indelible wounds on society. Labourers were said to have become disobedient to their masters, demanding higher wages and increased numbers of thieves and vagrants seemed to flood towns and cities. To many landowners it appeared they were living in anarchic times. Parliament introduced bills to tackle some of these issues in 1559, but none passed into law. It seems there was some coordination between central and local government to re-establish order in the realm. The Council of the North pushed towns to stop labourers taking high wages. In 1562 the York assizes show that 113 labourers were indicted for taking unlawfully high wages and similar patterns emerge elsewhere in the North.

The Act of Artificers in 1563 sanctioned compulsory labour during harvest time, but also imposed a minimum hire of one year for workmen, forced apprenticeships of seven years for craftsmen and ordered JPs to fix maximum rates for wages. The Act was only partially successful because most unemployment was caused by the ever-increasing inflation. By fixing wages, it artificially depressed wages at a time when the number of people looking for paid employment was rising. The Act therefore indirectly contributed to the growth of poverty. Inflation also made living in towns increasingly expensive as rates and taxes increased, which forced many people to move out to surrounding villages and provided the authorities with more concerns about a moving population causing unrest.

The government also tried to curb social unrest by passing legislation to prevent further enclosure of the land. The Act for Maintaining Tillage was passed in 1563 and stated that all land which had been under **tillage** for four years since 1528 must remain so. The Act also meant that no land under tillage could be converted

ACTIVITY 3.3

Create a mind map showing the problems Elizabeth faced in the early part of her reign. Then discuss with a partner which might have been the most important issues.

Key term

Huguenots: French Protestants inspired by the writings of John Calvin, who developed Christian doctrine dominated by the idea of predestination and absolute sovereignty of God in salvation. There were approximately two million Huguenots living in Catholic France by 1562 but they faced systematic persecution. Many fled France to England, Denmark and Sweden.

Key term

tillage: the preparation of soil for growing crops by farmers, including digging and overturning.

to pasture, which the authorities hoped would prevent depopulation of some rural areas.

Economic developments

In order fully to restore stability in the realm, the problem of debased coinage still had to be addressed. Northumberland's attempted reforms had been incomplete and plans formulated under Mary had been delayed. In 1560 a new commission issued a proclamation to reduce the value of debased coins by 25% or more. Holders of debased coins were encouraged to return them to the mint in exchange for new, good coins, in accordance with their reduced face value. Before these reforms the amount of currency in circulation was approximately £1 700 000 of which about £1 000 000 was debased. The government bought the debased coins back for less than their true value and issued £670 000 of new currency. The government made a profit of £50 000 as a result of this process of reminting, but it did restore the stability of the currency.

The other major financial problem facing Elizabeth's government was revenue. The reforms under Mary had brought ordinary revenue to a satisfactory level for peacetime, but wars had saddled the Crown with £300 000 worth of debt. In the first two years of her reign Elizabeth paid off £130 000 of her domestic debt that she inherited. In so doing, she increased her debt to foreign creditors, particularly in Antwerp, to £280 000 – although this was not an uncontrollable amount within the context of the period and government finances were on a firmer footing by 1563.

The impact of religious developments

The ecclesiastical history of Elizabethan England demonstrates that a political decision for Protestantism was taken in 1558. Yet as Haigh (1984) argues, although the Act of Settlement represented a legislative Reformation, evidence suggests that there had only been a very limited popular reformation by 1559: throughout much of the reign of Elizabeth I, the Church of England was a 'prescribed, national church with more or less protestant liturgy and theology but an essentially non-Protestant laity'.[10] Some London parish churches continued to celebrate the Catholic liturgy up until the last legal moment, although waves of **iconoclasm** spread through the city. In Canterbury however, 3000 people attended the last Corpus Christi procession in a gesture of public allegiance to the old faith.

The visitations carried out in 1559 demonstrate that perhaps lessons had been learnt from the Marian restoration. It was not enough to request the surrender of Catholic liturgical books or the removal of images: it was obvious in 1553 that parishes up and down the country had merely concealed their images and books, only to be brought out again at the accession of Mary. Commitment to the new order could only be fostered if the physical remains of Catholicism and monuments to superstition were removed. The commissioners were also concerned with parishioners leaving money, plate or ornaments in their wills. Historians of the period have tended to rely quite heavily on wills as evidence of shifting beliefs. Although recently historians have questioned the use of wills alone as evidence of belief, it certainly seems that commissioners at the time were

Key term

iconoclasm: describes the destruction of religious paintings stained glass windows and icons during the Reformation.

preoccupied with finding out if the clergy were discouraging parishioners from leaving any plate, money or ornaments for prayers or mass.

Although attempts to prevent the destruction of images was widespread, evidence suggests that the commissioners were equally determined to see images destroyed. People who had tried to conceal images were forced to destroy them publicly in London and Exeter. Duffy (2005) argues that the conformity of the majority of parishes was reluctant and partial. The removal of roods and altars were part of a 'weary obedience to unpopular measures'.[11] The royal visitations reveal that just 45 of the 180 parishes were reported to have complied promptly to remove the altars, rood and other images. The Reformation in this sense can be seen as a slow moving conformity that was imposed from above.

Conclusion

The reign of a minor, followed by the brief reign of a woman, was bound to cause a certain amount of instability. Coupled with the scale of religious upheaval that each of Henry VIII's children inflicted on their subjects, it is not surprising this period has often been described as one of turmoil. The people of England also witnessed terrible harvests, epidemics and population decreases, which were completely out of the government's control and had a devastating impact on many parts of the kingdom. Yet for all of the wearing away of ancient religious traditions and demographic changes, there were many aspects of Tudor England that remained virtually unchanged. The political centre of the kingdom remained in London, with many of the same personnel serving all three monarchs. The system of governance and legal foundations remained largely untouched during this period. England's position on the Continent was inevitably weakened after pursuing futile attacks on Scotland and France, culminating in the loss of Calais, which really symbolised the failures of the previous two decades of foreign policy. Elizabeth I, then, inherited a throne on stable foundations, but with many problems. She did not solve all of those problems by 1563, but by enacting a religious settlement that seemed to acknowledge a certain amount of personal choice in prayer and by beginning to tackle some of the financial weaknesses of the realm, she made a promising start.

Practice essay questions

1. 'The Tudors faced instability and crises between 1540 and 1563 primarily because of economic factors.' Assess the validity of this view.
2. 'The foreign policy of Tudor monarchs failed to achieve its objectives in the years from 1547 to 1563.' Assess the validity of this view.
3. Reread Extract A (in Speak like a historian: ML Bush), Extract B (in Speak like a historian: Fletcher and MacCulloch) and then read Extract C. Given your understanding of the historical context, assess how convincing these arguments are in relation to the threat posed by rebellions 1536–49?

ACTIVITY 3.4

Create a table with the heading 'What effect did their actions have on the religious settlement?' and complete the table for the following categories:
Elizabeth and the Privy Council
The House of Commons
The House of Lords
The Marian exiles.

Developing concepts

The following concepts have been very important in this section. For each one write a definition and give an example of what it means in the context of Tudor society in the period 1547–63:

- radical
- Protestant
- Catholic
- recusant
- nobility
- Privy Council.

ACTIVITY 3.5

Go back through your notes and create a timeline that highlights the key events in foreign policy 1547–63.

Extract C

The speed with which the protest movement spread suggests, furthermore, that the quantity of explosive material was such that it needed very little to set it off. While Catholic factionalism divided some members of the governing elite, the mobilization and solidarity of so many northerners cannot be taken for granted. Also there were lesser disturbances in southern counties: East Anglia, Somerset and Cornwall. So, while Court plotting shaped the form of the Pilgrimage to some degree, it does not sufficiently explain its force and extent.

Yet the rebels could only have toppled Henry VIII with the support of the leading nobility whom the king named as members of the 'emergency' Privy Council in the autumn of 1536: the dukes of Norfolk and Suffolk, the Marquess of Exeter, and the Earls of Shrewsbury, Sussex and Oxford … none saw any advantage in treason.

Source: Guy J. *Tudor England:* Oxford University Press; 1988: p. 152.

 Chapter summary

After studying this period, you should be able to:

- describe England's foreign policy failures during the period
- explain why England faced financial crisis during the 1550s
- assess whether this period could be fairly characterised as unstable
- evaluate the success of Elizabeth's religious settlement.

Further reading

Jennifer Loach's book *Edward VI* is detailed but accessible. She helpfully reviews traditional interpretations of Edward but clearly uses evidence to refute many of the older claims about the weakness of his reign.

Penry Williams's book *The Later Tudors: England 1547–1603* takes a narrative approach to the period but is clear and detailed. The chapter on Mary is much more detailed than other general overview books.

End notes

1   Pollard AF. *Cambridge Modern History, Vol II.* Cambridge: CUP; 1903. p. 499.
2   Duffy E. *The Stripping of the Altars: Traditional Religion in England 1400–1580.* New Haven: Yale University Press; 2005. p. 468.
3   Duffy E. *The Stripping of the Altars: Traditional Religion in England 1400–1580.* New Haven: Yale University Press; 2005. p. 484.
4   Elton GR. *England Under the Tudors.* London: Folio Society; 1903. p. 211.
5   Guy J. *Tudor England:* Oxford: OUP; 1988. p. 227.
6   Tittler R. *The Reign of Mary I:* Harlow: Longman; 1983. p. 73.
7   Davies CSL. *Peace, Print and Protestantism:* Colorado: Paladin; 1977. p. 299.
8   Williams P. *The Later Tudors: England 1547–1603.* Oxford: OUP; 1983. p. 230.
9   Somerset A. *Elizabeth I.* London: Phoenix; 1997. p. 105.
10 Haigh C. 'The Church of England, the Catholics and the People.' In *The Reign of Elizabeth I.* London: Macmillan; 1984. p. 196.
11 Duffy E. *The Stripping of the Altars: Traditional Religion in England 1400–1580.* New Haven: Yale University Press, 2005. p. 570.

4 The triumph of Elizabeth, 1563–1603

In this section we will examine the political authority of England's last Tudor and consider some of the changes that were taking place and how these began to affect the economy, people's religious beliefs and the stability of the kingdom. We will look into:

- Elizabethan government: court, ministers and parliament; factional rivalries.
- Foreign affairs: issues of succession; Mary, Queen of Scots; relations with Spain.
- Society: continuity and change; problems in the regions; social discontent and rebellions.
- Economic development: trade, exploration and colonisation; prosperity and depression.
- Religious developments, change and continuity; the English renaissance and 'the Golden Age' of art, literature and music.
- The last years of Elizabeth: the state of England politically, economically, religiously and socially by 1603.

Introduction

Elizabeth I has been widely regarded as the most popular monarch in English history. It is easy to see why. Some of the greatest literature, drama and poetry ever written was produced in her reign. Some of the most memorable portraits of a monarch ever made are of Elizabeth. Her skills in public display made her deeply admired by her public almost until the very end, and it is difficult to find historians who are highly critical of her. By choosing able ministers and remaining loyal to them, she provided England with the stability that her father, brother and sister had failed to do. She lived so long that her Anglicanism became the custom for the vast majority of the population. Her foreign policy has been criticised, particularly with regard to her procrastination and lack of strategy, yet she presided over one of the most celebrated military victories in history, the defeat of the Spanish Armada. She allowed royal revenues to fall due to inflation and sold off much of the Crown lands, yet her successor, James I, inherited a peaceful realm, arguably in no worse state than it had been in 1547 or 1558. Elizabeth I proved beyond doubt that a woman could control a Council, command an army and rule a country. In order to prove this Elizabeth sacrificed her own desires for a husband and a family. However, her lack of an heir provoked more threats to her life than any other Tudor had faced. The triumph of Elizabeth must surely be that she endured religious upheaval, assassination plots, attempted invasion, financial difficulties and warring factions to rule for over 44 years.

Elizabethan government

Elizabeth was clearly determined to rule her own house, as a result of which she kept her servants on their toes by taking a direct interest in all aspects of administration. She interfered in the minutiae of policies, much to her ministers' irritation. Traditional historians viewed her as a 'Great Queen' who struggled against a confident government, whereas revisionists perceive her government as stable and cooperative institutions, free of tension. Haigh (1993) argues that Elizabeth undermined her effectiveness by ruling through personal relationships. She has been credited by almost every biographer for choosing excellent counsel in William Cecil, Francis Walsingham, Francis Bacon and Walter Mildmay. As part of their role in the Privy Council they supervised a number of central agencies that existed to help preserve law and order, of which the King's Bench, Common Pleas, Star Chamber, Chancery and Exchequer and Navy Board played vital roles. Due to the queen's and her chief minister, Cecil's conservatism, very little was reformed in Elizabethan government and practices established by her father continued largely untouched.

By far the most significant element of Elizabethan government was the Privy Council. To Elizabeth, it was there to exercise administrative authority, carry out judicial work within the country and give counsel when she asked for it. The advice she obtained was rarely unanimous (see the section on Factional rivalries) and this allowed Elizabeth to consider differing arguments from her ministers before deciding on direction of policy. The Council was mostly preoccupied with the administration of the state, and pages of the Privy Council Register demonstrate the diverse range of issues its members dealt with. Councillors exercised detailed supervision over the work of JPs as well as the offensive and defensive operations when war with Spain came in 1585. The council also received floods of petitions from private suitors who claimed assistance in righting injustices they had suffered. Smith (1997) argues this was just one indication that the work of the Council grew considerably under Elizabeth.

Elizabeth has been praised by historians for her government's solvency, which has been seen in striking comparison to her predecessors Edward VI and Mary I and with her contemporary rivals on the Continent. William Cecil was appointed Lord Treasurer in 1572 and he oversaw a conservative approach towards finance, making very few alterations in terms of building greater efficiency. Nevertheless, Elizabeth's ordinary revenue increased from approximately £200 000 per year to £300 000 per annum by the end of her reign. This was at a time when food prices rose by two-thirds, therefore the queen's revenue seems to have kept pace with inflation. Of course, 18 years of war with Spain took their toll and she died about £350 000 in debt, which Smith suggests was a remarkable achievement. On the other hand, Cecil's conservatism meant that he neglected opportunities to increase ordinary revenue. For example, failure to reform the collection of customs duties meant that their value in 1603 was little more than it had been when Elizabeth acceded to the throne, a poor performance at a time of inflation. Cecil's lack of reform contrasts sharply with that of Winchester under Mary I. His conservatism was no doubt due to his desire to buttress the stability of the regime, but it meant that the landed classes grew accustomed to paying only small parts of their income to the Crown, and left Elizabeth's successors with little in the coffers to work with.

Court, ministers and parliament

Court

Most accounts of the Tudor Court have tended to emphasise factional strife and an atmosphere of ambitious enmity surrounding an imperious queen. However, as Adams (1984) asserts, factional conflict did not really emerge until the 1590s, when tensions arose at Court between the followers of Sir Robert Cecil and the Earl of Essex (see the section entitled Factional rivalries). The two main departments at court were the Chamber and the Household. Both saw their budgets increase over the course of Elizabeth's reign, much to the Queen's annoyance. Partly this was due to inflation, but Elizabeth's extended progresses to market towns across the country was the chief cause.

ACTIVITY 4.1

Study Figure 4.1, then carry out some research into what each department was responsible for.

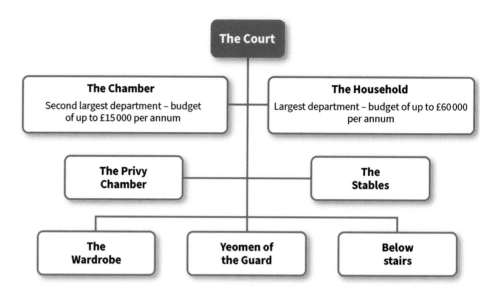

Figure 4.1: The Elizabethan Court. There was considerable overlap between the responsibilities of each department, and it is almost impossible to distinguish between bureaucrats and courtiers, as many of Elizabeth's servants played both roles.

The Privy Chamber was staffed by women, who were often daughters of important Councillors such as Sir Francis Knollys. The composition of the Court is more difficult to define as it followed no formal structure, but was adapted to the idiosyncrasies of the queen. Elizabeth effected barely any changes to the Court organisation, making it a static structure. A central feature of her Court was her conservative attitude to office and rank, which might explain why the peerage barely expanded during her reign. There was an established body of Household families that Elizabeth did not disrupt and the same appears to be the case in the Chamber. Elizabeth used offices at Court as a reward for service, rather than as a means to advance individuals. The queen also tended to leave offices vacant for significant periods of time, for example, between the death of Sir Francis Walsingham in 1590 and the appointment of Sir Robert Cecil, the secretariat was officially left vacant for six years. Most positions were held jointly by one person for long periods too, which compounded the static nature of the Court. For example, Sir Francis Knollys and Sir Christopher Hatton both combined the Vice-Chamberlaincy and the Captaincy of the Guard. This created fierce competition and created a gap between those who received the full benefit of the queen's favour, and those who did not.

Presence at Court was critical to political success because it was the only place to secure royal **patronage**. The system of patronage was a complicated web where lesser men attached themselves to courtiers in the hope of gaining grants or offices. A courtier's following outside Court was dependent on their ability to provide patronage, and that was dependent on the favour of the queen. Cecil received up to 100 letters a day from suitors requiring royal favour, making the management of royal favour a gigantic task. One example of a success story was Sir Christopher Hatton, who joined the Court in 1564, with no office and over £5000 of debt. By 1575 he had an annuity from the queen and the Bishop of Ely had given him his London house. By 1577 he became Vice-Chamberlain of the Household

Key term

patronage: the support, privilege or financial aid that an individual can bestow to another. Often patronage was given to musicians, painters or sculptors but Elizabeth I used it more systematically to ensure the loyalty of the gentry during her reign.

and in 1578 he became Receiver of First Fruits and Tenths, where he made his fortune. By 1587 he was Lord Chancellor, making him the envy of the Court.

Ministers

Elizabeth selected her 'inner ring' of ministers carefully and all had unique skills. Cecil was of course politically and administratively able – a true statesman. The Earl of Leicester has been criticised for using his skills for his own advancement, although much evidence suggests he cooperated with Cecil a great deal during the 1570s and 1580s. Walsingham was a versatile diplomat with a keen eye for detail, and was also extremely loyal. Hatton had strong links with Parliament and acted as the main channel between the legislature and the executive. The Earl of Essex, who came to prominence towards the end of Elizabeth's reign, was interested in military expeditions, although in this he has been considered ineffectual. The relationship between the leading ministers and the queen varied widely. Cecil shared Elizabeth's instinctive caution in policy, whereas Leicester, who had a closer personal relationship with the queen, was much more excessive, particularly in his early years. Walsingham probably had the least direct influence on the queen, yet she respected his professionalism because he only tended to speak his mind on matters of belief. The one servant who seemed to combine the queen's affection with her respect for his judgement was Hatton, who took a key role in persuading Parliament to apply pressure to Elizabeth to execute Mary, Queen of Scots. The partnership between Walsingham, Hatton and Cecil can therefore be seen as a key stabilising factor in the reign. Elizabeth, although subject to flattery and despite her weakness for favourites, retained full control over her ministers, despite their efforts to persuade, cajole and pressure her.

Walsingham became Secretary of State when Burghley was forced to step back, due to overwork. Walsingham specialised in diplomacy and espionage and was extremely able. He was an avowed Protestant and was largely responsible for the increasing number of Catholic recusants to be executed as Elizabeth's reign wore on. His Protestantism often made him feverishly alive to the perils of Catholic forces abroad. In this way he was a good balance to the cool and cynical monarch. Together with Burghley he wrote the 1585 Act for the Surety of the Queen's Person, which was effectively a counter-terrorism law that empowered ordinary citizens to take any conspirators against the queen into their own hands. He died in 1590.

Sir Christopher Hatton (1540–91) was gifted, industrious and loyal and rose to prominence through the court, where he was noticed by the young queen. When Elizabeth ascended the throne he was Vice-Chamberlain of the Household and a Privy Councillor. By the 1580s, without any legal training, he had become Lord Chancellor and was rewarded with lands and had gained a monopoly on the wine trade. He was the only one of Elizabeth's favourites who remained truly loyal to her and never married.

Robert Dudley, Earl of Leicester (1532–88) was the son of the Duke of Northumberland and had only just been released from prison for his part in the Lady Jane Grey affair when Elizabeth acceded to the throne. In 1558 he was appointed Master of the Horse. Described as dashing and flamboyant by contemporaries, he was rumoured to be Elizabeth's lover, and in 1560 when his

Figure 4.2: William Cecil, First Baron of Burghley, Elizabeth's close adviser for 40 years.

wife died from falling down the stairs he became an object of suspicion. Leicester often competed with Hatton for the queen's affections and she revelled in the attention they offered. Dudley was given a seat on the Privy Council and despite Cecil's objections to him marrying Elizabeth, evidence suggests they worked well together on matters of religion and foreign policy. Leicester was a prominent patron of overseas exploration and trade, literature and science. He was no intellectual but learnt Latin because it was in fashion and read science to better his understanding of the world around him. In 1567 he secretly married the Countess of Essex, which caused controversy at court, but he served Elizabeth loyally until his death in 1588.

Parliament

Elizabeth did not like Parliaments. Her father, brother and sister had summoned Parliament 28 times in the 30 years that preceded Elizabeth's accession. In contrast, Elizabeth called Parliament nine times in the first 30 years she was on the throne and only 13 times in a reign lasting 45 years. In the 1559 Parliament, only 54% of members of the Commons were present after a month-long session. By 1571 attendance had become such an issue that members were fined fourpence for each day they missed, and the proceeds were given to the poor. This failed to improve matters, so a new rate of fines was introduced in 1581.

 Voices from the past

Sir William Cecil

Sir William Cecil was appointed to the Privy Council on Elizabeth's accession to the throne. She indicated almost immediately that she would entrust him to be her chief adviser and told him:

'I give you this charge, that you shall be … content to take pains for me and my realm. This judgement I have of you that you will not be corrupted by any manner of gift and that you will be faithful to the state.'[1]

This speech began the trusting relationship that lasted throughout the 40 years of his diligent service. Cecil and Elizabeth held the longest partnership between sovereign and minister in the whole of English history. In William Cecil Elizabeth had the best available agent to fulfil her wishes in Parliament. He was conservative, skilful in managing Parliament and consistently loyal, although it is probably true that sometimes he employed Parliament to manipulate Elizabeth's options towards his own. Cecil was everywhere, on committees, drafting, debating, delivering official statements and always manipulating behind the scenes. Yet his real power derived from his personal relationship with the Queen:

in this way he approached the stature of the great ministers of Henry VIII. He had a rival in Leicester, undoubtedly one of the queen's favourites. However, countless bishops, nobles and men of the Commons became his lieutenants as he grew in stature and experience. He became Baron Burghley in 1571 and served Elizabeth until his death in 1598. Historians have debated how committed he was to Protestantism; recent research suggests he was pragmatic. He was committed to Protestantism but he did not let it cloud his judgement when it came to foreign policy or dealing with recusant Catholics. In 1583 Burghley made his feelings clear in *The Execution of Justice in England*, in which he argued that those priests who preached Catholicism were not martyrs, but traitors to their legitimate sovereign. Burghley was single-minded in his quest to maintain the security of Elizabeth's throne and everything he did must be seen in this light. His younger son, Robert Cecil, inherited his political mantle, taking on the role of Secretary of State following the death of Walsingham (although he was not officially confirmed in the title until 1596) and becoming Elizabeth's chief minister after the death of his father.

County members would be charged £20 for absence from a whole session and borough representatives £10. It was much the same in the Upper House. Linked to attendance, but perhaps even more important, was participation. Only about 10% of MPs were known to have spoken in each Parliament. This perhaps raises questions about why Elizabeth bothered calling them at all. The answer, unsurprisingly, was supply. Graves (1985) writes that out of 13 parliaments, 12 of them were called to raise a subsidy or introduce a new tax. In the first year of her reign, it was relatively easy to suggest that the realm was in need of greater defence and the threat of Mary, Queen of Scots loomed large.

However, the need for financial assistance was not the only reason Parliament was summoned. The problem of succession, religion and foreign policy were all discussed by parliaments in the early years of Elizabeth's reign. The argument that this is where Parliament grew in stature, and where the **Puritan** forces that would topple Charles I were fostered, has been challenged. Elizabeth's first three parliaments passed 122 Acts, which was highly productive considering the queen wanted to keep sessions short. The governing classes worked in harmony in these years to a large extent. Councillors would use Parliament to persuade Elizabeth to their point of view. Elizabethan parliamentary politicking was often an extension of Court and Council politics. Apart from a few Councillors like Cecil, Knollys and Mildmay, most of the great politicians, ministers and faction leaders sat in the House of Lords. The conflict between queen and Parliament was often the result of unresolved matters between the queen and Privy Councillors and not an overconfident Parliament. With the notable exception of their resistance in 1559, Privy Councillors avoided confrontation in meetings and preferred to collaborate with the Commons, or use their clients there as spokesmen. The session of 1566 exemplified this. The Council persuaded Elizabeth to call Parliament for another subsidy, but Cecil was able to use the session to put pressure on her to marry. Graves (1985) suggests that Cecil dominated the first three parliaments in this way and this is key in understanding how they worked.

The first major political crisis of the reign occurred between 1568 and 1572, when Mary, Queen of Scots fled to England, the earls rebelled in her favour, Elizabeth was excommunicated by the Pope and then the Ridolfi plot exploded. The parliaments of 1571–72 were responses to the initial crisis, but they marked a turning point in Elizabethan politics. Cecil was ennobled twice in 1571, becoming

Figure 4.3: Sir Francis Walsingham, who was known to be Elizabeth's spy-master.

 Key term

Puritan: a term coined in the 1560s to describe radical Protestants who criticised the newly established Elizabethan Church on the grounds that it needed further reform. Generally, 'Puritan' was a derogatory term.

 Voices from the past

Sir Francis Walsingham

Walsingham had known William Cecil in their days as students at Cambridge, but Walsingham was also well connected: his brother-in-law was Sir Walter Mildmay, who was appointed Chancellor of the Exchequer in 1566. Burghley had employed him on court business and ensured his election to the House of Commons in 1563. By 1567 Walsingham was supplying William Cecil with information about the movements of foreign spies in London. In a letter to one of his nephews,

Walsingham reveals how he judged men whom he would take into his service: 'Especially have regard … chiefly of the nobility [and] gentry … that you see the inclination of each man, which way he is bent, whether it be a marshal or counsellor, a plain open nature, [or] dissembling or counterfeit and what pension he has from abroad.'

Source: Cited in Hutchinson R. *Elizabeth's Spy Master: Francis Walsingham and the Secret War that Saved England.* London: Weidenfeld & Nicholson; 2007. p. 26.

ACTIVITY 4.2

Look back through your notes for signs of change and continuity between Henry VII's governance and Elizabeth I's. For example, William Paget, Henry VIII's secretary seems to have the same role as William Cecil under Elizabeth I. Draw a simple table with the headings 'Henry VIII', 'Elizabeth I' and 'similar or different?' and fill in notes on Court, Ministers and Parliament for each.

Baron Burghley, and from his new position in the House of Lords, he controlled Parliament's response to the crises. Burghley, through his clients in the Commons, applied relentless pressure on Elizabeth throughout the crises provoked by Mary and increasingly resorted to parliaments to implement new, harsh laws for combatting Catholicism. In this light, Graves (1985) argues Parliament can be seen as posing little threat to Elizabeth's authority. In 1581, Parliament was called to enact laws against recusants and missionary priests, which it did. In 1584 Parliament was called to enact legislation providing for the queen's safety, following the assassination of William of Orange (leader of the rebels in the Netherlands). When members tried to pass a law requiring stricter observation of the Sabbath, Elizabeth withheld her assent, as she did with eight other bills. These 'later' parliaments were all called for advice and new laws, rather than subsidies, but Elizabeth's actions demonstrate her retention of control.

Factional rivalries

It was an accepted truth for generations that Elizabeth's Court was riven with factional rivalries, yet some historians argue that there was little, if any factionalism before the war with Spain in 1585 (see the section on Relations with Spain). Brief feuding erupted between Cecil and the Earl of Leicester over the latter's romance with the queen and who Elizabeth should marry. But the major and sustained disagreements occurred over intervention in the Netherlands. Leicester and Walsingham favoured military intervention to develop a European Protestant coalition, but Cecil did not share their enthusiasm to commit England to war with Spain and opinion became increasingly polarised. However, even at this time battle lines were not drawn between 'moderates' and 'ideologues'. The Privy Council was agreed on the need to settle the succession and on the broad aims of Protestant foreign policy. Adams (1982) argues that Leicester, Burghley and Walsingham frequently liaised to organise their persuasion of the queen.

Real factional feuds began after the deaths of the Earl of Leicester in 1588, Sir Walter Mildmay in 1589, Sir Francis Walsingham in 1590 and Sir Christopher Hatton, Lord Chancellor and royal favourite in 1591. William Cecil was elderly and failed to relate to the younger men of the Council, instead relying on his son, Robert, who took on the functions of Secretary of State in 1590. The rising man at court was Robert Devereux, the Earl of Essex: he was young, handsome and ambitious, and quickly became a favourite of Elizabeth's. Essex loathed Cecil and his grip on ministerial power and frequently fought with him over appointments. When Cecil died it threw the political field wide open, as courtiers scrabbled for his political inheritance. The ambitious young Essex sought offices. Essex's main rival for favour with the queen was Sir Walter Raleigh, who was older but still handsome, and intellectually able too. He had made his name as a soldier, first in France and then in Ireland. Although he profited from royal favour, he failed to make it into the inner chambers of power, but always stayed loyal to the queen. Haigh (1993) suggests that as Elizabeth ran such a narrowly based government in her latter years, it is unsurprising the ambitious men at court gathered around men like the Earl of Essex and the queen could do little to compose the rivalries. For this reason he blames the Essex Rising (see the section on Social discontent and rebellions) on Elizabeth and her poor control of the Court.

Foreign affairs

Elizabeth's foreign policy priorities were similar to those of her predecessors: she needed to preserve trade, maintain a secure northern frontier and ensure the Channel coastline was well protected. Unlike her predecessors she was not dynastic in her approach; she accepted the loss of Calais and gave up claims to the French throne and refused to marry into a European family even though it would have buttressed national security. There is little evidence that Elizabeth was driven by religious concerns either, although religion was certainly a factor for her councillors. In fact, in the first half of her reign, Elizabeth's foreign policy was driven by domestic concerns, namely a lack of resources and a need to secure the religious settlement. Although Elizabeth was excommunicated by papal bull in 1570, it was the Netherlands that would play a decisive part in starting 18 years of war between England and Spain in 1585. Wernham (1966) suggests that Elizabeth's policy towards the Netherlands was consistent and was in large part successful in avoiding open confrontation with Spain. MacCaffrey (1993) has provided us with a more complex, and convincing view. He argues that Elizabeth had consistent principles, yet she was at the mercy of events rather than an initiator of policy and was often compelled to act in an ad hoc fashion.

Figure 4.4: The distribution of religion across Europe, c. 1560.

Issues of succession

The security of the realm depended ultimately upon the succession, therefore practical politics determined that Elizabeth should marry. The strongest candidate from abroad was the Archduke Charles, third son of the Emperor Maximilian. Philip II of Spain approved, even though evidence suggests he had designs on Elizabeth himself. Elizabeth clearly had no intention of marrying Charles, however, and ten years of wooing did not convince her. The Council were even less keen as he insisted he should be allowed to continue to practise his own religion in private. Elizabeth was more interested in Lord Robert Dudley, whom she had known since her childhood because of his father's connections. Dudley was adventurous, good looking but married. The suspicious death of his wife ended the affair, although Dudley never lost his political influence at Court and he was made the Earl of Leicester in 1564. Both Cecil and Throckmorton on the Council opposed the marriage, although they respected his political following at Court and never tried to oust him completely.

With marriage a distant prospect, the question of succession was discussed at length in Council meetings. There were two contenders: Lady Catherine Grey, sister of the ill-fated Lady Jane Grey, and Mary, Queen of Scots. (To see Mary's claim to the throne, look back at the Tudor family tree in Chapter 3, Figure 3.2.) Lady Catherine, although a Protestant, was in low standing with the queen. Against Elizabeth's wishes, she had secretly married the Earl of Hertford and had a child with him. The marriage was declared invalid, and Catherine was disgraced and banished from Court. The most likely candidate was therefore Mary, Queen of Scots. Although her religion made her unsuitable, she had accepted the Protestant settlement in Scotland. In 1565 she married Lord Darnley, thereby uniting two claims to the English throne. The marriage had momentous consequences for English politics (see the section on Mary, Queen of Scots).

In October 1562 Elizabeth I nearly died of smallpox and the political class glimpsed the shocking prospect of a civil war to decide the succession. The problem never faded from Cecil's mind. The security and stability of England depended on the survival of an unmarried woman who had no clearly recognised heir. Cecil and the Council were prepared to use Parliament to apply pressure on Elizabeth to marry or name an heir whenever it met. But Elizabeth would neither do this nor disavow Mary as her heir. The House of Commons petitioned Elizabeth in 1563 to name a successor and warned against the threat from Mary, but Elizabeth refused to be moved to answer. In 1572, Parliament passed a bill debarring Mary from the succession but Elizabeth withheld her assent. Despite Burghley's pressure she refused ever to name an heir.

Mary, Queen of Scots

Mary Stuart has been the subject of much historical debate, between those who see her as a tragic figure and those who think she was calculating and dangerous. She had a reasonable claim to the English throne, but it was her Catholicism and half-French lineage that really made her a threat to Elizabeth. By 1563 Mary Stuart had returned to Scotland after having lived in France since she was five years old. She returned to a Protestant country that was dominated by noble factions. Her main concern, however, was gaining recognition from Elizabeth as her rightful heir. She therefore accepted the Protestant ruling nobles and focused on remarrying, as her husband, the King of France, had died in 1560.

Elizabeth largely stood aside during the endless civil wars that took place in France during the 1560s. Despite their being fellow Protestants in need of support, Elizabeth viewed the Huguenots as rebels against their lawful sovereign, which she disapproved of. The real threat came from Mary Stuart's claim to the throne and whether the French king would support her. Mary married Lord Robert Darnley, a grandson of Margaret Tudor, in 1565. This marriage strengthened Mary's claim to the throne, but Darnley was reportedly an alcoholic, unstable and, at times, violent. In May 1566, Darnley and his supporters murdered David Rizzio, who was reputed to be Mary's lover, stabbing him 56 times in front of her. When Mary gave birth to a son, James, in June 1566, there were rumours the child was Rizzio's. Several months later, Darnley was recovering from smallpox at Kirk O'Field near Edinburgh when his house was blown up. His body was found in the grounds, apparently unscathed, and it was thought that he had been strangled after the explosion. The chief suspect was the Protestant Earl of Bothwell, whom Mary married later in the year. The scandal was too much for the Protestant Scottish lords and they raised an army against Mary. She established a regency under the Earl of Moray after she was forced to abdicate in favour of her infant son. Mary was subsequently imprisoned in the island fortress of Loch Leven. Somehow she managed to escape in 1568 and fled to England to seek support from Elizabeth. Elizabeth held a conference at York to determine whether Mary bore guilt for Darnley's murder. Mary refused to answer the charges and the conference was inconclusive, as Elizabeth did not wish to convict her. Moray was given £5000 in loans from England to restore the peace in Scotland and Mary was kept in confinement at one country house or another for the rest of her life.

Figure 4.5: The young Mary Stuart. She was praised for her beauty, although some historians have suggested she was a victim of poor marriages because of it.

Northern Rising

Once Mary was in England, she created a host of problems for Elizabeth. In 1569 the Northern Rising broke out (see the section on Social discontent and rebellions). The Duke of Norfolk had schemed to marry Mary with the support of some northern earls who had Catholic sympathies. Norfolk did not intend to oust Elizabeth, but had clear designs on Cecil's posts. When the scheme failed, the northern earls revolted, but Elizabeth raised a large force against them and they were defeated.

Ridolfi Plot

In 1570, Pope Pius V excommunicated Elizabeth and declared that her subjects owed her no allegiance, prompting her to see Catholics as enemies. Anti-Catholic fears multiplied when Cecil uncovered a plot to overthrow Elizabeth in 1571. The plan, led by Roberto Ridolfi, a Florentine banker, was to land 6000 Spaniards at Harwich in order to depose Elizabeth and enthrone Mary. Again Norfolk and Mary were involved in the plot. The would-be successor to the throne had become the focal point for conspiracies. Elizabeth was still reluctant to take any drastic action against Mary, despite the Council orchestrating a Parliament which pressed her to do just that. Twice Elizabeth signed Mary's death warrant, and twice she recalled it. Norfolk was not so lucky.

To combat the threat of Mary, negotiations opened in 1571 for a marriage alliance between Elizabeth and Francis, Duke of Anjou and Alençon, who was heir to the French throne and strongly allied with Protestant forces in the country. The proposal failed but a defensive Treaty of Friendship was signed at Blois in 1572, which quelled fears about Charles IX's support for Mary. However, the massacre of 3000 Huguenots in Paris in August 1572 rocked England. Elizabeth simultaneously authorised munitions to be sent to the Huguenots and allowed talks about marriage to the Duke of Alençon to resume the following year, as a way of maintaining peaceful relations with the French. Elizabeth gave unofficial help to the Huguenots in 1568 and in 1570 to ensure their military and political survival and continued to manipulate Alençon to support English interests in the Netherlands (see the section on Relations with Spain).

Throckmorton Plot

Throughout the 1570s, minor plots centring around Mary were uncovered by Walsingham's spy network, but few of them were ever likely to succeed. In 1583 Walsingham discovered more sinister plans, involving Mary, the French and Spanish ambassadors, Francis Throckmorton, who was a member of a Warwickshire Catholic family, and two Scottish Jesuits. They were supported by the Pope and Philip of Spain. There were devastating repercussions for Jesuits in England (see the section on Religious changes) and the episode pushed England further towards war with Spain (see the section on Relations with Spain). It was decided that Mary would have to be more closely guarded, and Sir Amias Paulet, a strict Puritan, was chosen to be her gaoler.

Babington Plot

In 1586 Walsingham discovered another plot involving Mary, the French ambassador, Châteauneuf, and a young Catholic, Anthony Babington. Government agents discovered that Mary had been smuggling letters in and out of her prison through a beer barrel. Walsingham's men sprang a trap by forging letters from Babington threatening to assassinate Elizabeth, which Mary implicitly approved in her written response. The letter from Mary was almost certainly genuine and her complicity constituted treason.

Execution 1587

The trial was held in September with 40 Privy Councillors present. They quickly reached a guilty verdict and left it to Parliament to petition Elizabeth to execute Mary. Elizabeth said she could give no speedy answer:

'We Princes, are set on stages, in the sight and view of all the world duly observed. The eyes of many behold our actions; a spot is soon spied in our garments, a blemish quickly noted in our doings … that I must give direction for her death, which cannot be but most grievous, and an irksome burden to me.'[2]

Although Elizabeth remained undecided, she did allow the public proclamation of the death sentence against Mary on 4 December. However, the warrant still required Elizabeth's signature and she put off the deed until 1 February. There was some controversy about the sealing of the warrant, Elizabeth claiming it had been done in haste without her permission: she clearly wanted another way out, other than executing a fellow queen. Elizabeth's vacillation on the matter has been much

Key term

Jesuits: members of the Society of Jesus, a Catholic missionary order founded in 1540. Excluded from England in 1584, they continued to enter the country secretly and became reviled as the embodiment of the Catholic threat-from-within.

debated, with Elton (1955) accepting that there was very little else Elizabeth could have done in the circumstances and MacCaffrey (1993) suggesting that although Elizabeth had done everything possible to taint Mary's reputation, England's monarch still respected her fellow queen. Unfortunately for Elizabeth, Mary's execution did not bring peace, for Philip II was preparing the largest fleet of ships in history to attack England's shores (see the section on Relations with Spain).

Scotland

During the 1570s, England had been secure on her northern borders due to the pro-English policies of the regent, the Earl of Morton. However, James resented the regent's authority and became attached to Esmé Stewart, Sieur d'Aubigny, kinsman to the Earl of Lennox. D'Aubigny built up his influence in court and had Morton executed for his supposed involvement in the murder of Lord Darnley. Both France and Spain were manoeuvring to set up Scotland as a client state. Elizabeth was unmoved by any of this and refused military support, and even refused Walsingham's suggestions to get James VI married off to a Protestant princess. Luckily the pro-English Earl of Angus toppled d'Aubigny. By the 1580s James VI of Scotland was taking a greater interest in governing his realm and he reinstated d'Aubigny, now the Earl of Arran. After painstaking negotiations, James VI eventually accepted a league with England in return for a pension of £4000 per annum. The northern border was once again secure.

Relations with Spain

The first decade of Elizabeth's reign saw fairly stable, positive relations maintained between England and the Habsburgs. Philip of Spain preferred to see a heretic on the throne of England to Mary Stuart, who was queen of France in 1559–60 and closely linked to the French royal family, and there was no open breach between England and Spain before 1568. Cordial relations were assisted by Guzman de Silva, as Spanish ambassador at Elizabeth's court: Elizabeth seemed to like him a great deal and he was highly skilled at easing diplomatic tensions as and when they arose. Several historians have pointed to events in the Netherlands between 1566 and 1568 as the cause of souring relations between England and Spain.

Problems arise 1566–71

From 1566, revolts against Philip II's rule broke out in the Netherlands. Philip responded by sending the Duke of Alva with 50 000 men to suppress them. Elizabeth was not initially worried, but by 1568 Alva had achieved a military victory over all his opponents, and fears grew that he might use the Netherlands as a springboard to an invasion of England. Guy (1988) suggests that the importance of Alva's arrival cannot be overplayed. War was out of the question for England after a military expedition to France in support of the Huguenots in 1562–63 had ended in failure and Elizabeth sought to demonstrate English power in other ways. High-ranking court officials backed John Hawkins (a cousin of Francis Drake) to make voyages to Africa to purchase slaves and sell them in Spanish America, which would break the Spanish trading monopoly. This failed when Hawkins's ship was destroyed by the Spanish in 1568. Next came the 'Bullion Affair' when 400 000 florins were seized from Spanish ships sheltering in English ports on their way to the Netherlands. The motives for the seizure are unclear but it prompted a total suspension of Anglo-Spanish trade for five years and can be considered a diplomatic blunder on Elizabeth's part.

Relations continued to deteriorate when Alva gave money to Catholics in northern England in 1569, and in 1571 Philip supported the Ridolfi Plot (see the section on Social discontent and rebellions) and instructed Alva to send 10 000 troops to support Catholics in England. In retaliation Elizabeth ordered the attacking and looting of Spanish ships until 1573, when it appears she saw the need to restore commercial relations at least. A limited agreement was reached the same year, which reopened Anglo-Spanish trade. This was followed in 1574 by the Convention of Bristol, which improved relations further and Elizabeth withdrew support for maritime ventures against the Spanish in the Caribbean.

Relations deteriorate 1572–84

Again, events in the Netherlands proved critical in 1572. More revolts broke out in revulsion against Spanish rule, the suppression of which aroused fears within England. Elizabeth tried to mediate and provided indirect aid to the rebels, all of which angered the Spaniards. By 1578, all 17 provinces of the Netherlands were in open revolt against the Spanish. Elizabeth was pressed by Walsingham and Leicester to intervene. Elizabeth erred on the side of caution, but could not leave the Netherlands to their fate, for it might mean total submission to the Spanish

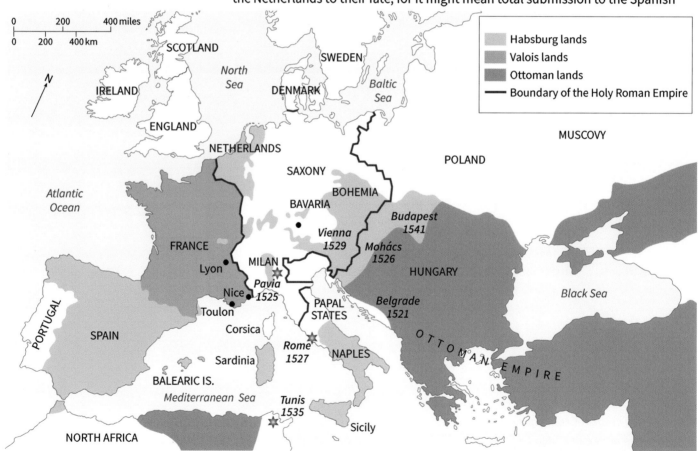

Figure 4.6: This map of Europe shows the great empires in 1563.

Discussion points:

1. Who would England's natural allies be?
2. Why did the Habsburgs start to become more of a threat in 1568?

or drive them into the arms of the French. By 1578 the Spanish government had repeatedly rebuffed her attempts to mediate and the rebels were drawing closer to the French. MacCaffrey (1993) suggests that Elizabeth was still pursuing carefully defined neutrality here. Elizabeth used marriage negotiations with the Duke of Anjou and Alençon to improve the situation in 1579. The negotiations failed to amount to marriage, but Elizabeth met the duke and sent financial assistance to his expedition to the Netherlands in 1580–81. Meanwhile, Philip II had become the King of Portugal, providing him with a rich colonial empire as well as a substantial fleet.

Elizabeth pursued more openly anti-Spanish policies, proposing an Anglo-French league and knighting Francis Drake for his maritime exploits against the Spaniards. The death of Alençon allowed France's Catholic League to conclude a treaty with Philip II (the Treaty of Joinville in December 1584), where he promised them protection. Elizabeth offered the Dutch informal aid in 1585 and supported privateering plans led by Drake. These actions culminated in a trade embargo and seizure of English shipping and goods in Iberian ports. Elizabeth, reluctantly and with great hesitation, finally committed foot soldiers to the Netherlands, although she still hoped for peace. Guy (1988) argues 'her policy – if the defensive expediency of 1572–85 can be dignified with that term – attempted to reconcile conflicting strategic, commercial, and religious interests at a minimum cost.'[3]

War and the Armada 1585–03

By August 1585 England was committed to fighting Spain, although as yet there had been no declaration of war and at least five parallel sets of negotiations continued right up until the sailing of the **Armada**. Philip had decided on war with England in 1584 and started to prepare this great war fleet, provoked no doubt by Sir Francis Drake's piracy. Philip's aims were to recover his reputation after the humiliating sea raids by the English and reduce England to accepting Catholicism. He was a devout man and had become convinced he was acting as God's instrument.

The defeat of the Spanish Armada, according to Doran (1986), owed much to the overambitious nature of the project, but also to the talents of Sir John Hawkins's work at the navy board. The English victory was spectacular, but solved nothing. In the next ten years Philip II commissioned 12 new 1000-ton galleons, but in contrast Elizabeth did little to strengthen her own navy. Perhaps even worse was Elizabeth's reaction to Lord Admiral Howard, who begged her for money to pay for food, shelter and care for sick sailors, who were falling ill in their hundreds. The Queen preferred to save her money, and many died for her realm without reward.

From 1588 to 1594 Elizabeth pursued a dual military strategy, which involved privateering at sea to finance the expensive land war in France and the Netherlands. Elizabeth also kept her soldiers as auxiliaries in the Netherlands, sending 20 000 men to France from 1589 until 1595 to halt the Spanish invasion. MacCaffrey (1993) argues that these years saw foreign policy slip from Elizabeth's control, but that 1593 must be considered a turning point for Elizabeth's foreign policy. This can partly be explained by Elizabeth's belief that England's security was no longer at risk, and partly because she needed to divert more troops to settle Ireland. Even after Calais fell to the Spaniards in 1596 she would only

Key term

Armada: the Spanish and Portuguese word for naval fleet.

Speak like a historian: Susan Doran

Extract A

Susan Doran has written extensively about Elizabeth I, challenging views that all of the Queen's problems were linked to her gender. In this extract she discusses Elizabeth's foreign policy.

Elizabeth's caution and parsimony were in large measure due to a realistic assessment of the military resources at her disposal. She was only too well aware, however, of the limitations of her purse and the unpopularity of expedients to raise necessary sums, and she cut her royal cloth accordingly. She insisted that her allies should pay their share of the cost of campaigns, and she avoided ambitious ventures. The decision to pursue a privateering war rather than to attack the Spanish navy can be seen in the same light. Dependent as she was on private enterprise for her fleets, she had to allow her captains and investors to pursue the type of warfare that would bring her profit as well as strengthen national security. Nonetheless, Elizabeth did not allow her parsimony to dictate her policies to the extent that she did everything by halves; for her campaigns in France in 1589–92 she raised levies to recruit new men and continually overspent her budgets … From the beginning of 1589 until 1595 the total cost of the Continental war reached £1 100 000.

Source: Doran S. *England and Europe 1485–1603*. New York: Longman Press; 1996. p. 90.

Discussion points:
1. What is Doran arguing here?
2. Can you find evidence from your notes to support her arguments?
3. How convincing is her argument?

commit 2000 troops to France to be placed on garrison duty. Only two major naval campaigns against Spain were launched in 1595 and 1596. Drake and Hawkins led the first, attempting to capture Panama, but this ended in failure and the deaths of both commanders. The second was a strike on the Spanish fleet at Cadiz, led by the Earl of Essex (a new favourite at court) and Lord Admiral Effingham. This was partly successful: 57 ships were burned and looted, but the merchant fleet was not captured and no garrison was stationed there for the future creation of a naval base. A major reason for the missed opportunity at Cadiz was Elizabeth's reluctance to spend money.

In 1598 the Franco-Spanish war came to an end and Philip II died, opening the way for peace negotiations. Elizabeth's terms for peace reflected her war aims; she demanded neither territory nor financial compensation, but insisted the Netherlands be virtually independent. The Spanish would not agree to those terms and for the rest of the reign, low level talks continued. Doran (1996) argues that ultimately Elizabeth achieved her objectives, 'Spain was bloodied but undefeated'.[5]

Discussion points:

1. Pick out the symbolic references included in this portrait (Hint: Look at the windows behind Elizabeth and the globe she rests her hand on).
2. This is an example of masterful propaganda. What is the message of this painting?

Society

Continuity and change

The major factors causing social upheaval throughout the Tudor period, but significantly during Elizabeth's reign, were population increases and price rises. Wrigley and Schofield (1981) suggest that the population had reached 3 000 000 by the 1550s but had climbed to almost 4 200 000 by the time of Elizabeth's death. Along with the growth of the population came increased mobility. A good deal of the movement can be accounted for by young men and women who left their villages to seek employment in towns or neighbouring villages; some may have even ventured to London, which grew considerably throughout the 16th century. Kerridge (1969) claims there was an agricultural revolution given the transformation in production techniques, more efficient use of labour force and improvement in some methods at this time, although this view is still being challenged today. Population increase was accompanied by agricultural price rises. The harvest failures of the 1550s and 1590s were certainly significant in creating inflationary pressures. Production was unable to keep up with the expanding population, and in these circumstances, the numbers of poor and vagrants grew. It is important to note that 'vagrants', as determined by contemporary sources, were probably not criminals but migrants in search of subsistence.

In some respects the Elizabethan era continued to be one of social fluidity. The pattern of newly risen councillors such as Paget under Henry VIII was repeated by Sir Thomas Smith under Elizabeth I. However, when political stability had been truly restored by 1570, social conservatism prevented any recurrence of this. Elizabeth did not appoint anyone who could be considered humbly born in the latter half of her reign and created almost no new peerages. MacCaffrey (1993) claims that Elizabeth did not want to tax the rich for fear of alienating

Voices from the past

Sir Francis Drake

Francis Drake (1540–96) was a remarkable figure, who successfully circumnavigated the world between 1577 and 1580. From humble beginnings he rose to prominence due to his successes in slaving voyages, making vast amounts of money. He continued to privateer, plundering Spanish ships and taking the treasures for himself and his queen. He was knighted by Elizabeth aboard his ship *The Golden Hind*. In 1587 he led an attack on Cadiz in 1587. This incident sometimes known as the 'singeing of the King of Spain's beard'. In a daring raid, over 30 ships were sunk. Of even greater importance, though, was the destruction of supplies intended for King Philip's planned Spanish Armada.

them. Palliser (1992) argues that the nobility did not decline but the gentry expanded. Law and government office, like trade and marriage, were avenues to social advancement. The Bacons and the Cecils both profited well enough from government office to found great noble mansions such as Burghley House in Lincolnshire. However, although some were fortunate, many members of the gentry sank into poverty, due to poor harvests or mounting debts.

The social divide between the gentry and the rest of the population was a political one. The gentry comprised the 'political nation' who took an interest in the running of the country and often sought to influence how it was governed. For those at the bottom of the heap, the numbers of poor and vagrants were increasing. Smith (1997) maintains that socially some degree of change was occurring but this cannot be classed as revolutionary as the change was not consistent and not universal. Historians have also acknowledged that England witnessed change both at the top of society and at the bottom. At the top end we witness the expansion of the social elite to incorporate more groups, while at the bottom the numbers of poor and vagrants were increasing. The government had now to deal with problems of vagrancy produced by the policies of Henry VIII. The government did not welcome this, and in fact the Elizabethan government attempted to maintain social hierarchies as part of a belief in divine order, or 'the Great Chain of Being', where everyone had their place. Of course there were practical reasons too, whereby the government sought to prevent disorder and Elizabeth's ministers feared that social change could precipitate a breakdown in law and order. The government believed that enclosures were responsible for the worst economic ills of the country and therefore tried to limit the depopulation of the countryside and reverse conversions from arable to pastoral farming.

Voices from the past

Elizabeth I

On 8 August Queen Elizabeth went to Tilbury to encourage her forces, and the next day gave to them what is probably her most famous speech:

My loving people, we have been persuaded by some that are careful of our safety, to take heed how we commit ourselves to armed multitudes for fear of treachery; but, I do assure you, I do not desire to live to distrust my faithful and loving people. Let tyrants fear, I have always so behaved myself, that under God I have placed my chiefest strength and safeguard in the loyal hearts and goodwill of my subjects; and, therefore, I am come amongst you as you see at this time, not for my recreation and disport, but being resolved, in the midst and heat of battle, to live or die amongst you all – to lay down for my God, and for my kingdoms, and for my

people, my honour and my blood even in the dust. I know I have the body of a weak and feeble woman; but I have the heart and stomach of a king – and of a King of England too, and think foul scorn that Parma or Spain, or any prince of Europe, should dare to invade the borders of my realm; to which, rather than any dishonour should grow by me, I myself will take up arms – I myself will be your general, judge, and rewarder of every one of your virtues in the field.[4]

Discussion points:
1. How does Elizabeth refer to herself?
2. How does Elizabeth refer to her subjects?
3. What does Elizabeth promise to do?
4. Why is this such a powerful speech?

The government also sought to help the 'deserving poor' and punish sturdy beggars and vagabonds, an enormous task given the increasing numbers of people who fell into this category. Guy (1988) argues that the official response to harvest failures and associated problems was quite remarkable. The Poor Law legislation of 1598 and 1601 summed up over 50 years of local initiative and placed responsibility for the poor firmly with churchwardens, **overseers of the poor** and ratepayers of every parish. The costs of providing for the poor were to be met by a parish rate, and begging was prohibited unless licensed by the parish. Vagrants, on first offence, were to be whipped and returned to their place of residence, with the punishment to be carried out by local constables or other officers. If judged incorrigible, beggars could be sent to a House of Correction or even prison. Pauper children would become apprentices. The law offered relief to people who were

> ### Key term
>
> **overseer of the poor:** an official who administered poor relief in the form of food, money and clothing in England and various other countries that derived their law from England.

Figure 4.7: This portrait was painted after the Armada victory and is arguably one of the most famous paintings of Elizabeth I. Philip II sent over 20 000 men in 130 ships into the English Channel, with some 30 000 waiting in the Netherlands to be ferried to England. Some have suggested that bad weather played a major role in the defeat of the Armada, but Parker (1988) argues that the tactics of Drake, Effingham and Hawkins must surely have played a significant part. Only 67 of Philip II's ships and fewer than 10 000 men of the men who sailed survived. It was a humiliating defeat for the Spanish king.

unable to work – the impotent poor (for example, maimed soldiers returning from duty, the old and the blind) were to be given money or food or cared for in almshouses. The able-bodied poor were to be set to work in 'houses of industry'. The laws were implemented by local parishes and there was much variation in their application.

Problems in the regions

Elizabeth faced a great deal of opposition in the North and in Ireland. In both cases this was closely tied not only to the religious question, but also to the oppressive policies undertaken since Henry VIII. The northern nobility demonstrated their disgust in the Northern Rising (see the section on Social discontent and rebellions), while Ireland suffered civil and religious strife, murder bordering on genocide, clan warfare and disorder throughout Elizabeth's reign.

Wales

Cromwell's Act of Union in 1536 had marked the end of a thorough and lengthy pacification of Wales. It is significant that Wales provided no resistance to the Reformation and no support for the kind of rebellions that had taken place in the South West in 1549 and in the North in 1569. The Welsh accepted the Elizabethan settlement without demur and Welsh Bibles were produced for all the region's churches. The peaceful acceptance of religious change can be explained by the availability of Church lands, the beneficiaries of which were high-born freemen. Gaining the support of men who could dominate the political landscape in Wales was vital for the Tudor regime in ensuring the majority of people attached themselves to the tenets of the new faith.

Ireland

Elizabeth had inherited a disastrous situation in Ireland. The administration had little if any control outside the Pale. Thomas Radcliffe, the Earl of Sussex, became Lord Deputy in 1556 and began an aggressive policy. He wanted to expel the major lords from Ireland altogether and extend English colonies (known as plantations) throughout the province of Leinster. If it had been carried out, this policy would have been excessively expensive. Nevertheless, Sussex did try to settle Ulster, leading several campaigns through the north, but proving ultimately unsuccessful. The problem was Elizabeth, who, as Williams (1995) argues, 'alternated between half-hearted conciliation and inadequate military response'.[6]

By 1565 the weakness of the government was evident when the Earl of Desmond fought against the Earl of Ormond. Elizabeth took a sterner line and sent Sir Henry Sidney to be Lord Deputy. The rivalries between the Anglo-Irish factions were intense and both Desmond and Ormond allied themselves to a different member of Elizabeth's Council to try to gain her support. Elizabeth, probably under the influence of members of her Council, signalled that she would support Ormond. Sidney was rebuked for trying to provide impartial justice and Desmond was arrested in 1567. Meanwhile, Shane O' Neill, the Earl of Ulster, had begun negotiating with Charles IX of France and Mary Stuart for military support. Elizabeth told Sidney to extirpate O'Neill, but Sidney needed no urging. Using Gaelic and Scottish forces, Sidney marched through Ulster and convinced the region of the strength of royal power. In the course of the conflict, O'Neill fell into the hands of an enemy family, who killed him.

Sidney tried to instigate political and social reforms through the Dublin Parliament in 1569, but they met widespread opposition. It is perhaps no surprise that a rebellion broke out in the South in 1569, led by the Catholic James Fitzmaurice Fitzgerald, who asked Spain for support to rid Ireland of the English. He was an ineffective leader, but the timing of it made the government fearful, as relations with Spain were deteriorating (see the section on Relations with Spain). Ormond supported the queen and Sidney initiated a brutal campaign of suppression across Munster. All who resisted – men, women and children – were killed. The English were victorious, over 800 rebels were executed and Sidney could retire back to England with the threat of Spain using Ireland as a base against England diminished. In 1571 Sir William Fitzwilliam became Lord Deputy.

Between 1573 and 1576 a series of English lords attempted to colonise parts of Ireland for themselves. All attempts ended in the deaths of Irish men, women and children and led to the disgrace of the English earls. Fitzwilliam's approach was the perennial English policy of ruling the Irish by the sword rather than by the law. Sidney returned to Ireland as Deputy in 1575 in order to make Ireland financially self-sufficient. However, Elizabeth quickly grew tired of his expensive attempts to reform taxation and, once again, she abandoned him. Once again James Fitzmaurice Fitzgerald stirred a rebellion, this time with a force of Italians, Spaniards and support from the Pope. Although Fitzmaurice was killed within a few weeks, the rebels gained the support of the Earl of Desmond. The government acted firmly and Ormond was appointed to burn Desmond's castles and devastate his land. It would have ended there but other Irish lords were prompted to join the rebels, along with 600 Italian and Spanish troops. The new Lord Deputy, Arthur Grey Wilton massacred them to a man. Conflict in Ireland was becoming increasingly brutal. From 1581–83 control was re-established by a brutal pacification of the Pale and surrounding counties. Nobles were imprisoned or executed, land was burned and civilians massacred or starved. Sir John Perrot became Lord Deputy in 1584 and confiscated the lands of Desmond and 130 other rebels. It was decided that the lands, which took up the majority of Munster, should be colonised. The plan was to encourage 15 000 English settlers to work the farmland there. However, by 1592 only 3000 had arrived and 4000 in 1598, and so Irish farmers were allowed to settle there too. In 1595 a bloody rebellion broke out again in Ulster; this time the Earl of Essex thought he could do better than others before him, but he wasted his time marching around and then discharged himself back to England (see the section on Social discontent and rebellions). It was left to James I to resume the plantation policy.

Social discontent and rebellions

All of the Tudors faced rebellions and social discontent, but Elizabeth perhaps faced the greatest number of threats to her life. With the arrival in England of Mary, Queen of Scots, a large rebellion and countless plots were formed to depose Elizabeth and replace her with a Catholic queen (see the section on Mary, Queen of Scots). At first Elizabeth acted with clemency against those who conspired against her but as tensions with Spain increased, the threat to the queen's security became too great and the overwhelming force of the state was used against those who sought to disrupt the natural order of things.

The Northern Rising

The Northern Rising of 1569–70 grew out of a plot to marry Mary, Queen of Scots to the Duke of Norfolk. This was orchestrated by Thomas Percy, the Earl of Northumberland, and supported, for a time at least, by a number of the nobility including the Earl of Leicester. Protestant nobles supported the venture at first because it seemed to settle the problem of Mary entering England and solved the succession issue. However, Elizabeth refused to countenance the idea of a nobleman of her realm marrying the most dangerous claimant to her throne. The Duke of Norfolk panicked at the queen's reaction and fled the court in the summer of 1569. This prompted the earls of the North to muster their forces, expecting him to march on London. In fact, Norfolk threw himself on the mercy of the queen, and was promptly sent to the Tower.

The main agitators in the Northern Rising were acting in the name of Catholicism. Northumberland was deeply religious, but also had a bitter, personal grievance against the queen. Elizabeth had deprived him of his wardenship of the Middle March and, as a result, he had declined in wealth and status. The Earl of Westmorland, a major figure in the rebellion, was also suffering from poverty. The rebellion was easily quelled, as the earls seemed to lose their resolve upon hearing of the Earl of Warwick's forces amassing in the South. Elizabeth dealt with the rebels harshly, executing no fewer than 450 men for their actions, including Westmorland. In comparison with the Pilgrimage of Grace and Kett's Rebellion, which genuinely threatened the regimes of her father and brother, Elizabeth killed twice as many rebels and confiscated so much land that feudal structures broke down in the North. Elizabeth restored the Council of the North, appointing the Puritan Earl of Huntingdon as leader. He effectively ruled in her name. By choosing Protestant councillors, refusing to marry, imprisoning Mary, Queen of Scots, and allowing relations with Spain to break down, Elizabeth effectively allowed Catholicism to threaten England's stability.

Oxfordshire Rising 1596

The Oxfordshire Rising reveals the inadequate nature of any challenge from commoners during the 1590s, known as a decade of starvation and disease. The handful of rebels were roused by class-based anger, uttering threats specifically aimed at the rich. Impoverished, they hoped to seize weapons and march on London, gathering hundreds as they marched. The state used overwhelming force to crush the rebellion. Elizabeth employed military force, torture and the death sentence on the leader, Bartholomew Steer, along with four others. Whereas she procrastinated long and loud over the death of a nobleman, she seemed to insist on the most savage of punishments for the commoners who threatened to challenge the order of things. It was the local gentry, men of property who were particularly threatened by this rising, reflecting the poor social conditions and growing inequality between the richest and poorest.

Essex Rising 1601

The Earl of Essex had been one of Elizabeth's favourites and had used his courtly skills to gain her confidence. He was the stepson of the Earl of Leicester and therefore expected the same position as he had had. This is not so surprising given that Robert Cecil had been handed power by his father when he became a Privy Councillor in 1591. Essex had built up considerable patronage at court and was well known in his locality for his generosity. During the decade of the 1590s he built himself a faction with which to challenge the Cecils. He fought to get his own men appointed; for example, when the post of Attorney-General became vacant, Essex lobbied to obtain the position for his supporter Francis Bacon. Cecil had other ideas, and he was victorious.

Essex displayed dangerous qualities of ambition and military ardour and disenchantment with the court, but Elizabeth protected him. After Burghley died, Essex hoped to acquire some of the deceased's political inheritance. However, also in search for glory, Essex volunteered for service in Ireland to quell a rebellion in Ulster. Once there, he disobeyed the queen's orders in setting up negotiations with the rebels, and then discharged himself of his own accord. For this, Elizabeth put him under house arrest, much to the anger of his supporters. Sympathy for Essex became more pronounced when news spread that he had fallen ill. Elizabeth decided to call the JPs together to explain her treatment of Essex, which reveals a lot about her dependence on the gentry for maintaining the peace. Over the next few months it appears Robert Cecil tried to reconcile Essex back to court, but Elizabeth was still resentful over his disobedience in Ireland and suspended him from his offices. Deeply in debt, Essex's sorrow shifted to rage and he planned to seize the Court, the City of London and the Tower. He believed he would acquire the support of James VI, who had responded very cautiously to Essex's requests for soldiers.

With 140 followers, Essex expected to win over Londoners on 8 February 1601 to his cause, but by 9 p.m. was forced to surrender. Essex was condemned to death along with six of his conspirators. Many more were reprieved, or sentenced to a fine and imprisonment. His followers were the 'visible tip of a larger range of discontent' according to Williams (1998).[7] Many soldiers, courtiers and country gentlemen resented the power of the Cecils, but they were too disorganised and personally greedy to form any serious opposition to the government.

Economic development

Traditional historians claim that this period witnessed the birth of capitalism and great economic improvement. Internal trade expanded rapidly during the Tudor period. This was due primarily to the growing population, which was bound to create an expanding internal market. England also had a considerable river network and extensive coastline, making it easier to transport heavier cargoes within England than it was in her European counterparts. England's overseas trade probably accounted for a much smaller proportion than internal. But overseas trade had expanded rapidly, probably due to the falling value of English currency, and by the 1560s, exports in woollen textiles accounted for 80% of England's total exports. The Elizabethan period saw a change in direction of overseas trade, partly due to the experience of the trade slumps under Edward VI, but mostly because of the growing enmity with Spain. Palliser (1992) claims that England was in desperate need of new markets due to the stagnation of trade with Germany and the Netherlands.

Trade, exploration and colonisation

At first, England played a small part in the exploration and colonisation of the New World, allowing the Portuguese and Spanish to establish a **hegemony** over the whole region. The revival of interest in exploration perhaps owes something to the increasing uncertainty of the Antwerp cloth market and the need to broaden England's trade base. The first major exploration ventures began just before Edward VI died, due to the patronage of the Duke of Northumberland. Its purpose was to find a north-east passage to the Indies and was inspired by Sebastian Cabot, by now an old man. It failed to find a northerly route to the Orient, but opened up a commercial route to Moscow through the White Sea. This expedition prompted others, such as those of John Hawkins, who began trading slaves across the Atlantic in 1562. Hawkins took advantage of the need for labour in the new Spanish colonies, by collecting slaves from the Guinea coast and shipping them across to the Caribbean. Eventually the Spanish attacked his ships off the coast of Mexico, destroying three of them and forcing Hawkins to abandon slaving.

Expeditions for plunder and exploration marked the next 20 years, led by Francis Drake. His voyage around the world gave confidence to other English sailors and marked England's entry into the Asian world, although he failed to establish a colony in South America. Many further failed explorations followed, for example that of Frobisher and Davis to find the Northwest Passage (the sea route that connects the Atlantic and Pacific Oceans along the northern coast of North America). Although these men contributed much to geographical knowledge, they were not able to add to English trade or colonisation. However, by this time Sir Walter Raleigh's half-brother, Humphrey Gilbert, had embarked on an ambitious scheme to colonise North America. With backing from Walsingham he set out with ten ships, reaching Newfoundland, but drowned when his own ship sank. Sir Walter Raleigh was more successful, carrying the notion of plantations in Ireland across to America. In 1585 he sent a fleet to Roanoke Island in the territory he named Virginia (after Elizabeth, who was known as the Virgin Queen), which established a short-lived colony there. The Armada limited any further expeditions to America as the war diverted funds that might have been provided by the Crown and were essential to success.

Williams (1998) argues that the most positive achievement overseas between 1568 and 1588 was the least dramatic. An English merchant, William Harbone, set out to negotiate privileges for English merchants with the Ottomans. In 1581 the queen granted sole right to trade with the Ottoman ports, selling English woollen cloth in return for raw silk and currants. This Mediterranean trading route was probably the most profitable branch of commerce aside from the traditional cloth trade. Following the Armada, English overseas enterprise was dominated by the war at sea. As well as major naval expeditions – to Portugal in 1589, the Caribbean in 1595 and Cadiz in 1596 – there were many little wars of privateering, funded by London merchants. Between 1585 and 1603 there were 74 separate expeditions, involving over 180 ships. They brought English merchants considerable profit, which they invested later in the trade to Asia.

The major colonising expeditions of the Elizabethan era were mostly failures, although they laid the foundations for a future overseas empire. Dutch merchants

Key term

hegemony: the dominance of one nation over another.

were more successful than their English counterparts in the East Indies, although the latter inspired the founding of the East India Company, which was granted its charter in 1600. Although its beginnings were small and voyages were delayed until 1604, the company went on to account for half of the world's trade. Sir Walter Raleigh also led an expedition to Guyana in 1595 in an attempt to found a colony to rival the Spanish, but he failed to gain Elizabeth's support to make it successful. Other signs of the 'new worlds' being discovered were the appearance of tobacco in 1560s and the potato. Although Raleigh will always be associated with the introduction of potatoes and tobacco to Britain, these had already reached Europe via the Spanish. Raleigh did, however, help to popularise smoking at court. But it was only with the establishment of a colony on Roanoke in 1607 that England really took on colonisation.

Prosperity and depression

One of the most striking features of the Elizabethan economy was inflation. When Elizabeth ascended the throne inflation had slowed, but there was a rapid increase towards the end of her reign. There were several reasons for this. Contemporaries certainly regarded the key factor as the debasement of coinage that had taken place extensively under Henry VIII, Edward VI and Mary I. The debasements certainly did affect the purchasing power of the coinage and thereby acted as a catalyst for further increases in prices. Historians such as Nef (1940) suggested that inflation was caused by the impact of bullion from the New World, via the Spanish market, on Europe's economy. Although these factors would almost certainly have caused periodic fluctuations, there were other issues at play in the latter half of the Elizabethan period. Coleman (1978) argues that bad harvests in 1594 and 1598 drove up food prices, which were often slow to recover. Second, the cost of warfare from 1581 disrupted the normal flow of the economy by causing rises in taxation and the cost of imports. A knock-on effect of this was often rent increases coupled with falling wages. Third, enclosures required investment, so to cover the costs farmers increased the prices of grain and meat, which had a significant impact on the cost of living. Finally, population growth was a key factor as it created pressure on agricultural production and forced prices up. Those who suffered from inflation were wage-earners and rent payers, which covered the majority of the population. There was therefore a significant increase in poverty and a widening of inequality between rich and poor.

Religious developments, change and continuity

The Elizabethan religious settlement had apparently settled nothing. Some of its concessions led English Catholics to believe Elizabeth might still be won to their cause. Rumours of religious change circulated and in 1565 Catholic exiles in Antwerp dedicated books to the queen. In contrast, Protestants wanted further reform to rid the settlement of the concessions such as the attire of priests. In 1566 and 1571 Parliament applied pressure for ecclesiastical reform but Elizabeth forbade discussion of some of the bills presented. This was repeated again in 1584 and 1586 when more militant Protestants tried to apply pressure for reform in Parliament, but Elizabeth, the most committed Anglican in the country, was unmoved. Many Protestant clergymen balked at the more Catholic aspects of the settlement, leading Elizabeth to demand that Archbishop Parker enforce the conformity of the clergy in ceremony and doctrine. In 1576 Elizabeth intervened again, asking Archbishop Grindal to proceed against non-conformists in London, resulting in the suspension of 37 ministers who refused to wear the prescribed dress. It is not clear why Elizabeth cared so much about these particular ceremonies. Haigh (1993) suggests it was probably because she disliked invasion of her prerogative and was reluctant to weaken her authority by allowing deviation from the settlement, although a major factor has to be her fear of provoking Catholic dissent.

Some historians have claimed that Elizabeth was determined not to drive Catholics into outright opposition, something evidenced in her liturgical conservatism, her enforcement of clerical conformity and her moderation in the persecution of Catholics. There are examples of her trying to ingratiate conservatives into her regime, by keeping some of Mary's councillors such as Winchester and Arundel. Elizabeth visited Catholic nobles such as Lord Montagu on her summer progress and allowed a Catholic circle at Court. When Catholics were prosecuted, Elizabeth claimed it was for their disloyalty to the nation, rather than their beliefs. Elizabeth's rhetoric suggested an even-handedness against Protestant or Catholic deviation and she has been credited with a deliberate policy of toleration against Catholic non-conformists. Evidence for this claim can be cited in 1563 when a statute prescribed execution for a second refusal of the Oath of Supremacy. The queen ordered that no one should be asked twice. She also vetoed bills that sought to punish absence from Communion in 1571, 1572 and 1581.

However, Elizabeth's toleration of Catholics was limited. She allowed men and women to believe what they liked, as long as they did nothing about it, but she never intended Catholicism to live on in England, and indeed attempted to stifle the old religion. Elizabeth was tolerant when to be intolerant would have put her or her realm in danger. This can perhaps explain the toleration of Catholics in the 1560s and early 1570s, for example recusancy was only punished after political scares such as the Northern Rising in 1569 (see the section on Social discontent and rebellions) and following the papal bull excommunicating Elizabeth in 1570. Limited toleration of Catholics made political sense, while repression would have been costly and administratively difficult, given the number of **Church papists** among the justices and clergy. However, English Catholics began to pose both political and religious threats to the queen. The political threats at first centred around plots to depose Elizabeth and replace her with Mary, Queen of Scots (see the section on Mary, Queen of Scots) and of course the threat of war with Spain. Most of the Catholic laity regarded these threats as terrible and disloyal.

More serious for Elizabeth was the religious threat. The influx of **seminary priests** from 1574 and Jesuits from 1580 demonstrated a hardening of attitudes and it was clear the old religion was not fading away as the government had hoped. Poor church attendance, the papal bull and Philip's increasing hostility provoked a Treasons Act, based on the one passed by Cromwell (see Chapter 2), which made it a capital offence to call the queen a heretic or usurper. Fines were raised for non-attendance at church, anyone saying Mass would be fined and imprisoned and anyone employing a **recusant** schoolmaster could be fined too. In 1582 Elizabeth went further and issued a proclamation that declared all seminary priests and

Key terms

Church papists: loyal to Elizabeth but maintained Catholic beliefs and practices (such as Mass) and thought the sacraments were necessary for salvation.

seminary priests: English priests who had been trained in Flanders. They were taught to work for the salvation of souls and, if necessary, that they should seek martyrdom to restore Catholicism in England.

recusants: refused to attend church services, though some did take the Oath of Supremacy. Doctrinally they supported the Roman Catholic Church and would not compromise on aspects such as Mass given in Latin.

Presbyterians: emphasises the sovereignty of God, not the monarch, and governance of the Church by groups of elders, not bishops. Doctrinally, Presbyterians are heavily influenced by Calvin.

prophesyings: local meetings where ministers expounded biblical texts. They were effectively training sessions to encourage a more effective preaching ministry. Lay people were often invited in the hope of evangelising them too.

Jesuits to be traitors. From 1583 the Council created recusancy commissions to root out non-conformists, Catholics were fined, imprisoned and 180 were even executed between 1581 and 1603; the tide had turned. The government insisted they were executed because they opposed the Crown on temporal matters, while Catholics suggested they died for their faith. Of course, both sides were right as politics and religion were so closely entwined. This might explain why most lay Catholics were not threatened, and persecution only spiked in the crisis years immediately before and after the Armada.

Although Elizabeth had ascended the throne as the Protestants' queen, she soon came into conflict with them too. Her early attempts to conciliate Catholics offended Protestants. Elizabeth had recruited Protestants into her Council, most of whom would have been happy with further reforms to the Church, including Leicester, Walsingham and Mildmay. However, Elizabeth was deeply suspicious of Puritans, whose **Presbyterianism** she saw as subversive of royal authority, and she began to take a hard line against them. In 1574 Elizabeth attempted to suppress **prophesyings** in London and Lincoln of their radical Puritan tone. When, in 1576, she extended her attempts at suppression by asking Grindal to limit the number of licensed preachers within each diocese, it seemed Elizabeth was determined to stifle evangelistic efforts. Grindal, however, produced a written defence on the necessity of preaching and argued that bishops knew best. Elizabeth was furious and suspended Grindal, but did not dare to replace him, so until his death in 1583 England had no active Archbishop of Canterbury. Elizabeth criticised bishops in 1585 for allowing variety in preaching and ritual, yet she controlled appointments and milked their revenues by appropriating episcopal lands, depriving them of the necessary attributes to carry out her wishes. Only one bishop secured her affections, John Whitgift, who was Archbishop of Canterbury from 1583 to 1604: he was the pillar of conservatism and conformity and persecuted radicals of both persuasions. He oppressed Puritans, and in 1593 was responsible for the execution of Henry Barrow, John Greenwood and John Penry for setting up a congregation separate from the Church of England. Neale (1953) asserts the traditional view that the Puritans were a growing force within Elizabethan England that posed a genuine threat to the settlement. However, others claim that the Puritans, for various reasons, posed no significant threat.

Guy (1988) argues that parish Catholicism had been eroded by the 1590s and the new Church had begun to put down roots. The efforts of the 471 seminary priests were thwarted; over a quarter were executed, and the rest were ill-informed about pastoral needs. However, Haigh (1984) suggests that the Jesuits failed because they concentrated their efforts on the South-East, near the ports where they entered the country, but this area had already converted to Protestantism in the main. The treason laws also meant that any priest ordained by papal authority since 1559 could be convicted and no more proof of wrongdoing was needed. Even the recusant priesthood that had been active in Yorkshire, Lancashire and Peterborough in 1571 were unable to have a significant effect. By 1590 perhaps only a quarter of the Marian clergy were still alive, and no more than a dozen by 1603. Catholicism could not have endured in the mainstream without Catholic priests willing to administer the sacraments. It was only the gentry who allowed Catholicism to survive at all in England. Many built 'priest holes' in their houses

Hidden voices

Edmund Campion

Father Edmund Campion (1540–1581) was an English Roman Catholic **Jesuit** priest and martyr. He joined the College of Douai in Flanders, founded by the English Catholic, William Allen. The college developed into a missionary college or seminary, to supply England with priests as long as the schism with Rome persisted. Campion taught there for a while and then travelled to Rome, on foot, disguised as a pilgrim. There he joined the Jesuits and taught rhetoric and philosophy. Campion finally entered England arriving in London on 24 June 1580, disguised as a jewel merchant, and started preaching shortly after. He made many converts during this brief period, but soon attracted the attention of the authorities. During the time that he was delivering illicit sermons and holding Masses, Campion started to write his *Decem Rationes* (Ten Reasons), in which he set out the Catholic faith and his case against the Anglican Church. It caused a great sensation, and the hunt for Campion was stepped up. Captured in July 1581, he was taken to the Tower of London where he refused to renounce his beliefs when offered rich inducements to do so. He was subsequently tortured and then hanged, drawn and quartered on the technical charge of treason, but in reality because of his beliefs.

where they could hide Jesuit priests and protect them from royal visitations. Yet it was not the threat of persecution that forced Catholicism into a minority status, but the steps made by Protestantism to challenge it that made the difference.

As Collinson (1984) points out, there were two distinct processes occurring during the age of Elizabeth: on the one hand, a growing diversity in religious culture; on the other, the adoption by the majority of Protestantism, which was closely connected to national identity and civil obedience, edged with hostility to Catholic foreign powers and the Pope. By the 1600s, Elizabeth presided over an outwardly Protestant nation containing deep tension. This is partly because of the limited aims of the settlement itself, as Bacon spoke of a queen reluctant to make windows into men's souls. What Elizabeth sought was outward submission to an established religion rather than knowledgeable and conscientious assent to its content.

Year	Events	Government reaction
1568	Mary, Queen of Scots arrives in England. William Allen founds college for seminary priests in Flanders.	
1569	James Fitzmaurice Fitzgerald rebellion in Ireland. Northern Rising	
1570	Pope Pius V issues bull, *Regnans in Excelsis* – excommunicating Elizabeth.	
1571	Ridolfi Plot	

Year	Events	Government reaction
1572	Protestants are massacred in France on St Bartholomew's Day. Bill introduced in Parliament to remove many rites and ceremonies from the Prayer Book. The *Admonition to Parliament* is published, attacking the Church for its continuing links with Catholic practices.	The Queen vetoes the bill and forbids bishops from discussing the matter. The authors, John Field and Thomas Wilcox, are imprisoned. Puritan printing presses are destroyed and bishops ordered to enforce uniformity.
1574	First seminary priests arrive in England.	
1577	Edmund Grindal, Archbishop of Canterbury, refuses to suppress prophesyings.	
1578	Pope Gregory XIII pledges support to James Fitzmaurice Fitzgerald's rebellion in Ireland.	
1580	Edmund Campion, Father Parsons (Jesuits) arrive in England.	
1583	Throckmorton Plot John Whitgift becomes Archbishop of Canterbury.	
1585		England pledges assistance to the Protestants in the Netherlands in their revolt against Spanish rule.
1586	Small group of Puritans, led by Robert Browne, leaves the established Church to set up their own congregation. Babington Plot Philip II plans an invasion of England.	
1587	Peter Wentworth MP argues that Members of Parliament should have the right to discuss religious matters.	Wentworth is imprisoned. Mary, Queen of Scots is executed.
1588	Spanish Armada	31 Catholic priests are executed.
1593		Separatists Robert Browne, Henry Barrow and John Greenwood are executed.

ACTIVITY 4.3

1. Look at the Timeline: the threat of religious radicals and use two colours to highlight threats from Catholics and threats from Puritans.
2. Use your notes to complete the 'events' section in the Timeline – refer to your notes on foreign policy and religious change only.
3. Use your notes to complete the government reaction section.
4. How did the government respond to the threat from religious radicals?
5. How far did religion affect the stability of England?

Year	Events	Government reaction
1594	Father Parsons (Jesuit) publishes a document supporting the claim of the Spanish Infanta to the English throne.	
1602		Royal proclamation orders all Jesuits to leave the country immediately. Other Catholic priests given two months to leave.

Timeline: the threat of religious radicals

The English renaissance and 'the Golden Age' of art, literature and music

The Elizabethan 'Golden Age' has been much written about. Yet it was not entirely an age of 'high' culture. Nobles and commoners alike delighted in cock-fighting, bear baiting and bulls fighting dogs and the queen enjoyed this as much as reading Greek with her old tutor Ascham whenever he was at Court. The overlap between elite and popular culture is most obviously seen in the works of Shakespeare, however. Some have attributed the flourishing of cultural achievements to the spread of the **Renaissance**, which began in Florence in the late 15th century. It was highly fashionable among the nobility to appreciate Italian art and French literature. However, the artists and craftsmen of England were slow to take on the Italian style and ideas, and displayed a strong continuity with their medieval English past.

Two major and permanent changes caused what can fairly be described as a revolution in popular culture. The growth of printing and the increase of books printed in English had an incalculable impact on the population. Some 2760 books were printed in the first half of Elizabeth's reign and 4370 in the second; in fact the numbers are likely to be higher, as these figures are based on surviving texts. Even though those who owned books were in the minority, the impact on the greater population was enormous. The Puritan preacher, John Foxe, gave thanks to God for printing and Bacon named it one of the three greatest inventions of the age, along with gunpowder and the mariner's compass. The educated and the wealthy started to build large private libraries, for example John Dee of Mortlake owned over 4000 books by the time of his death. Most books had been published in Latin at the beginning of the century, but more and more books were published in English for a wider readership, although the majority of these were translations of classical texts.

Art and architecture

The artists of the Tudor Court in the Renaissance and those who followed until the early 18th century came mostly from Europe, often from Flanders. These included Hans Holbein the Younger (Henry VIII's great court painter) and the Flemish painter Peter Paul Rubens. The Reformation had a significant impact on

Key term

Renaissance: meaning 'rebirth', refers to the historical period dating from approximately 1450 to 1750. This period saw cultural and artistic movements characterised by an interest in Classical scholarship and values.

English art, in that Italian artistic influence was greatly diminished, because of the close connection of Italy with Catholicism. The iconoclasm associated with the Reformation destroyed much medieval religious art and the skills of painting and making stained glass windows were all but lost in England. In contrast, there grew up a strong tradition for the portrait miniature, as exemplified by Nicholas Hilliard, who had learnt his craft from European artists. Elizabeth appointed him official miniature painter and he painted a number of miniatures of the queen, as well as some larger panel portraits. Hilliard enjoyed his position throughout Elizabeth's reign and into that of her successor, James I. His paintings exemplify the visual image of Elizabethan England, very different from that of most of Europe in the late 16th century. His tiny portraits are exquisitely painted although technically he was very conservative by European standards. The queen had her own collection of miniatures, reportedly her favourite being one of the Earl of Leicester. The portraiture of Elizabeth I was carefully controlled, and developed into an elaborate iconic style, which has succeeded in creating enduring images, such as the Armada portrait (see the section on Relations with Spain).

It was not until the Elizabethan architecture of the end of the century that a true English Renaissance style emerged, despite some buildings in a partly Renaissance style from the reign of Henry VIII, notably Hampton Court Palace, and later, Somerset House under Edward VI. Palliser (1992) argues that the Marian reaction of 1553 broke up this architectural trend. Instead, the houses of the Elizabethan era owed their influence more by northern Europe than Italy. The most famous buildings were large show houses constructed for courtiers and, at a time when glass was very expensive, characterised by extremely large windows, as at Hardwick Hall in Derbyshire and Burghley House in Lincolnshire. Urban housing, farmhouses and many manor houses remained in the more traditional perpendicular style, which was characterised by mullioned windows, vaulted roofs and the use of ornament to decorate.

Literature

Without doubt when most people speak of a 'golden age' in literature the first name that springs to mind is William Shakespeare – one of the founding fathers of English cultural heritage. Great literature was written in language that was increasingly rich as the century advanced, due to the importation of foreign words and competition between contemporary writers such as Francis Bacon, John Foxe, Christopher Marlowe and, of course, Shakespeare. Many of these writers were influenced by both Tyndale's and Cranmer's Bible translations, which were fine examples of prose. Notable pieces, such as Spenser's *Fairie Queene*, probably written in 1590, celebrates the Elizabethan age using marvellous imagery. Owing much to English medieval allegories, although it also imitated the Italian poet Ariosto, it is both a great work of art and a political commentary. The queen favoured Spenser so much she gave him a pension of £50 a year, even though there is a good chance she never read the poem. Another great, arguably the greatest tragedian before Shakespeare, was Marlowe. His two most famous pieces, *Tamburlaine*, the story of the Tartar hero, and *Dr Faustus*, the tale of a magician who sold his soul to the Devil in return for universal knowledge, contain some of the finest examples of blank verse.

Figure 4.8: Hardwick Hall, in Derbyshire, was built by the formidable Elizabeth Talbot, Countess of Shrewsbury, better known as Bess of Hardwick. She was married four times, each husband wealthier than the last.

Discussion point:

1. What aspects of the house reveal Renaissance influence?

Dramas were performed privately for the court and nobility, while the crowded theatres drew the widest public in Europe. The first theatre, aptly named 'The Theatre' was built in 1576 followed by the Rose and the Swan and the more famous Globe, which opened in 1599. The flourishing of theatres in London reflected both official encouragement and the broadening of popular culture. Writers and dramatists of the period observed the change in Elizabethan government and society after 1585. The themes of kinship, authority and the acquisition and retention of power came to fascinate writers after 1591. These themes were debated within the humanist definitions of 'virtue' in governance in an effort to explain how 'vice', 'flattery' and 'ambition' had come to supersede the traditional values of 'wisdom' and 'service'. One example of this was Ben Jonson's *Sejanus His Fall* in 1603, which seemed to represent the queen's capriciousness and her troubles with Essex and Raleigh.

Voices from the past

William Shakespeare

Shakespeare's historical plays provided a magnificent literary view of 15th-century English history, which had such an influence that it is only in the last 60 years or so that historians have challenged these views. His *King Richard III* for example, is a caricature, but one that has become absolutely synonymous with any representation of the former king.

I, that am rudely stamp'd and want love's majesty

To strut before a wanton ambling nymph;

I, that am curtail'd of this fair proportion,

Cheated of feature by dissembling nature,

Deform'd, unfinish'd, sent before my time

Into this breathing world, scarce half made up,

And that so lamely and unfashionable

That dogs bark at me, as I halt by them;

Why, I, in this weak piping time of peace,

Have no delight to pass away the time,

Unless to see my shadow in the sun

And descant on mine own deformity:

And therefore, since I cannot prove a lover,

To entertain these fair well-spoken days,

I am determined to prove a villain,

And hate the idle pleasures of these days.

Plots have I laid, inductions dangerous,

By drunken prophecies, libels and dreams,

To set me brother Clarence and the king

In deadly hate the one against the other.

Source: *King Richard III*, (ed.) Lull J. In *The New Cambridge Shakespeare*. Cambridge: CUP; 2009. Act I, Scene I, lines 16–35.

Discussion point:
Consider why Shakespeare portrays Richard III as a villain. (You may want to refer back to Chapter 1 to remind yourself of his family background.)

Music
The Elizabethan period was a great age for music, with notable achievements in both secular and sacred music. The great Thomas Tallis along with Christopher Tye and Robert White produced sacred music still played today and William Byrd is considered one of the greatest European composers of the time. The madrigal, a musical form introduced from Italy, was extremely popular in England by the 1590s and the first completely English collection was produced in 1594. Both Tallis

Voices from the past

John Donne

John Donne (1572–1631) is known as one of the finest poets of his time. He followed a traditional route of going to Oxford, although did not receive a degree because, as a Catholic, he refused to swear the Oath of Supremacy. He then became a lawyer but when he married the niece of Sir Thomas Egerton without her uncle's permission, his career was ruined.

His earliest poems criticised Elizabethan society as many other poets did. His satires dealt with corruption in the legal system and pompous courtiers. Perhaps his most famous works deal with eroticism or the problem of true religion. He argued that it was better to examine one's religious convictions than to follow any established tradition.

ACTIVITY 4.4

For each of the headings in Figure 4.9, make notes to explain how it helped cultural developments under Elizabeth I. You may want to carry out some extra research into some of these aspects.

and Byrd were patronised by Elizabeth, who was an elegant singer and talented player of the lute and lyre herself.

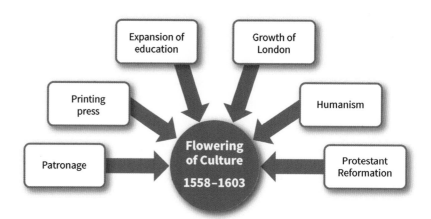

Figure 4.9: The reasons for a flowering in English culture between 1558 and 1603.

The last years of Elizabeth

Guy (1988) has convincingly argued that there were 'two reigns' of Elizabeth, the second beginning in 1585 with the reversal of a non-interventionist foreign policy and subsequent execution of Mary, Queen of Scots in 1587. He suggests that even though Mary's death solved one political and constitutional issue, it precipitated another. The wars that followed in France, the Netherlands, the Atlantic and Ireland cost England dearly. In politics the anxiety of courtiers and the poverty of the Crown kindled factionalism, self-interest and instability, culminating in Essex's attempted coup. The turmoil of poor harvests, outbreaks of influenza and rising prices provoked resistance to the Crown's military needs and demands for levies. This in turn triggered an increasingly authoritarian reaction from Privy Councillors against religious nonconformity. The deaths of four major figures at court: Robert Dudley, Earl of Leicester in 1588, Sir Walter Mildmay in 1589, the Earl of Warwick in 1590 and Sir Francis Walsingham in 1590 left a political vacuum that Elizabeth declined to fill. This led to years of overcaution and conservatism. Elizabeth's own shrewdness deserted her in the 1590s and she persistently dithered, allowing decisions to be taken for her. In Parliament too, there were deep-seated anxieties about crime, poverty and unemployment, prompting the Elizabethan Poor Laws (see the section on Society). There was no slide to disaster, however, and the political elite remained united in their fears of rising crime and fostered values of authoritarianism.

The state of England politically, economically, religiously and socially by 1603

The last two years of Elizabeth's reign were dominated by three great matters of state: finance, military campaigns and the succession. By 1601 the government

Speak like a historian: Wallace MacCaffrey

Extract B

Wallace MacCaffrey's seminal biography of Elizabeth I explores the queen as a practising politician. In this extract he discusses Elizabeth's foreign policy and the impact it had on her reign.

She was forced to take up the role of warrior queen who could not evade the grand responsibilities of high strategy, where and by what means to assail the enemy … Events quite beyond her control foreclosed the possibilities of choice or the luxury of delay. Moreover, the very nature of the decisions to be made was conditioned by military and naval expertise which Elizabeth necessarily lacked. She was compelled to submit to the judgement of men whose purposes she more than half distrusted, soldiers and sailors whose martial ambitions for professional renown, countered her own fear of risk-taking and her despair at the wasteful expenditure of her slender means.

It is not surprising that these were years when the Queen's political indisposition to act, her instinctive inclination to procrastinate, became more marked than ever. Armies dispatched to the Low Countries or to France, ships sailing away to the Azores or the West Indies, slipped away from her control. The companies sent to Holland or Brittany dwindled away; the demand for more men, more money, more supplies was unending … The image of the beneficent goddess whose reign was to be a golden era of peace and prosperity faded as the war dragged wearily on, year by year.

Source: MacCaffrey W. *Elizabeth I*. Princeton University Press; 1994. p. 243.

Discussion points:
1. What is MacCaffrey arguing here?
2. Can you find evidence in your notes that supports his view?
3. How convincing do you find his argument?

was in desperate need to pay for the continuing wars in Ireland and therefore called a Parliament as soon as they could be sure the Essex rising had been dealt with. Members of Parliament agreed to three subsidies, but Francis Bacon and Walter Raleigh criticised how they were assessed. Raleigh thought that the estates of the rich were massively undervalued while an unfair burden fell on the poor. Although Raleigh and Bacon aired their views, nothing was done to remedy this ill. In the same Parliament, religious debate was mild and the Poor Law Act of 1598 was re-enacted, forming the basis of laws on the matter until the 19th century.

The second major issue for the Crown was the military campaigns continuing in Ireland and that English soldiers were still heavily engaged in the Netherlands. Elizabeth had sent nearly 8000 troops since 1600 to help the Dutch defend Ostend. The support given to the Dutch put considerable strain on English resources at a time when the government was trying to maintain peace and stability in Ireland. A massive rebellion had broken out in Ulster in 1599 and the Earl of Essex had failed to quell the disturbances. Lord Mountjoy became Lord Deputy of Ireland and Sir George Carew, the new Lord President of Ulster. Mountjoy was given an army of 14 000, which was slightly smaller than Essex, but the new Deputy was determined to succeed. Together they made some formidable advances and only Spanish support could have saved the Irish, but Philip III wanted disengagement from war. Philip gave limited support and did not listen to advice from the Irish commanders, resulting in their forces being overwhelmed by Mountjoy's. The Irish disturbances imposed a heavy burden on England. Over 55 000 men were sent to fight in Ireland from 1594 onwards and paying for their arms, munitions, food and wages cost the Exchequer an astounding £2 000 000 – about the same amount as had been spent on defeating the Armada. Half the money had come from parliamentary subsidies, but the rest came from surpluses that had accrued during times of peace and sales of land. The Exchequer's balance had fallen to £9000 in 1599 and the Crown was hard pressed to meet the financial demands being placed on it.

The people of England resented the local taxes imposed on them for coastal defence and purchase of weapons and continual requests for men. Until the Armada, these demands had been light, but then rose quickly. Of these taxes, **Ship Money** was probably hated most. In Suffolk, JPs refused to collect it, and in London opposition was so strong that the government was forced to drop its demand. By 1601 shires and towns were appealing for relief from these taxes, while officers commanding troops were concerned about the quality of men being recruited. It was not the weight of the levy so much as the regularity with which the requests came during the 1590s that so irked the people. Luckily, peace in Ireland was restored a few days before Elizabeth's death and the Council had managed to finance the war and supply the armies for 18 years without provoking a rebellion.

By 1588 the Church of England, despite many difficulties, had put down roots in the country. Among the difficulties were the debates between clerics concerning the Calvinist doctrine of predestination, which was the idea that God had preordained some men and women to eternal bliss and some to eternal damnation, irrespective of their piety on earth. Some clerics expressed anti-Calvinist views that suggested man had free will to work out his own salvation on earth. Of course these debates only affected those in universities and a small number of clerics engaged in theology, but it does reveal the delicate balance Anglicanism was trying to maintain, by providing a broad church to a whole range of views, which were evolving over the century. There was always a danger of a theological split. Archbishop Whitgift had been appointed as Archbishop of Canterbury in 1583 and had begun an assault on Puritans to attempt to reduce them to conformity. He had no sympathy with the developing theological trends. He demanded that all clergy subscribe to the 39 articles, acknowledge the Royal Supremacy and affirm the Prayer Book. The penalty was deprivation of office. Due to pressure applied by Leicester, Walsingham and Burghley, who had sympathy for Puritan beliefs, only a few lost their titles. Whitgift's actions alienated those clergy who wanted reform and one of them, John Field, attempted to build a secret network of Presbyterian synods within the Church of England. Field died in 1588, the year of the Armada victory, which provided a favourable atmosphere for

Key term

Ship Money: a tax that monarchs could levy without the approval of Parliament. Traditionally it was only levied when a monarch needed to furnish the navy with ships.

attacking more radical religious elements. In 1589 papers of leading Presbyterians were collected and nine ministers were prosecuted under laws relating to sedition. Although none was found guilty, the ordeal drove Presbyterianism underground until the end of Elizabeth's reign. The Catholics of England were quietened by England's victory in the Armada and many became Church papists who accepted the queen's supremacy, while continuing to practise their traditional ceremonies behind closed doors.

The succession

The problem of Elizabeth's successor had been heightened following the death of Mary, Queen of Scots, in 1587. Henry VIII had nominated successors should his own children fail to produce heirs, which had now become the case. Henry VIII had nominated the Greys, giving lower priority to the Stuart line. James VI of Scotland was the most legitimate hereditary heir, but he was foreign and his mother had been condemned for treason. He was a Protestant, however, and had successfully ruled Scotland for some time. Despite the claims to the throne lodged by Philip II's daughter, Catherine Grey's son and the Earl of Derby, Elizabeth would not be moved on naming her successor. Robert Cecil was in favour of James and advised him to choose a few honest men to advise him. Williams (1998) suggests this was to ensure his own political survival and remove Raleigh and Northumberland from any future appointments James might make as king.

Accounts of Elizabeth's death suggest she decided, with her dying breath, that James VI should be her successor, although contemporary accounts do not offer a definitive narrative here. In reality the succession depended on the Privy Council, who guessed at the unspoken consensus of the nation. A rider galloped north to James VI to inform him of his new role, and James made his leisurely progress south. There could hardly have been a greater contrast between the accession of the first of the Stuarts and the first Tudor, 118 years before. Where Henry VII had to win his crown on the battlefield, James succeeded without dispute, the decision made ultimately by a group of courtiers. Perhaps this in itself demonstrates one major change that had occurred during the Tudor dynasty: the transfer of power from magnates with militia to courtiers with pens who administered the government.

Practice essay questions

1. 'Elizabeth failed to control her ministers effectively throughout her reign.' Assess the validity of this view.
2. 'Elizabeth's failure to solve the succession question provided her with the greatest threat to her reign.' Assess the validity of this view.
3. 'Elizabeth presided over a "Golden Age" for the people of England.' Assess the validity of this view.
4. Read Extracts A, B and C (Extracts A and B are within this chapter and Extract C appears here). Using your understanding of the historical context, assess how convincing the arguments are in these three extracts in relation to how successful Elizabeth's foreign policy was.

Extract C

Christopher Haigh has written about Elizabeth's power in England and how she survived as a ruler. Here Haigh discusses her foreign policy.

Elizabeth's control of her commanders was limited by her attempts to hold down costs. By taking financial partners into her initiatives, she shared her own authority and left her associates freedom of action … Problems also arose because there was no general agreement on the strategy to be followed, and the two main approaches, land campaigns and naval strikes, were adopted by different Court factions … But all these reasons do not quite explain the repeated and flagrant disregard of royal instructions … In Council, Court and Parliament, Elizabeth could show her competence; she could beat men at their own game – if necessary by using feminine tactics. But in war she was at the mercy of her generals, who thought they knew better – and she never succeeded in persuading them that they did not. In no other area of activity or policy was there such blatant disobedience to her express orders, such scorn for her authority, such contempt for monarchical dignity. A woman could browbeat politicians and seduce courtiers, but she could not command soldiers. Try as she might, Elizabeth could not quite escape from her sex.

Source: Haigh C. *Elizabeth I.* New York: Longman; 1993. p. 142.

Chapter summary

After studying this period, you should be able to:

- list the ministers who advised Elizabeth I
- describe the religious developments that took place during her reign
- assess the impact of the economic developments on the people of England
- evaluate the strengths and weaknesses of Elizabeth I as a monarch
- explain the flourishing of art, literature and music during Elizabeth's reign.

Further reading

Christopher Haigh has edited a collection of essays from the key historians on the Elizabethan era in a book called *The Reign of Elizabeth.* It is well worth reading because it outlines new interpretations and reports on recent research.

For a biography of the queen, Anne Somerset's book *Elizabeth I* is a lengthy but incredibly detailed look at aspects of her character as well as key domestic and foreign conflicts.

End notes

1 Cited in Smith AGR. *The Emergence of a Nation State: The Commonwealth of England 1529–1660.* Harlow: Pearson; 1997. p. 115.
2 Neale JE. *Elizabeth I and her Parliaments, Volume 2, 1584–1601.* London: Jonathan Cape; 1957. p. 119.
3 Guy J. *Tudor England.* Oxford: OUP. p. 283.
4 Damrosh D et al. *The Longman Anthology of British Literature, Volume 1B: The early modern period.* (3rd edn). New York: Pearson Longman; 2006. p. 115.
5 Doran S. *England and Europe 1485–1603.* New York: Longman Press. p. 91.
6 Williams P. *The Later Tudors: England 1547–1603.* Oxford: OUP; 1998. p. 266.
7 Williams P. *The Later Tudors: England 1547–1603.* Oxford: OUP; 1998. p. 376.

Glossary

A

Act of Attainder Statute (law) used by monarchs to punish without trial nobles or magnates who had committed an act of treason or serious crime against the Crown. Punishment could include revoking their property and hereditary titles, and typically the right to pass them on to their heirs. Attainders (meaning 'corruption of blood') could be reversed upon promises of loyalty: for example, Edward IV had reversed 86 of 120 when he claimed the throne.

Act of Indemnity Statute (law) passed to protect someone who has committed an illegal act from legal penalties. Acts of indemnity were used by monarchs to show clemency to those who had fought against them.

Annates Taxes levied by the Pope on recently appointed clergy.

Annuities A fixed sum of money paid to someone each year, often acting as pensions or rewards for loyal servants of the Crown.

Anticlericalism Opposition to the Church. At the turn of the 15th century this focused on the Church's independent jurisdiction, its wealth and abuses such as payment of fees for spiritual services.

Armada The Spanish and Portuguese word for naval fleet

B

Benefit of Clergy Enabled clerics to be tried in an ecclesiastical court. By the 16th century it was being successfully claimed by those who could simply read a couple of verses of the first psalm, enabling them to escape severe punishment.

C

Chantry A form of a trust fund that provided for payment for priests to sing masses for a soul after death. People believed it would enable the soul to make its way to heaven more quickly.

Church plate The name given to Church objects made of precious metal.

Church Papists Although loyal to Elizabeth, they maintained Catholic beliefs and practices (such as Mass) and thought the sacraments were necessary for salvation.

Clemency Term used to describe mercy or lenience shown by a monarch or leader when punishing enemies or traitors.

Conciliar Relating to a council, for example when policies are generated by a council.

Convocation Held either at Canterbury or at York, these were large gatherings where representatives from the Church (mostly bishops) would meet to discuss and decide on Church policy.

Council of Trent A council of the Catholic church that was organised in response to the Protestant Reformation. The Council issued key statements and clarifications on Catholic doctrine and teachings, addressing a wide range of subjects. It is said to have begun the 'Counter-Reformation', a period of Catholic revival across Europe.

D

Defender of the Faith One of a number of similar titles bestowed on European monarchs who had provided protection for Rome or had promoted Catholicism in some way. Henry VIII was given this title in 1521 by Pope Leo X.

Demesne Refers to the land held by the king or nobles not let out to tenants, effectively their great personal estates.

Doctrine Stated set of beliefs held and taught by the Church.

E

Enclosure The fencing off of common land. Once enclosed, use of a piece of land was restricted to its owner and the members of the community who had previously shared rights to it could no longer use it.

Engrossing A practice that consolidated two or more farms to increase the profit of a unit.

Eucharist — Rite considered by most Christian churches to be a sacrament. During the Last Supper, Jesus gave his disciples bread and wine and said they should eat and drink in his memory. Catholics believe in transubstantiation, that is, the bread and wine is changed into the blood and body of Christ, whereas Protestants believe they are symbolic.

Evangelical — Refers to members of a loose movement, united by an emphasis on the transformative power of the word of God. Opponents referred to them in a disparaging way as those who promoted 'new learning' – though some of their ideas had long been discussed among Lollards.

Exchequer — A court that specialised in collecting the king's revenues. Only small amounts of litigation stemmed from this court since its primary function was administrative.

F

Fifteenth and Tenth — A subsidy based on a fraction of the value of moveable, personal goods from each community. These were based on one fifteenth for rural inhabitants and one tenth for urban areas and royal demesne lands.

First Fruits and Tenths — The clergy were obliged to pay a portion of their first year's revenue from their benefice and a tenth of their income every year thereafter.

Five Wounds of Christ — Refers to the five wounds Jesus suffered during the crucifixion.

Fraternities — Lay organisations allied to the Catholic Church. They provided opportunities for people to become involved in the work of the Church and offered support for the poor within the congregation.

G

Gothic style — The Gothic style characterises much of the architecture developed in the medieval era. Key features include pointed arches, heavily buttressed tower walls, ornate façades and vaulted ceilings.

H

Hegemony — The dominance of one nation over another.

Huguenots — French Protestants inspired by the writings of John Calvin, who developed Christian doctrine dominated by the idea of predestination and absolute sovereignty of God in salvation. There were approximately two million Huguenots living in Catholic France by 1562 but they faced systematic persecution. Many fled France to England, Denmark and Sweden.

Humanism — Refers to a movement that promoted the study and recovery of Classical texts and teaching of grammar, rhetoric, poetry, history and moral philosophy.

I

Iconoclasm — Describes the destruction of religious paintings, stained glass windows and icons during the Reformation.

Indemnity — A statute passed to protect those who have committed an illegal act that would normally see them become the subject of legal sanctions.

J

Jesuits — Members of the Society of Jesus, a Catholic missionary order founded in 1540. Excluded from England in 1584, they continued to enter the country secretly and became reviled as the embodiment of the Catholic threat-from-within.

L

Lancastrians — Often associated with a red rose. The Lancastrians were descended from John of Gaunt, who was the third son of Henry III and made the Duke of Lancaster. They were a powerful family with claims to the English throne. Henry of Bolingbroke (later, Henry IV) was the first Lancastrian to assert his claim when he deposed Richard II in 1399. The Lancastrian throne was weakened when Henry VI succeeded the throne as an infant. Another family, also descended from Henry III's first and fourth sons, challenged the Lancastrians for the throne in wars that became known as 'The Wars of the Roses'.

Litany — A form of prayer used in some services where the people at the service respond to lines spoken by the priest.

Liturgy	The customary form or pattern of public worship carried out by congregations.
Livery	Distinctive uniform or badge relating to a family.
Lollardy	A heretical movement, originating in the 1380s under the Oxford scholar John Wycliffe.
Lutheran	Denotes a follower of Protestant Christianity who subscribes to the teachings of Martin Luther. The main way in which Luther differed from the Catholic tradition was his belief in justification by faith alone: that is, only God can grant passage into heaven and forgive sins.

M

Maintenance	The practice of upholding a retainer's interests.

N

New World	The term applied to the Americas and Caribbean islands. Although a few Vikings had set foot there, the Americas were essentially unknown to Europeans until the voyage of Christopher Columbus in 1492.
Non-residence	Refers to an abuse by clerics who held positions in several parishes or bishoprics but never visited their congregations, and merely lived off the proceeds. This issue was linked with pluralism – where clergy held multiple ecclesiastical offices. Wolsey is one such example as he held the Bishopric of Lincoln and the Archbishopric of York.

O

Overseer of the poor	An official who administered poor relief in the form of food, money and clothing in England and various other countries that derived their law from England.

P

'The Pale'	The region of Ireland directly controlled by England – the area this encompassed varied across time but it always centred on Dublin.
Papal bull	An official letter or document issued by the Pope.
Papal legate	An authorised representative of the Pope. Legates were frequently commissioned to carry out foreign diplomacy on the Pope's behalf.

Parliament	The highest court in the realm. Parliament's decisions were binding on all other courts and parliamentary statute overrode a judge's ability to interpret the law
Patronage	The support, privilege or financial aid that an individual can bestow to another. Often patronage was given to musicians, painters or sculptors but Elizabeth I used it more systematically to ensure the loyalty of the gentry during her reign.
Praemunire	A law prohibiting the assertion of papal jurisdiction over that of the monarch.
Presbyterians	Emphasises the sovereignty of God, not the monarch, and governance of the Church by groups of elders, not bishops. Doctrinally, Presbytarians are heavily influenced by Calvin.
Primogeniture	A principle by which the first-born son inherits the estate or title of the father.
Prophesyings	Local meetings where ministers expounded biblical texts. They were effectively training sessions to encourage a more effective preaching ministry. Lay people were often invited in hopes of evangelising them too.
Purgatory	According to Catholic doctrine, it is a form of temporary punishment for the soul immediately after death, for those who are not entirely free of faults or who have not fully paid for their sins to undergo purification before they can enter heaven.
Puritan	Term coined in the 1560s to describe radical Protestants who criticised the newly established Elizabethan Church on the grounds that it needed further reform. Generally, 'Puritan' was a derogatory term.

R

Recognisances	Sums of money pledged to fulfil an obligation.
Recusants	Refused to attend church services. Some did take the Oath of Supremacy. Doctrinally they supported the Roman Catholic Church and would not compromise on aspects such as Mass given in Latin.
Regnant	A Queen Regnant reigns in her own right, not through marriage to a king.

Renaissance

Meaning 'rebirth', refers to the historical period dating from approximately 1450 to 1750. This period saw cultural and artistic movements characterised by an interest in Classical scholarship and values.

Retaining

A medieval practice in which nobles maintained bands of followers who would take up arms for them if necessary. Retainers wore livery (a uniform or badge) to show which noble family they served.

Retrenchment

Act of reduction, particularly in the realm of public expenditure.

S

Sacrament

Christian rite of particular importance. The Catholic Church teaches that there are seven sacraments. During the 16th century, Protestants argued that there were only two sacraments instituted by Christ – the Eucharist and Baptism.

Sanctuary

A safe haven, usually in a Church. Fugitives from the law could take refuge in a sanctuary because the Church laws forbade anyone to be arrested within their walls. The right to sanctuary was limited in cases of treason.

Scholasticism

Refers to a medieval movement that taught arithmetic, geometry, astronomy and music.

Seminary priests

English priests who had been trained in Flanders. They were taught to work for the salvation of souls and, if necessary, that they should seek martyrdom to restore Catholicism in England.

Ship Money

Tax that monarchs could levy without the approval of Parliament. Traditionally it was only levied when a monarch needed to furnish the navy with ships.

Synod

Traditionally denotes a council meeting of a church, designed to determine a doctrine, for example.

T

Tillage

The preparation of soil for growing crops by farmers, including digging and overturning.

Tithes

Annual payments of an agreed proportion of the yearly produce of the land. Tithes were payable by parishioners to their local parish church, to support it and its clergyman.

Transubstantiation

Catholics believe that the bread and wine are changed into the blood and body of Christ, whereas Protestants believe they are symbolic.

Y

Yorkist

The Yorkist family were descended from a branch of the Plantagenet family tree. They claimed the English throne and three of its members became English kings in the 15th century. The last Yorkist king was Richard III who lost his life in battle to Henry Tudor in 1485.

Note about the value of money

The money used in England in the 15th century was the pre-decimal currency of pounds, shillings and pence (12 pence in a shilling, 20 shillings or 240 pence in a pound).

The value of £1 in 1500 is roughly equivalent to £486 today, though it should be stressed that due to inflation and other fluctuations this is a very approximate multiplier.

A nobleman had an income between £1500 and £3000 per annum.

A merchant had an income of £300 per annum.

A carpenter had an income of £20 per annum.

A labourer had an income of £10 per annum.

Bibliography

Chapter 1

Arthurson I. *The Perkin Warbeck Conspiracy 1491–1499*. Stroud; Sutton Publishing Ltd; 1998.

Carpenter C. 'Henry VII and the English polity'. In B Thompson (ed.) *The Reign of Henry VII*, Stamford; 1995.

Carpenter C. *The Wars of the Roses: Politics and the Constitution in England 1437–1509*: Cambridge: CUP; 1997.

Chrimes SB. *Henry VII*. New Haven: Yale University Press; 1977.

Currin JM '"Pro Expensis Ambassatorum": diplomacy and financial administration in the reign of Henry VII.' *English Historical Review*, 108; 1993. p. 589–609.

Davies CSL. 'Bishop John Morton, the Holy See and the Accession of Henry VII.' *English Historical Review*, 102; 1987. p. 2–30.

Elton GR. *England under the Tudors*. London: Folio Society; 1955.

Fletcher A and D MacCulloch. *Tudor Rebellions*. Harlow: Pearson; 2004.

Grant A. *Henry VII*. London: Routledge; 1985.

Gunn SJ. *Early Tudor Government, 1485–1558*. London: Palgrave Macmillan; 1995.

Guy J. *Tudor England*. Oxford: OUP; 1988.

Jones MK and M Underwood. *The King's Mother: Lady Margaret Beaufort, Countess of Richmond and Derby*. Cambridge: CUP; 1993.

Lander JR. *Government and Community: England 1450–1509*. London: Edward Arnold; 1980.

Loades DM. *Politics and Nation: England 1450–1660* (5th edn). Oxford: OUP; 1999.

Lockyer R. *Henry VII* (2nd edn). Harlow: Pearson; 1983.

Penn T. *Winter King: The Dawn of Tudor England*. London: Penguin; 2012.

Pollard AJ. *The Wars of the Roses: British History in Perspective*. London: Palgrave Macmillan; 2001.

Storey RL. *The Reign of Henry VII*. London: Blandford Press; 1968.

Williams PP. 'A Revolution in Tudor History: The Tudor State.' *Past and Present*: 1963, 25(1). p. 39–58.

Wood A. *Riot, Rebellion and Popular Politics in Early Modern England*. London: Palgrave Macmillan; 2002.

Chapter 2

Bernard GW. *The King's Reformation: Henry VIII and the Remaking of the English Church*. New Haven: Yale University Press; 2007.

Coby P. *Thomas Cromwell: Machiavellian Statecraft and the English Reformation*. Lanham; Lexington Books; 2009.

Dickens AG. *The English Reformation*. London: BT Batsford Ltd Publications; 1964.

Doran S. *England and Europe 1485–1603*. New York: Longman Press; 1996.

Duffy E. *The Stripping of the Altars: Traditional Religion in England 1400–1580*. New Haven: Yale University Press; 2005.

Ellis S. *Tudor Ireland, 1470–1603*. Harlow: Longman; 1985.

Elton GR. *England under the Tudors*. London: Folio Society; 1955.

Elton GR. *Reform and Reformation: England 1509–1558*. Cambridge, MA: Harvard University Press; 1977.

Everett M. *The Rise of Thomas Cromwell: Power and Politics in the Reign of Henry VIII*: New Haven: Yale University Press; 2015.

Fletcher A and D MacCulloch. *Tudor Rebellions*. Harlow: Pearson; 2008.

Gunn SJ. *Early Tudor Government, 1485–1558*. London: Palgrave Macmillan; 1995.

Gunther K and EH Shagan. 'Protestant Radicalism and Political Thought in the Reign of Henry VIII.' *Past & Present*, 194; Feb 2007. p. 35–74.

Guy JA. 'Henry VIII and the Praemunire Manoeuvres of 1530–1531.' *The English Historical Review*, 97(384); July 1982. p. 481–503.

Guy J. *Tudor England*. Oxford: OUP; 1988.

Gwyn P. *The King's Cardinal: The Rise and Fall of Thomas Wolsey*. London; Pimlico; 1990.

Haigh C. *English Reformations: Religion, Politics and Society under the Tudors*. Oxford: OUP; 1993.

Hutchinson R. *Thomas Cromwell: The Rise And Fall Of Henry VIII's Most Notorious Minister*. London: Weidenfeld & Nicholson; 2007.

Ives EW. 'Henry VIII's Will – A Forensic Conundrum.' *The Historical Journal*, 35(4); Dec. 1992. p. 779–804.

Ives EW. 'Faction at the Court of Henry VIII: the Fall of Anne Boleyn.' *History*; 1972. p. 169–88.

Ives EW. 'Henry VIII: The political perspective'. (ed. D MacCulloch). London: Palgrave Macmillan; 1995.

Ives EW. *Very Interesting People – Henry VIII*. Oxford: OUP; 2007.

Lipscomb S. *1536: The Year that Changed Henry VIII*: London: Lion Hudson; 2009.

Lipscomb S, 'Who Was Henry VIII?' *History Today*, 59(4); April 2009. As of 16 October 2015: http://www.historytoday.com/suzannah-lipscomb/who-was-henry-viii#sthash.nXcgcg01.dpuf

Loades DM. *Politics and Nation, England 1450–1660*. (5th edn) Oxford: OUP; 1999.

Loades DM. *Thomas Cromwell, Servant to Henry VIII*. Stroud: Amberley Publishing; 2013.

MacCulloch D. (ed.). *The Reign of Henry VIII: Politics, Policy and Piety*. London: Palgrave Macmillan; 1995.

Marius R. *Thomas More: A Biography*. New Haven: Yale University Press; 1999.

Marshall P. *Reformation England 1480–1642*. London: Bloomsbury; 2012.

Morris TA. *Europe and England in the Sixteenth Century*. London: Routledge; 1998.

Penn T. *Winter King: The Dawn of Tudor England*. London: Penguin; 2012.

Rex R. *Henry VIII and the English Reformation*. London: Palgrave Macmillan; 2006.

Richardson G. 'Good Friends and Brothers? Francis I and Henry VIII.' *History Today*, 44(9); 1994.

Scarisbrick JJ. *Henry VIII*. New Haven: Yale University Press; 1997.

Smith LB. *Henry VIII: the Mask of Royalty*. London: Jonathan Cape; 1971.

Starkey D. *The Reign of Henry VIII: Personalities and Politics*. London: Vintage; 1985.

Wernham RB. *Before the Armada: The Growth of English Foreign Policy 1485–1588*. London: Jonathan Cape; 1966.

Wilkie WE. *The Cardinal Protectors of England: Rome and the Tudors Before the Reformation. Cambridge*: CUP; 1974.

Wilson D. *The Uncrowned Kings of England: The Black Legend of the Dudleys and the Tudor Throne*. New York: Carroll and Graf Publishers Inc; 2005.

Wood A. *Riot, Rebellion and Popular Politics in Early Modern England*. London: Palgrave Macmillan; 2002.

Chapter 3

Bush ML. *The Government Policy of Protector Somerset*. London: Edward Arnold; 1975.

Davies CA. *Religion of the Word: The Defence of the Reformation in the Reign of Edward VI*. Manchester: Manchester University Press; 2002.

Davies CSL. *Peace, Print and Protestantism 1450–1558*. Colorado: Paladin; 1977.

Dickens AG. *The English Reformation*. London: BT Batsford Ltd Publications; 1964.

Doran S. *England and Europe 1485–1603*. New York: Longman Press; 1996.

Duffy E. *The Stripping of the Altars: Traditional Religion in England 1400–1580*. New Haven: Yale University Press; 2005.

Elton GR. *England under the Tudors*. London: Folio Society; 1955.

Fletcher A. and D. MacCulloch. *Tudor Rebellions*. Harlow: Pearson; 2008.

Gunn SJ. *Early Tudor Government, 1485–1558*. London: Palgrave Macmillan; 1995.

Guy J. *Tudor England*. Oxford: OUP; 1988.

Haigh C (ed.). 'The Church of England, the Catholics and the People.' In *The Reign of Elizabeth I*. London: Macmillan; 1984.

Haigh C. *English Reformations: Religion, Politics and Society Under the Tudors*. Oxford: OUP; 1993.

Jones NL. 'Elizabeth's First Year: The Conception and Birth of the Elizabethan Political World.' In C Haigh (ed.) *The Reign of Elizabeth I*. London: Macmillan; 1984.

Jordan WK. *Edward VI: The Threshold of Power*. London: Allen and Unwin; 1970.

Loach J. *A Mid Tudor Crisis?* London: Historical Association; 1993.

Loach J. *Edward VI*. Norfolk: St Edmundsbury Press; 2002.

Loades DM. *Politics and Nation, England 1450–1660*. (5th edn). Oxford: OUP; 1999.

MacCaffrey W. *Elizabeth I*. London: Edward Arnold; 1993.

Neale J. *Elizabeth I and her Parliaments*, 2 vols. London: Jonathan Cape; 1953.

Neale J. 'The Elizabethan Acts of Supremacy and Uniformity.' *English Historical Review*, 65; 1950. p. 304–24.

Pollard AF. *Cambridge Modern History, Vol II*. Cambridge: CUP; 1903.

Smith AGR. *The Emergence of a Nation State: The Commonwealth of England 1529–1660*. Harlow: Pearson; 1997.

Somerset A. *Elizabeth I*. London: Phoenix; 1997.

Starkey D. *Elizabeth I*. London: Vintage; 2001.

Tittler R. *The Reign of Mary I*. Harlow: Longman; 1983.

Wernham RB. *Before the Armada: The Growth of English Foreign Policy 1485–1558*. London; 1966.

Williams P. *The Later Tudors: England 1547–1603*. Oxford: OUP; 1998.

Wizeman W. *The Theology and Spirituality of Mary Tudor's Church*. Aldershot: Ashgate Publishing; 2006.

Chapter 4

Adams S. 'Faction, Clientage and Party: English Politics, 1550–1603.' *History Today*, 32 (Dec. 1982). p. 33–39.

Adams S. 'Eliza Enthroned?' In *The Reign of Elizabeth I* (ed. C Haigh). London: Macmillan; 1984.

Coleman DC. *The Economy of England, 1450–1750*. Oxford: OUP; 1978.

Collinson P. 'The Elizabethan Church and the New Religion.' In *The Reign of Elizabeth I* (ed. C Haigh). London: Macmillan; 1984.

Doran S. *England and Europe 1485–1603*. New York: Longman Press; 1996.

Doran S. *Queen Elizabeth I (British Library Historic Lives)*. London: British Library; 2003.

Graves MAR. *The Tudor Parliaments: Crown, Lords and Commons, 1485–1603:* New York: Longman; 1985.

Guy J. *Tudor England:* Oxford: OUP; 1988.

Guy J. (ed.). *The Reign of Elizabeth I, Court and Culture in the Last Decade*. Cambridge: CUP; 1995.

Haigh C. *Elizabeth I*. New York: Longman; 1993.

Jones NL. 'Elizabeth's First Year: The conception and birth of the Elizabethan political world.' In *The Reign of Elizabeth I* (ed. C Haigh). London: Macmillan; 1984.

Kerridge E. 'The Agricultural Revolution Reconsidered.' *Agricultural History:* Agricultural History Society. 43(4); Oct. 1969. p. 463–76.

Loades DM. *Politics and Nation, England 1450–1660* (5th edn). Oxford: OUP; 1999.

MacCaffrey W. *Elizabeth I*. London: Edward Arnold; 1993.

Neale JE. *Elizabeth I and her Parliaments, Vol. 1. 1559–1581*. London: Jonathan Cape; 1953.

Neale JE. *Elizabeth I and her Parliaments, Vol. 2. 1584–1601*. London: Jonathan Cape; 1957.

Nef JU. *Industry and Government in France and England, 1540–1640:* Ithaca: New York: Cornell University Press; 1940.

Palliser DM. *The Age of Elizabeth, England Under the Later Tudors 1547–1603:* New York: Longman; 1992.

Parker G. 'Why the Armada Failed.' *History Today*, 8(5); May 1988. p. 26–33.

Smith AGR. *The Emergence of a Nation State: The Commonwealth of England 1529–1660*. Harlow: Pearson; 1997.

Somerset A. *Elizabeth I*. London: Phoenix; 1997.

Wernham RB. *Before the Armada: The Growth of English Foreign Policy 1485–1558*. London; Jonathan Cape; 1966.

Williams P. *The Later Tudors: England 1547–1603*. Oxford: OUP; 1998.

Wilson C. *Queen Elizabeth and the Revolt of the Netherlands*. London; 1970.

Wrigley EA and RS Schofield. *The Population History of England 1541–1871*. Cambridge: CUP; 1981.

Acknowledgements

The authors and publishers acknowledge the following sources of copyright material and are grateful for the permissions granted. While every effort has been made, it has not always been possible to identify the sources of all the material used, or to trace all copyright holders. If any omissions are brought to our notice, we will be happy to include the appropriate acknowledgements on reprinting.

The publisher would like to thank the following for permission to reproduce their photographs (numbers refer to figure numbers, unless otherwise stated):

Cover Image: Adam Woolfitt/ Corbis**, Chapter 1 Opener Alamy Images:** Stefano Ravera; **Figure 1.2** Bridgeman Images: Stefano Baldini; **Figure 1.6 Alamy Images:** Stefano Ravera; **Figure 1.9 Alamy Images:** Mary Evans Picture Library*;* **Chapter 2 Opener Alamy Images:** Niday Picture Library; **Figure 2.1 Alamy Images:** Active Museum; **Figure 2.2** Bridgeman Images: National Portrait Gallery, London; **Figure 2.4 Alamy Images:** Active Museum; **Figure 2.5 Alamy Images:** Niday Picture Library; **Figure 2.9 Alamy Images:** GL Archive; **Figure 2.10 Alamy Images:** Lebrecht Music and Arts Photo Library; **Chapter 3 Opener Alamy Images:** World History Archive; **Figure 3.3** Bridgeman Images: National Portrait Gallery, London; **Figure 3.4; Alamy Images:** Pictorial Press Ltd, **Figure 3.5 Alamy Images:** World History Archive; **Chapter 4 Opener Corbis: Alamy Images:** Archivart; **Figure 4.2 Corbis:** The Print Collector; **Figure 4.3** Bridgeman Images: National Trust Photographic Library; **Figure 4.5** Bridgeman Images: Bonhams, London; **Figure 4.7 Alamy Images:** Archivart; **Figure 4.8 Shutterstock:** Phil MacD Photography

The publisher would like to thank the following for permission to reproduce extracts from their texts:

Chapter 1 Henry VII and the English Polity by Christine Carpenter in The Reign of Henry VII Edited by B. Thompson © 1995 Paul Watkins Publishing with permission; **Chapter 2** Cromwell and the Reform of Government by John Guy © 1995 reproduced with permission of Palgrave Macmillan; **Chapter 2** The Rise of Thomas Cromwell: Power and Politics in the Reign of Henry VII by Michael Everett © 2015 Yale University Press; **Chapter 3** Elizabeth's First Year: The conception and birth of the Elizabethan political world by NL Jones in The Reign of Elizabeth I edited by C Haigh © 1984 reproduced with permission of Palgrave Macmillan and The University of Georgia Press; **Chapter 3** Tudor England by J Guy © 1988 Oxford University Press; **Chapter 4** Elizabeth I by Wallace MacCaffrey © 1994 Bloomsbury.

Index

Printed in Great Britain
by Amazon